COMEDY
TECHNIQUES FOR WRITERS AND PERFORMERS

The HEARTS Theory of Humor Writing

by
MELVIN HELITZER

LAWHEAD PRESS
Athens, Ohio

Comedy Techniques for Writers and Performers, Copyright 1984 by Melvin Helitzer. Printed and bound in the United States of America. All rights reserved. No part of this book may be reproduced in any form or by electronic or mechanical means including information storage and retrieval systems without permission in writing from the author, except by a reviewer who may quote brief passages in a review. Published by Lawhead Press, P.O. Box A, Athens, Ohio 45701. First edition.

Library of Congress Catalog Card Number 83-83368

Helitzer, Melvin
   Comedy Techniques for Writers and Performers
   Includes Index.
   1. Wit and humor — Authorship. I Title.

ISBN 0-916199-00-2

Assistant Editor Lowell Verheul
Cover Design by Patrice Kroutel

*"The world is a comedy to those that think;
a tragedy to those that feel."*

*Horace Walpole
December 31, 1769*

ACKNOWLEDGEMENTS

The author is grateful for the permission to reprint edited condensations of the following copyrighted material:

"Eight Humor Theories" from "Early Concepts of Humor: Varieties and Issues," by Patricia Keith-Spiegel in *Psychology of Humor,* edited by J.H. Goldstein and P.E. McGhee, (C) 1972, The Academic Press, 111 Fifth Avenue, New York, N.Y. 10003.

"Sick Humor and the Function of Comedy," by Jesse Bier from *The Humanist,* (C) Jan/Feb 1979, 7 Harwood Drive, Amherst, N.Y. 14226.

"Saturday Night Live: Nihilism or Ethical Absolutism?" by Robert G. Pielke from *American Humor: An Inter-disciplinary Newsletter,* (C) Spring 1980, published by the American Studies Program, University of Maryland.

"Fourteen Varieties of Humor," by Roy Paul Nelson, School of Journalism, University of Oregon, from the author's book *Articles and Features,* (C) 1978, Houghton Mifflin Company, Boston, Mass.

"A Philosophy for Beginning Comedy Writers," by Gene Perret, from *Gene Perret's Round Table,* a newsletter for comedy writers and humorous speakers, P.O. Box 13, King of Prussia, Pa., 19406.

"Confessions of a Speechwriter," by Daniel Lynch, from *Dun's Business Month* (formerly Dun's Review), (C) November 1965, Dun & Bradstreet Publications Corporation, New York, N.Y.

"How to Spice Up Those Dull Speeches," by Robert Orben, from *Enterprise Magazine,* (C) 1980 by Robert Orben, The Comedy Center, 700 Orange Street, Wilmington, Dela. 19801.

"How to Tell a Joke," by Fred Ebel, from *Better Communications,* a newsletter published by Information Plus, Inc., 1165 Long Hill Road, Sterling, N.J. 07980.

"Tips for Beginning Professional Speakers," by Ed Hercer and Gene Perret, from *Gene Perret's Round Table,* a newsletter for comedy writers and humorous speakers, P.O. Box 13, King of Prussia, Pa., 19406.

"The Light Touch," by Roy Paul Nelson, School of Journalism, University of Oregon, from the author's book *Articles and Features,* (C) 1978, Houghton Mifflin Company, Boston, Mass.

"How to Write Humor Fillers for the *Reader's Digest,"* by Betty Johnston, from *Writer's Digest,* (C) 1975, Writer's Digest Publishing, 9933 Alliance Road, Cincinnati, O. 45242.

"Now Let's Write a Complete Monologue," by Ron Carver from the author's book *How to Write Jokes,* (C) 1964, Hollywood School of Humor Writing.

"Ethnic Humor," by Larry Wilde from *The Complete Book of Ethnic Humor,* (C) 1978, Pinnacle Books, Inc., 1430 Broadway, New York, N.Y. 10018.

"Television Comedy Techniques," by Daniel E. Garvey and William L. Rivers from their book *Broadcast Writing,* first edition, (C) 1982 by Longman, Inc., New York, N.Y. 10036.

"Gag Writing for Cartoons," by Jack Markow from the author's book *Cartoonists and Gag Writer's Handbook* (C) 1967, Writer's Digest Books, 9933 Alliance Road, Cincinnati, Ohio 45242.

"Write Studio Cards and Still Have Time for Sex," by Bob Hammerquist from the book *A Guide to Greeting Card Writing* by Larry Sandman, (C) 1980, Writer's Digest Books, 9933 Alliance Road, Cincinnati, Ohio 45242.

"Humor Writing for Greeting Cards," by Larry Sandman from the author's book *A Guide to Greeting Card Writing,* (C) 1980, Writer's Digest Books, 9933 Alliance Road, Cincinnati, Ohio 45242.

DEDICATED TO:

My students and faculty associates without whose helpful suggestions and frank criticism this book would have been finished three years ago.

PREFACE

Since 1972 — or the end of America's Vietnam involvement — comedy's growth has been inching steadily upward.

Today, it is on the march. And the Pied Piper of the parade is none other than the President of the United States. When Reagan jokes, the press reports them as if they were recapping last night's Johnny Carson monologues. Nothing seems to faze this "ha to the chief." He gets shot and he quips to his wife. On the campaign tour, he uses self-deprecating humor to deflect criticism about his age.

Never before have so many public figures been using humor, and never before has there been such a need for writers who are able to consistently "gag it out."

As an example, look at television, a monster which is gulping up comedy material faster than professional writers can produce it. Of the full complement of prime time network programs, fully three quarters of them are sitcoms or adventure programs which rely heavily on humor content. Six of the top ten rated tv programs are sitcoms, and so are fifteen of the top rated twenty.

Comedy is the theme of the most popular variety shows like Carson's *Tonight* show, *Saturday Night Live*, *Benny Hill* and Bob Hope's annual farewell appearances. The channels are filled with wise-cracking, Bugs-Bunny-type animated heroes, quiz show MCs, celebrity guest panelists and a host of talk shows and exercise classes. Top rated *60 Minutes* ends most programs with witticisms by Andy Rooney, and news anchormen, sportscasters and even weathermen are encouraged to spice up their delivery with Dick Cavett-style material.

But all material must first be written — there are few ad-libs — and the problem is that there are just not enough experienced comedy writers in Los Angeles, and to a lesser extent New York, to meet the demand. Top writers (generally in teams of two) are demanding up to $35,000 for a half-hour sitcom script, plus extras that come from being "hyphenated" (a writer-producer or a writer-director). To ease the crunch, some of the networks and major tv studios are conducting talent search workshops for young writers, enticing them with short-term contracts of $3,500 per sitcom treatment if they show promise.

Hollywood is in even more desperate straits. Box office grosses of multi-million dollar budgeted films are off sharply. On the average, two movies in ten make a profit, two more break even and the rest are losers. And of this year's financially most successful movies, seven are comedies.

Studio executives know the demographics better than they do *The Talmud*. Sixty percent of today's audiences are under 24, and they want fun, fun, fun . . . mixed with escapist excitement, adventure or sexual fantasy.

Like the situation in TV, there are not enough comedy film writers to go around. Pros start at $50,000 per accepted script, and at the other end of the spectrum, writers Mel Brooks, Woody Allen, Neil Simon and Alan Alda produce, direct and sometimes star in their own films, which gives them four places on the production budget.

When you shuffle in the deals that playwriters of *stage comedies* get (10 to 20% of gross) and the fact that writers for *professional entertainers,* who start at $1,000 for one page of material, have been known to receive up to 10% of the comedian's gross income for special performances, the rewards for big league comedy writing can equal those of name performers, sport stars and business tycoons. That's only the tip of the good humor stick. There are also tremendous financial rewards for the ability to write humor or wit for business and political speeches (at $100-$300 per minute of speech), advertising (at $1,000-$1,500 per 30-second commercial), public relations releases ($200 per page), greeting cards, posters and buttons ($50 per idea), cartoons ($500-$3,500) and even anecdotes and fillers for newspaper and magazine columns ($10-$100). Book publishers smile on humor books, because they consistently do well on best seller lists and have a long market life.

In the past 10 years, there has been a proliferation of *comedy clubs* which feature professional and amateur comedy talent. Over 100 clubs, playing to capacity young audiences five nights per week, are currently operating. New clubs are opening at the rate of one a week.

The need to use *therapeutic humor* is increasing on every front: psychotherapy, medicine, photography, even space science. Every speaker and lecturer, whether he be educator, politician, businessman or religious leader, knows the effectiveness of humor at the right time.

Every journalist (articles, essays, columns, fillers), every author of fiction and non-fiction, every writer of drama, films, etc. needs humorous effects at one time or another.

Humor breaks down sales resistance for car dealers, insurance, real estate and door-to-door salesmen. Sooner or later everyone sends a humorous congratulatory or get well telegram or, as a committee chairman, announces awards or accepts them with remarks hopefully a bit more original than "I want to thank the Academy. . . ."

Despite this, there are only five books on how to write humor currently available. There are a small number of books on writing for magazines, television, and greeting cards which devote from one paragraph up to one chapter on humor techniques. No one has yet fully explained why this subject is so vastly underrated and overlooked. Perhaps, because of the historic attitude that humor in trivial, higher education has rarely attempted to teach it in a systematic fashion. More likely, however, may be the fact that few communications or English instructors have had experience or training in this area —

and the writing pros are making too much money keeping up with demand to devote time to this speculative endeavor.

This is unfortunate. The public's appetite for creative humor instruction is overwhelming. And universities and schools which institute humor courses find registration running at capacity.

This is the first humor *textbook* to appear on the market. It is divided into three major sections: (1) humor theory, (2) humor technique, and (3) eight humor markets, namely, writing comedy for speeches, magazines, newspapers, stand-up comedians, tv sitcoms, cartoons, greeting cards and advertising. What has unfortunately been left out, because of space limitations, are markets of equal value: humor writing for the stage, films, books, music, poetry, mimes and clowns.

It is hoped that this material will whet the appetite of the student to the tremendous range, as well as opportunity, available to budding humor talents. Isn't it great to have a hobby that makes people laugh and get paid for it, too!

Ohio University   Melvin Helitzer
Athens, Ohio

CONTENTS

	PREFACE	7
	PART I - HUMOR THEORY	15
Chapter 1	Eight Humor Theories Patricia C. Keith-Spiegel condensed from *Psychology of Humor*	17
Chapter 2	The HEARTS Theory: the Anatomy of Humor	23
Chapter 3	Sick Humor and the Function of Comedy Jesse Bier condensed from *The Humanist*	49
Chapter 4	*Saturday Night Live*: Nihilism or Ethical Absolutism? Robert G. Pielke condensed from *American Humor: An Inter-disciplinary Newsletter*	54
	PART II - HUMOR TECHNIQUE	63
Chapter 5	Fourteen Varieties of Humor Roy Paul Nelson condensed from *Articles and Features*	65
Chapter 6	An Outline of Satire Dylan Williams	70
Chapter 7	Switching: Cliches, Synonyms & Truism	79
Chapter 8	Ask the Pros: Professional Advice on Humor	92
Chapter 9	Funny Words: The Sparkplugs of Humor	118
Chapter 10	A Philosophy for Beginning Comedy Writers Gene Perret condensed from *The Roundtable*	141
	PART III - HUMOR MARKETS	147

Chapter 11	Speechwriting -
	• Confessions of a Speechwriter
	  Daniel Lynch
	  condensed from *Dun's Review*
		149

12 COMEDY TECHNIQUES

- How to Spice Up Those Dull Speeches   152
  Robert Orben
  condensed from *Enterprise*

- How to Tell a Joke   157
  Fred Ebel
  condensed from *Better Communication*

- Tips for Beginning Professional Speakers   159
  Ed Hercer & Gene Perret
  condensed from *The Roundtable*

Chapter 12   Writing for Magazines and Newspapers   168

- The Light Touch
  Roy Paul Nelson
  condensed from *Articles and Features*

- How to Write Humor Fillers for the   173
  Reader's Digest
  Betty Johnston
  condensed from *Writer's Digest*

Chapter 13   Writing for Stand-up Comics

- Now, Let's Write a Complete Monologue   176
  Ron Carver
  condensed from *How to Write Jokes*

- Ethnic Humor   183
  Larry Wilde
  condensed from *The Complete Book of Ethnic Humor*

Chapter 14   Writing for Sitcoms

- The Do's and Don'ts of Sitcom Writing   190

- Television Comedy Techniques   200
  Daniel E. Garvey & William L. Rivers
  condensed from *Broadcast Writing*

- NBC Fact Sheet: The Marketing of Television   210
  Properties
  Submission Department, NBC-TV

- Looking for Mr. Right: Writer's Guide to   211
  Agents
  Oscar Millard
  condensed from *The Los Angeles Times*

- Writer's Representatives   214
  The Screenwriter's Handbook

	• Contracts and Rights condensed from *Scriptwriter's News*	224
Chapter 15	Writing for Print Cartoons	226
	• Gag Writing for Cartoons Jack Markow condensed from *Cartoonist's & Gag Writer's Handbook*	
	• Cartooning: Style and Marketing Robb Winwood	239
	• The Cartoon Writer's Agents condensed from *The Writer's Market*	242
Chapter 16	Writing for Greeting Cards	246
	• Write Studio Cards and Still Have Time for Sex Bob Hammerquist condensed from *A Guide to Greeting Card Writing*	
	• Humor Writing for Greeting Cards Larry Sandman condensed from *A Guide to Greeting Card Writing*	252
Chapter 17	Writing for Advertising	257

PART I
HUMOR THEORY

1

Eight Humor Theories
by Patricia C. Keith-Spiegel
Condensed from *The Psychology of Humor*

> *What does laughter mean? The greatest of thinkers, from Aristotle downwards, have tackled this little problem which has a knack of baffling every effort, of slipping away and escaping only to bob up again, a pert challenge flung at philosophic speculation.*
> — Henri Bergson (1911)

    Some of the major types of early assumptions about the nature of humor fall into more than one category.
    Many statements are actually descriptions of conditions under which humor may be experienced rather than attempts to explain humor. There have been relatively few attempts to relate laughter to general psychological and biological principles.

1- Biological, Instinct, and Evolution Theories

Laughter and humor potentials are "built-in" to the nervous mechanism of the organism and serve some adaptive function. That laughter appears early in life, before any complex cognitive processes have been formed, and that laughter and humor are universal phenomena are often used as points to support the hypothesis that we are dealing with behaviors that have survived for some utilitarian purpose.

Laughter and humor have been hailed as "good for the body" because they restore homeostasis, stabilize blood pressure, oxygenate the blood, massage the vital organs, stimulate circulation, facilitate digestion, relax the system, and produce a feeling of well being.

A number of theorists have taken the stand that what we regard today as laughter and humor are but vestiges of archaic adaptive behaviors. Gradually laughter and humor became a substitute for actual assault. The similarity of bodily stance (exposed teeth, contorted face, sprawling movements of the limbs, etc.) in both fighting and laughing is pointed to as evidence. Present-day ridicule can be terraced to the primitive thrashing of enemies. Laughter has also been viewed as the means of maintaining group standards in primitive times.

Laughter gradually became pleasureable as it blended with sympathy and affection.

2- Superiority Theories

The roots of laughter in triumph over other people (or circumstances) supplies the basis for superiority theories. Elation is engendered when we compare ourselves favorably to others as being less stupid, less ugly, less unfortunate, or less weak. According to the principle of superiority, mockery, ridicule, and laughter at the foolish actions of others are central to the humor experience.

Hobbes (1651) defined laughter as a kind of "sudden glory" which we achieve primarily by observing the infirmities of others and comparing them with the "eminency" in ourselves. Bain (1888) extended Hobbes's theory by including ideas, political institutions, and inanimate objects as targets for ridicule. Bergson (1911) viewed humor as a punishment inflicted on unsocial persons. Thus humiliation becomes a social corrective. Ludovici (1932) believed humor to be a case of superior adaptation whereby a person feels himself to be better adapted to a situation than someone else. The greater the dignity of the victim, the greater the resulting amusement.

Other theories incorporating superiority-related concepts as central to the nature of humor stress elation in triumph or victory; pleasure in outstripping one's competitors; joy of getting another at a disadvantage; delight in the sufferings and misfortunes of others or in the ugliness, deformity, or mental afflictions of others; and amusement at the stupid actions of others.

Not all theorists who include the element of superiority as part of humor believe that laughter is always contemptuous or scornful. Sympathy, congeniality, empathy, and geniality may be combined with the laughter of superiority.

3- Incongruity Theories

Humor arising from disjointed, ill-suited pairings of ideas or situations or presentations of ideas or situations that are divergent from habitual customs form the bases of incongruity theories.

Beattie (1776) believed that laughter arose when two or more inconsistent or unsuitable circumstances were united into one complex assemblage; and Priestley (1777) viewed the cause of laughter to be the perception of contrast. According to Schopenhauer, the realization of the accuracy of a perception over a thought leads to pleasure.

Not all incongruities, then, cause laughter. For example, in ascending incongruity, when an insignificant entity develops unexpectedly into something great, the emotion resulting is "wonder."

Bergson (1911) viewed the underlying cause of humor as "something mechanical encrusted on the living." A person is laughable when he behaves in a stiff, rigid, or automatic manner — the more mechanistic the behavior, the greater the laughter. Furthermore, "a situation is invariably comic when it belongs simultaneously to two altogether independent series of events and is capable of being interested in two entirely different meanings at the same time."

Leacock (1935) described humor as the contrast between a thing as it is or ought to be and a thing smashed out of shape, as it ought not to be. Koestler (1964) described the pattern underlying humor as the perception of a situation or event in two habitually incompatible contexts. The abrupt transfer in the train of thought to different rules or logic cannot be followed quickly by certain emotions, which work themselves off along the channel of least resistance — laughter.

4- Surprise Theories

The elements of "surprise," "shock," "suddenness," or "unexpectedness" have been regarded by many theorists as necessary (though not necessarily sufficient) conditions for the humor experience. There is some similarity between the concepts of surprise and incongruity in that both involve an instantaneous breaking up of the routine course of thought or action. It is, therefore, not unusual to find many theorists utilizing a blend of surprise and incongruity in explanatory concepts.

One of the most striking aspects of reactions to humor is adaptation to a given stimulus. When novelty of surprise is eliminated, or if a joke is remembered, the reaction to a humorous situation is altered. Thus writers incorporating surprise into their theories have the advantage of being able to account for the decline in appreciation level on repeated exposures to the same situation.

5- Ambivalence Theories

Ambivalence theories hold that laughter results when the individual simultaneously experiences incompatible emotions or feelings. "We laugh whenever, on contemplating an object or a situation, we find opposite emotions struggling within us for mastery. Although there is obvious similarity between ambivalence and incongruity theories, incongruity theories tend to stress ideas or perceptions whereas ambivalence theories stress emotions or feelings.

Other clashing feelings or emotions proposed as resolving themselves through laughter include love modified by hate, mania alternating with depression, playful chaos mixed with seriousness, sympathy and animosity, and conflict engendered by blocking the behavior associated with an instinct drive. With adults the typical funny situation is one providing a playful appeal plus an antagonistic response to reinforce it.

6- Release and Relief Theories

The functions of humor as affording relief from strain or constraints, or releasing excess tension, are the bases of these theories.

The excess-energy theory of humor: purposeless nervous energy in search of an outlet takes the most yielding course. This is illustrated by the actions of the organs of speech and muscles of respiration with the resultant vocal-respiratory phenomenon known as laughter.

The tension accompanying thought occasionally exceeds the capacity for controlled thinking causing a wave of emotion. Sometimes this leads to humorous experiences which serve the useful purpose of alleviating the strain involved in sustained attention. Gregory (1924) viewed relief as pervading all humor:

> *Relief is not the whole of laughter, though it is its root and fundamental plan. No discussion of laughter that ignores relief or makes it of little account can hope to prosper.*

7- Configurational Theories

That humor is experienced when elements originally perceived as unrelated suddenly fall into place is the basis of theories placed into this category. There is clearly some relationship between the notions behind both incongruity and configurational theories. Each stresses the cognitive and perceptual attributes of humor, but the main difference lies in the point at which humor emerges. As maintained in incongruity theories, it is the perception of "disjointedness" that somehow amuses. In configurational theories, it is the "falling into place" or sudden "insight" that leads to amusement. The configurational theories either anticipate or reflect the broader theoretical model of Gestalt psychology.

The appreciation of a joke must be instantaneous regardless of how long it takes to prepare for that appreciation. A joke must be understood clearly and completely as opposed to dimly or in parts.

When material is presented, we start ordering it in a certain way. A humorous incident encourages a certain direction or point of view but concludes (that is, organizes the facts presented) differently than expected. The unexpected configuration is a surprise. What differentiates humor from other forms of thinking or reasoning is that the ridiculous is logical only within certain bounds, so we take it lightly. Maier summarizes his theory as follows:

> *The thought-configuration which makes for a humorous experience must (1) be unprepared for; (2) appear suddenly and bring with it a change in the meaning of its elements; (3) be made up of elements which are experienced entirely objectively . . .; (4) contain as its elements the facts appearing in the story, and these facts must be harmonized, explained and unified; and (5) have the characteristics of the ridiculous in that its harmony and logic apply only to its own elements.*

8- Psychoanalytic Theory

Freud presented his theory of humor in two publications which dealt primarily with the distinctions among "the comic," "wit," and "humor" and their processes.

Freud contended that the ludicrous always represents a saving in the expenditure of psychic energy. When energy built up for occupation in certain psychic channels (cathexis) is not or cannot be utilized (owing to the censoring action of the superego), it may be pleasurably discharged in laughter. (Thus Freud could be characterized as the most eminent of the release theorists.) The pleasure in the comic is due to economy in the expenditure of thought. The comic may be found in many situations, and some contrast or deceived expectation is involved. In wit, the pleasure derives from economy in the expenditure of inhibition. Wit can be "harmless" as in the enjoyment of nonsense or childishness, or it can express inhibited tendencies. Social restrictions (introjected in the form of the superego) do not permit the acting out of regressive infantile sexual and aggressive behavior in a direct manner. The wit is a camouflage which functions to deceive the superego temporarily as repressions are being suddenly released. In humor there is an economy in the expenditure of feeling. Humor turns an event that would otherwise cause suffering into less significance. Energy is displaced onto the superego, and the ego is thereby allowed to return to an infantile state. Freud elaborated this "triumph of narcissism" in his later (1928) paper. Humor "signifies the triumph not only of the ego, but also of the pleasure-principle, which is strong enough to assert itself here in the face of the adverse real circumstances."

2

The HEARTS Theory:
The Anatomy of Humor

Many articles on humor begin with E.B. White's famous observation: "Humor can be dissected, as a frog can, but the thing dies in the process."

But students of comedy writing, like medical students, must dissect in order to comprehend anatomy — and, therefore, they must kill.

One of the first things killed is the overall attitude that the primary purpose of humor is entertainment.

Our instinctive perception of humor is that it is fun, it is harmless and, therefore, it can be forgiven if used harmfully ("It was only a joke," immediately followed by "But seriously now . . .").

Some practitioners agree. James Sully: "Laughter is a refusal to take things seriously. It allows us to regress temporarily to an infantile state of mind." Bill Mauldin: "Humor is really laughing off a hurt, grinning at misery." Woody Allen: "There's something secondary about comedy. It teases a problem, it pokes fun at it, but it really never confronts it."

Allen is wrong, this time. Humor not only defines a problem, it cuts into it with a serrated edge, so razor sharp that no one sees the incision, just the blood. A string of one-liners is not a necklace of pearls but a crown of thorns, designed to scratch your head with sharp, prickly things. As Gregory wrote, "Laughter is a response to pain rather than pleasure." Humor is group therapy for performer, writer and audience. It reduces our anxiety and aggression, through an entertainment format. It attempts to get others to join our cause through laughter, thereby reassuring us that our hostility is acceptable and free from individual guilt.

Whether it be high comedy (satirical wit) or low comedy (slapstick), "humor is," as Louis Kronenberger once said, "criticism." Noel Coward went one step further, "Wit is social criticism and the object is to deflate."

To others, humor is anguish. Said Peter Prescott: "Most comedy is at least partly cruel, which is why we like it so much, and most comedy writers of intelligence have let some of their disenchantment with humanity color their work."

In comedy the words cruel and ridicule not only appear frequently, but appear to be closely associated. It is my feeling that the true spelling of ridicule, when used in a comedic format, should be spelled rid-a-cruel.

It is important to accept and comprehend this concept of the thrust of humor — to rid-a-cruel, to combat with mental agility, rather than physical agility, that which challenges and threatens to defeat us most often.

Freud said: "By bringing ridicule to bear on 'sacred' aspects normally immune from social criticism, humor is used as a weapon by the 'have nots' against the 'haves.'"

Mark Van Doren wrote, "Humorists are serious. They are the only people who are." And we must take humor seriously.

After years of study, I believe that there are six criteria — like ingredients in a recipe — that are essential for humor to be most effective. Whether the material is a four-word one-liner ("Take my wife — please!") or a lengthy anecdote or theatrical piece, these same six elements consistently appear and, with few exceptions, the absence of any one of them so disturbs the formula that the humor is not only less effective but in danger of complete failure.

In cognitive order, they are (1) hostility, (2) aggression, (3) realism, (4) tension, (5) exaggeration, and (6) surprise. When I first put these words together, for my students, the first letters spelled what appeared to be a name — HARTES. This encouraged me to coin an even more memorable acronym. I took a bit of dramatic license and changed the above order of importance, which is arguable in any case, and suggested that the acronym become HEARTS. It helped!

It permitted the students to easily remember the theory: when it came to my final exam, their *hearts* beat as one.

"H" - HOSTILITY

To a humorist, no quote is more laudatory than Horace Walpole's "The world is a comedy to those that think; a tragedy to those that feel." Mark Twain agreed, "The human race has only one effective weapon and that is laughter."

All of us have hostility toward some person, thing or idea — unless we are St. Francis of Assisi (or, as Robert Benchley once speculated, "unless I am getting him mixed up with St. Simeon Sylites, which might be easy to do since both their names begin with St.").

Humor is a powerful pesticide which helps eradicate many of the hostile feelings in our daily life: the most common are (1) sexual frustrations, (2) intrusion of authority into our private lives, (3) family problems, (4) financial concerns, (5) angst, (6) the seeming impossibility of controlling technology and our environment and, (7) finally, human characteristics or foibles which trigger our prejudices and taunts.

1. *Sex* Close to 50% of all humor is based upon sexual activity, and the reason seems to be that all of us, male and female, young or old, are more concerned with sexual adequacy than any other single subject, and perhaps all other subjects combined.

According to Alexandra Penney *(How to Make Love to a Man)* men's greatest sex fears are size, temporary impotence, erection, premature ejaculation, secret homosexuality and aging. Shere Hite *(The Hite Report on Male Sexuality)* reported that while men like and treasure sexuality, "they also dislike and feel very put upon by it." Her report suggests that many of the 7,239 men who participated in her study said that they felt trapped by sexual stereotypes and found themselves unable to talk openly about their sexual angers, anxieties and desires. Many complained about the escalating pressures to initiate sex, to achieve and maintain frequent erections, to control the timing of ejaculations and to understand, let alone to satisfy, their partner's orgasmic needs.

Woody Allen said: "I finally had an orgasm and my doctor told me it was the wrong kind."

Females, while much more in control of their bodies, share sexual fears far more than has been commonly supposed. Research on sexual humor indicated that student joke tellers were more likely to select jokes with sexist content discriminating against males regardless of the gender of the performer or the audience. And the most common subjects were those which denigrated bodily parts and sexual performance. It is, therefore, hostility against male sexual inadequacy, more than sexism against women, that appears to be the dominant theme of most sexual humor.

In addition, women seem intrigued by the open discussion of sexual activity because it was always considered, for them, a taboo subject.

Flugel said, "a subject who is sexually aroused but has no means of expressing this motivation will prefer humor material with sexual content."

> *Three young boys were reading magazines in a dentist's office. During a break, the dentist said to one, "I see you're reading* Popular Mechanics. *I guess you'd like to become an engineer?" The boy nodded. He said to the second, "I see you're reading* Country Gentleman. *I assume you'd like to be a farmer?" The second boy nodded. He turned to the third, who was reading* Playboy. *"Well, well, well," he said, "What would you like to become?" "I don't know for sure," answered the boy, "but I can hardly wait to get started."*

To cover their fear of homosexuality, many men use deviants from the sexual norm as their second most common target. Woody Allen wrote: "Bisexuality immediately doubles your chances for a date on Saturday night."

Sexual jokes, in particular, are enjoyed most readily among those of comparable age, sex and social status. It is difficult, perhaps unwise, for a professor to attempt sexual jokes in a classroom of young students. It is even more difficult, and definitely unwise, for parents to swap risque material with their children.

2. *Authority* Hostility against authority is international, but particularly an American heritage. Since Revolutionary days, we have enjoyed pricking the bloated arrogance of authority, intending to deflate it and hopefully to watch it bleed. As we become more nihilistic, less and less of an authoritative nature is beyond criticism: government, religion, motherhood, social graces and even respect for the handicapped and the aged.

"Authoritarianism in any form is inimical to humor," said Flugel. As a subject, it is second only to sex as the most common fodder for much of today's publically performed humor. "A humorist," said Alan Coren, "tells himself every morning, 'I hope it's going to be a rough day.' When things are going well, it's much harder to make the right jokes."

The humor that came out of Watergate was a result of the fury that comes when we discover that an elected official is a liar and a crook. Jackie Mason said: "Nixon was a crook who knew his business. Everytime he got caught, somebody else went to jail."

Matty Simmons, publisher of the *National Lampoon,* credits the anti-establishment climate of Vietnam and Watergate with the birth and success of his magazine. "Nixon and Agnew had as much to do with the *Lampoon's* success as I did," he said. "We came along when marvelous people for satire were running the country. They were just so unlikeable."

> *A couple were leaving a party at the White House. The woman said, "I'd like to say goodbye to the President." Her husband said, "Who wouldn't?"*

Next to government, we frequently feel hostility toward successful people. This is especially true of comedy writers. La Rochefoucauld: "It is not enough to have a success, your best friend must fail." It's the same today. Johnny Carson: "Comedians and comedy writers talk about friendship, but a lot of us would kill each other. There's something bizarre about guys who do comedy . . . they hate to see other comedians get laughs."

Celebrities such as Jacqueline Kennedy Onassis, Elizabeth Taylor, Nancy Reagan and especially Frank Sinatra are constant targets of hostile humor. When Sinatra was elected Abbot (president) of the Friars Club, Milton Berle said, "I wish that they had elected him Pope instead. Then I'd only have to kiss his ring."

And celebrities, in turn, direct their hostility through humor against other authoritative groups. Said Sinatra: "If I had as many love affairs as the press has given me credit for, I would now be speaking to you from a jar in the Harvard Medical School."

There's also a performer's hostility to his own audience. When a comedian comes on stage, they are his adversary. He feels threatened and outnumbered. Humor is his only weapon. Robert Orben wrote: "Some people suffer from stage fright. I don't. The stage doesn't frighten me. It's the audience that scares the hell out of me."

That's why comedians speak in such violent terms about the audience. When he does well and gets a big audience response, he may say out loud, "I love you," but what he is really thinking is "I killed them," or "I fractured them." Other similar hostile expressions are "I murdered them," "They died laughing." People say that when a funny line triggers a laugh, this comedy was "explosive," or that the comedian had a "rapid-fire repartee," "a rapier wit," that he was a "smash hit" and that he "laid them in the aisles," which is most uncomfortable.

There is a difference between hostility and hatred. Hate can rarely produce humor. Writers were not very successful about writing humor which mocked Hitler. They hated him too much. Max Beerbohm said, "Satire should be based on a qualified love for the original." I don't know if I'd go that far, but satire that is based upon hatred is seldom funny, seldom attractive.

Abe Burrows said the biggest compliment he ever got regarding his artistry was a critique in *Time Magazine,* which was reviewing the Broadway version of *How to Succeed in Business Without Really Trying,* and wrote, "Burrows could have poured vitriol on big business; instead, he painted a moustache on it."

3. *Family Affairs* It is probable that the first anti-family joke you ever heard was a version of "Who was that lady I saw you out with the other night. . .etc." Other versions have asked, "Who was that lady I saw you *out wit* last night, "to more hostile answers such as "That was no lady, that was your wife," or "that was your mother," or even "that was my brother, he just walks that way."

The hostility that is felt against the confinement, responsibilities and conflicts of family life needs no elaboration here. What is happening, however, is the growing expansion of family targets to include no longer just wives and mother-in-laws, but the grey-haired venerable mother, the revered father figure, and even little children who are no longer just cute, they're stupid!

Parents are unburdening themselves wittily, if they are not able to do it financially:

> *They once asked my father what he wanted me to do when I grew up, and he said, "Leave home!"*

And young people are expressing more hostile humor against their parents:

> *My father's car can go 90 miles an hour, and Dad has it in writing — from a highway patrolman.*

Henny Youngman can do two solid hours of jokes on his wife:

> *She said that for our anniversary she wanted to go somewhere she had never been before. I said, "How about the kitchen?"*

★ ★ ★

> *My parents had a meaningful relationship and stayed together for 40 years. Out of love? No, out of spite. (Woody Allen)*

And as the employment rate of married women continues to grow:

> *"Stick to your washing, ironing, scrubbing, sewing and cooking," the husband yelled at his wife; "no wife of mine is going to work."*

4. *Money* Closely allied with family problems, and frequently

the cause of them, is our concern with finances, employment, investment, inflation and the general economic condition of the country. They are a constant thorn of irritation, and rich or poor, none have total control over their financial well-being.

> *I have a serious investment problem.*
> *I don't have any money.*

Humor is a way to keep from killing yourself. And, when you can look at material discomforts, as compared to health, with a funny slant, it helps to remove your mental anxiety. If you are a good humor writer, it might even alleviate your financial anxieties as well. Said Joe E. Lewis: "I've been rich and I've been poor. Believe me, rich is better."

This thesis is so well documented that it might be far more important to concentrate here on the method which humorists use to best accommodate this universal hostility. William Zinsser wrote that the function of the humorist is to represent himself as the victim or the dunce, enabling the audience to feel superior or, at least, to identify with a fellow victim. A recitation of your financial problems is unwelcome unless there is particular interest, like from your heirs:

> *"Being of sound mind," it was written in the will, "I spent every cent before I died."*

There's an old Confucius-type proverb which predicts that no one is going to give you much sympathy when you tell them your problems. Fifty percent of your friends don't care and the other fifty percent are glad you're getting what you deserve.

It is necessary, therefore, to identify with your audience's problems, to share their concerns about coping and to personalize your solutions and bizarre schemes. While this is equally true of humor on practically any subject, money has a wider age and sex interest than do such subjects as sex, family, fear of death, and the battle to control technology.

It is tempting to yell, "Good!" when Henny Youngman whines: "I've got all the money I'll ever need — if I die by four o'clock."

Much more effective, as a textbook example of humor involving your audience with this common hostility, is Peter Passell's observation: "There is a way to make money in the stock market. Unfortunately for most of us, it is the same way to lose a lot of money in the stock market."

> *As you all know, our firm's accounting department has a little red box on the wall with a sign saying "In case of emergency, break glass." Inside are two tickets to Brazil.*

5. *Angst* There is a growing acceptability of a nihilistic use of comedy, where nothing is so sacrosanct as to be beyond criticism. This has encouraged a dramatic increase in humor directed against anxieties so personal that, in the past, we carefully avoided discussing them even in private: the fear of death, coping with deforming health problems, deprivations, analytical interpretations of symptoms resulting from paranoia, rejection, narcissism, and a long list of psychotic neuroses.

A famous philosopher once said, "The best thing that could happen to a person is not to have been born at all. But, unfortunately, this happens to very few."

Angst is clearly an intellectual observation and its devotees found their mascot in the person of Woody Allen, whose understated humor is simply a way of looking at life through Woody Allen's glasses: "I merchandise misery. When I named my movie *Love and Death* the commercial possibilities were immediately apparent to me: sight gags and slapstick sequences about despair and emptiness, dialogue jokes about anguish and dread, finally, mortality, human suffering, anxiety. In short, the standard ploys of the funnyman."

> *A woman suddenly gets off a psychiatrist's couch with a gun in her hand, turns to the analyst and says, "And now you know too much!"*

In this category, our biggest dread is death — postponing it, understanding its inevitability, and rationalizing its effect on ourselves and our loved ones. Humor, once again, seems to be an effective intellectual weapon. It is certainly Woody Allen's. He once wrote: "I'm obsessed with sex and death. Everybody is. That's what people are usually talking about, even if the conversation seems to be about something else. . . . I don't believe in the after life, but I am bringing a change of underwear."

Nobody, it seems wants to live to be 100 — that is until they're 99. Humorists have written as many stories about the way to achieve longevity as they have on how to achieve orgasm.

> *"The way to live as long as I have," the old man said on his 100th birthday, "is to never smoke, drink liquor, fool around with women and be sure to get up at six every morning. I had a brother who did the same thing but he only lived to be eighty. He just didn't keep at it long enough."*

6. *Technology* Among the early humorists to fully exploit the universal hostility against machines and our inability to control, let

alone understand, rapidly growing technology, were Charlie Chaplin, Harold Lloyd and a handful of early film makers. Chaplin's *Modern Times* film featured assembly line schedules, Rube Goldberg appliances, the explosion of chemical substances, the race of car against the locomotive, the exasperation of keeping heavy machinery under control, and dozens of other comedy shticks still seen today.

It's not just machinery, but chemicals that lead to pollution, drugs that lead to suicide, advertising that leads to nonsensical fads, and more recently, the fear of nuclear war, of an invasion of spooks from outer space and attempted laboratory mutation of our body and mind.

The possibilities of a nuclear catastrophe grow daily. Here's a Cheech and Chong version:

> *"I like Pres. Reagan. He takes time off. I wouldn't trust a guy who worked 20 hours a day, not when his hand is right next to that little red button. I mean a month of hassles, 20 hours a day, comes home, wife won't fuck him, — boom — , nuclear war!"*

Humor, in any form, is an attempt to lessen the frustrations of the problem. Ogden Nash once wrote about his poetry: "My verse represents a handle I can grasp in order not to yield to the centrifugal forces which are trying to throw me off the world."

They asked astronaut John Glenn what he thought about just before his first capsule was shot off into space, and he said, "I looked around me and suddenly realized that everything had been built by the lowest bidder."

The need to constantly be updated becomes frustrating as new machines soon make obsolete those which we have only recently learned to control: home computers replace typewriters, radar ranges replace electric ovens, electronic synthesizers replace pianos, and video tapes replace live lectures. Even automobiles continue to add on new electronic gadgets while the most important gadget — the nut behind the wheel — remains as volatile as ever. As George Segal claimed: "New York is a city where there is no room for amateurs, even in crossing the street."

Television, its use and misuse, is a never ending subject. Said Clive Barnes: "TV is the first truly democratic culture — available to everyone and entirely governed by what the people want. The terrifying thing, unfortunately, is what the people want."

7. *Human Characteristics* Here is one of humor's most controversial subjects because it caters to our most primitive instincts — prejudice and fear. We hope to maintain some sense of superiority by ridiculing other's characteristics which appear — to the majority in that place and at that time — abnormal. Freud wrote: "A good bit of

humor is oriented to maintaining the status quo by ridiculing deviant social behavior and reassures the majority member that his way of life is proper and free from ridicule."

We fear control and intimidation by groups of different color or religion and so, by derision, we attempt to stereotype their physical appearances, their mannerisms, their colloquial speech, their hypocritical social attitudes — any abnormality to the accepted norm which offers a possible target for criticism.

As Victor Borge said: "I think that everybody is entitled to my opinion."

And so we are quick to point out the grotesque, those features which are easily understandable, obvious to eye or sound, and unacceptable to "our crowd."

These characteristics need not be permanent, as we tease the man with a broken leg in a cast. They need not be "in good taste," as we ridicule the handicapped: "Hire the handicapped. They're fun to watch." They need not be necessarily "inferior," as we scorn the blacks "who've got rhythm." We focus on abnormal size, feeble eyesight and hearing, mental and physical ineptitude, personal fetishes, over-indulgence, pomposity in fashion and manners, differences in nationality, personal hygiene, use of drugs, preferences in music, literature, education and profession, and hundreds of other characteristics in addition to those previously discussed: sex, psychological anxieties, family affairs and fear of authority.

We conduct these sins, in the name of humor, without conscience. As Harry Hershfield said: "A conscience cannot prevent sin. It only prevents you from enjoying it."

We attempt not only individual release from tensions, but also group therapy, since the humorist must perform his material for audiences which share the same conditioned logic. It is also the source of all impersonations.

Cheech and Chong, whose financial successes have outstripped every other comedy team in film history, concentrate on grass jokes:

> "Our jokes may be 50 years old, but our audience, the youth, ain't seen shit. To them, it's brand new. If you're white you can be afraid of people of different color, religious fanatics, but if you're black or brown, you're afraid of other things, like starvation and not having a place to live. By incorporating the basic humor of drugs and poverty into our appeal, it makes it universal — the underdogs against the world. We know the humor of these rough and ready . . . we pander to the worst instincts in people — caricaturing swishy gays, dumb blondes, illiterate Mexicans, greedy Jews. We're shameless panderers. We give them hope. Nobody ever put a gun to a guy's head and said, 'You gotta go down and see a Cheech and Chong

movie, or else.' Our fans must have two qualities: a sense of humor and five dollars."

It used to be mainly the whites who regurgitated the most hostile humor. Today, it's the blacks, sensing both an ever-widening standard of freedom for acceptable humor and an ever-widening, more affluent public of both blacks and whites. In other words, it is also commercially profitable to "kick'em in the ass."

Redd Foxx, for example, tries to be as outrageous as possible by, admittedly, being dirty, vulgar, low and nasty: "That's the humor I hear in the ghettos. They don't pull punches, and they don't want to hear about Little Boy Blue and Cinderella. . . . And if you don't like my shit, then fuck off!"

A common urban folk tale, which often crops up in various renditions, not only ridicules racial stereotyping and urban paranoia, but is told by whites as a way of offering relief from all the talk of racial crime:

> *Four doctors' wives from a small midwestern city decided to brave the streets of Manhattan for a shopping trip. Their husbands were apprehensive about crime. "If someone wants your pocketbook or jewelry, don't put up a fight. Do what they ask." As they descended in the hotel elevator on their very first morning, a well-dressed black man got on leading a large Doberman pinscher. He looked at the women only a moment, then commanded the dog, "Sit!" Immediately all four women sat on the floor.*

"Impropriety is the soul of wit," wrote W. Somerset Maugham. He should have added . . . so is hostility. When we all think alike there will be a lot less humor.

"A" - AGGRESSION

Hostility is the impetus for aggression. In humor, we use aggressive elements in order to degrade vexations beyond our immediate control.

For example, you do not attack a sacred cow with a bulldozer. You just sting her on the rump, then back off and watch her dance, and then sting her again. Nor can we sting every raging bull in the herd. There seem to be too many of them and, if anything, the raging ones are increasing in number.

Anything that goes wrong makes a good subject for humor. Aggression means vitriolic. For example, as we become more affluent we purchase more goods, which increases our anxieties four-fold (1) by trying to decide whether to buy the product, (2) by trying to decide which brand or style to buy, (3) by trying to decide how to allocate limited funds (and frequently we compound even that problem by agreeing to a costly, long-term installment plan), and (4) by enduring the additional cost and aggravation which results when the product breaks down . . . as they all do.

"Humor is a reduction of anxiety and aggression," wrote Flugel. "Laughter is a temporary relief." By adding aggressiveness to humor, we put the sting into our anger and frustration. It directs our shaft toward the most immediate, the most common, and perhaps the safest target we can find.

For example, as parents we are frequently annoyed by some of the expensive, time consuming, unproductive habits of our children. Threats and anger get only short-term results and very little appreciation from our children or sincere respect from our peers. We retaliate by telling friends (who should also be parents in order to get maximum response) that "the best way parents can assist in the education of our children is by pulling a few wires — television, telephone, radio and ignition." Hopefully, through humor, we make serious points in a memorable — not necessarily malicious — way while achieving, for ourselves, appreciative laughter. Mendelssohn wrote: "At an entertainment audience climate, laughter from the group assures the individual that his experience is being shared and he can enjoy a wide variety of tabooed phenomena without feelings of shame or punishment. That is why humor, wit and comedy are the keystone of mass entertainment."

"A laugh," says Abe Burrows, "is one of the most profound things that can happen to a human being. When you make a man laugh, you have evidently hit him right where he lives — deep. You've done something universal. You've moved him in an area that he probably didn't dare even think about and he laughs explosively."

All humor, with minor exceptions, contains aggressive elements and the more aggressive it is, the more effective it is. Slapstick is acted-out aggression.

> *If you asked me which three books most helped my daughter through life, I would have to say (1) the Bible, (2) her mother's cookbook and (3) her father's checkbook.*
>
> ★ ★ ★
>
> *As a child he was always taking things apart. His parents thought he'd grow up to be a mechanic . . . but instead he grew up to be a critic.*

Charlie Chaplin used primitive, unmotivated aggression — like pulling other men's beards and blowing into their bowls of soup — which are things we would like to do, but dare not.

Abe Burrows noted: "A good writer of comedy is as serious as anyone else. Comedy is his way of looking at things. Some kids throw rocks. He makes jokes. James Reston sits down and writes a profound, serious analysis of a particular world problem. Art Buchwald looks at exactly the same thing, thinks the same way about it as Reston does, has the same opinions, yet Buchwald cloaks his opinions in comedy. That's his way of coping."

> *This politician knew you can't fool all the people all the time, he just wanted a sizeable majority.*
>
> ★ ★ ★
>
> *I'm happy to announce that this year's ladies' auxiliary bake sale netted a profit exceeding that of Lockheed, Chrysler and International Harvester combined.*

By being aggressive against yourself, called self-deprecating humor, you can defuse your critics before they can get started. As noted previously, President Reagan was the first to joke about his age. By the time others tried to do it, it was old news.

Just as Woody Allen uses angst for his humor format and Rodney Dangerfield uses man's inability to cope with the world, so Don Rickles and other merchants of venom use aggression as their springboard. His stand-up put-down antics slice precariously between the rude and the crude. Wrote Tom Buckley of *The New York Times:* "Rulers have always had jesters to provide a kind of psychic vaccination against the overdoses of sycophancy to which they are inevitably exposed. In show business, the comic insult goes back to Aristophanes, but it doesn't always work, as Shakespeare's Lear, who had a biting Rickles sort of fool, discovered."

Rickles, who looks like a mean, snapping turtle, is at his raging best when he uses aggression to attack authority figures: (Frank Sinatra) — "Come right in Frankie. Make yourself at home. Hit somebody." (Dean Martin) — "You're Italian, right? What in the hell do we need Italians for? Oh, yeah, to keep the cops busy." (Sammy Davis) — "you should be proud of your race. A great Negro, Emerson Johnson Jones, once said in Mobile, Alabama, 'All aboarrrrd!'"

Each member of the audience will suffer gladly the maligning of others and, sometimes, even when this karate chop humor focuses on them. At least, it's a way of getting attention.

Aggression is helping a new greeting card company, Anonymously Yours, Inc., become a success. It publishes nasty greeting cards that permit the anonymous sender to throw a caustic barb rather than a broken beer bottle at a designated recipient. Some are funny, some are bitter and some just say, "Dear Boss. Drop Dead."

To feel mentally superior, we can work hard to improve our own intelligence or we can work at ridiculing others. For those who feel this need, it seems easier, or more convenient, to attack the intelligence of some group, like the Poles. And each group has their own arsenal of ethnic humor which ridicules others and is approved, through laughter, by those who share this insecurity. Each group has a favorite target — one color attacks the other, one religion disparages a second, the people in Ohio tell jokes about the good people of West Virginia, who tell tales about the hillbillies of Kentucky. Whom do the Poles joke about? — the citizens of Finland!

"R" - REALISM

"Most good jokes state a bitter truth," said Larry Gelbart.

The inclusion of realism into the humor formula is the most universally accepted and the easiest to understand. Without some fundamental basis of truth there is little with which the audience can associate.

The basic ingredients of a two-line joke are (1) to state some commonly acceptable statement such as a cliché, and then, (2) in the last word or two, change the expected ending to a surprise.

> What a lucky guy. He's got everything. A home, a family and a private parking space.

Now, if we add realism to a common hostility, plus the surprise ending, we get:

> People who lose sleep over the stock market are lucky. I lose money.

Then, there's Abe Burrow's version of the first two lines of Irving Berlin's song, "There's No Business Like Show Business."

> "Yesterday they told you, you would not go far. Last night you opened, and they were right!"

The incongruity theory, discussed previously, bases its premise on two or more realistic but contrasting circumstances united into one thought. Leacock wrote, "Humor results from the contrast between a thing as it is or *ought to be*, and a thing smashed out of shape, as it ought not to be." And Jack Kroll wrote, "Laughter is an orgasm triggered by the intercourse of reason with unreason."

> A baby polar bear, standing on an iceberg along side of mother polar bear, turns to her dejectedly and says, "I don't care what they say, I'm cold!"

Another variation is to state a truth as a basis of illogical comparison:

> *If you think the world is normal, then how come hot dogs come in packages of ten and hot-dog buns come in packages of eight?*

★ ★ ★

> *We shouldn't criticize potholes. They're among the few things left on the road that are still being made in the U.S.A.*

A truism, a self-evident, generally accepted attitude, is frequently written into witty bits of philosophy:

> *What can you expect from a day that begins with getting up in the morning?*

★ ★ ★

> *To entertain some people, all you have to do is listen. But nothing is quite so annoying as to have someone go right on talking when you're interrupting.*

The humor of children, frequently a combination of truth and simplistic naivete, delights us primarily because it gives us a feeling of superiority.

> *A 5-year-old was fascinated by his grandfather's false teeth. He watched as gramps removed his dentures, washed them and replaced them. He asked to see it done over and over. "Okay," said the grandfather, finally, "Anything else?" "Yeah," said the kid, "now take off your nose."*

★ ★ ★

> *A woman and her teen-age daughter were watching an old Clark Gable-Claudette Colbert movie on tv, which ended with the usual clinch and fade-out. "Gee, mom," said the daughter, "your movies end where ours just begin."*

To be most effective, the "facts" of the humor should be logical — the relationship between people clear and predictable, the time and the locale of the story, if applicable, reasonable, the hostility common to the audience and the aggression commensurate to the irritation. In essence, then, it should be as realistic as possible.

> The Prime Minister of Russia (insert real name) asked a soldier in Afghanistan, "How's everything." The soldier said, "I can't complain," and the Prime Minister answered, "You bet your life you can't!"

Major deviations from realism do not prevent humor, they only reduce a cognitive appreciation and — the payoff! — uninhibited laughter. By the way, applause is money, too!

There are many skeptics who can quickly find a selection of humor which has no realism. Despite these exceptions, humor is continually more appreciated when believable. As Dorothy Parker once wrote: "The difference between wit and wisecracking is that wit has truth to it, while wisecracking is simply calisthenics with words."

"E" - EXAGGERATION

It could be argued that exaggeration is the antithesis of realism, that it is ludicrous to have both within the framework of one piece of humor. But good humor is a paradox, the juxtaposition of putting the reasonable next to the unreasonable. The opening premise is frequently a factually honest statement. The wit comes from a second thought that is an audacious absurdity.

> The only way I'll ever be as trim as Robert Redford is if Robert Redford swallows a steel-belted radial tire.

We have often heard the expression "poetic license," the "permission" granted by this public to poets and lyricists to use words of soaring imagination and unabashed metaphors. Without such a linguistic license, humorists, too, are encouraged to use overstated or understated facts and figures, absurd hyperbole and blatant distortions. Nothing is impossible in comedy:

> See this watch. This is an absolutely fantastic, very fine, elegant gold watch, which speaks of breeding and was sold to me by my grandfather on his deathbed. My grandfather had a wonderful funeral . . . It was a catered funeral, with accordion players and a buffet table, and there was a replica of the deceased in potato salad. (Woody Allen)

The audience, in accepting humor, conveys its "willingness to suspend disbelief." This is not a double negative. When we are told a story by a colleague, even one highly respected, our instincts are to "believe it when we see it," i.e., to disbelieve it. In humor, however, we willingly give up normal skepticism for abnormal concepts.

> *It is written that he who has the best recipe for egg salad shall rule over heaven and earth. (Woody Allen)*

We understand that there will be exaggeration and we are willing to suspend our disbelief in order to enjoy the fabrication. It is this element which causes critics to classify humor as second-class art — and only one humorist has ever won a Pulitzer Prize. "How," critics ask, "can anything so obviously distorted be of value?"

> *Have you noticed how all the congressional candidates want to blow the whistle on government spending? This country could go broke just buying whistles.*

★ ★ ★

> *We always hang our jack-o-lantern on the front porch, and every year at Halloween the big kids run up and smash it with their fists. So this year, I painted my bowling ball orange . . .*

★ ★ ★

> *And speaking of pumpkins, here's Dolly Parton.*

Exaggeration may come in one of two styles: (1) overstatement or (2) understatement. Woody Allen, who is a master of non-sequitors, uses both of these techniques in one gulp: "For this the Rabbi bashes his head in, which, according to the Torah, is one of the most subtle methods of showing concern."

According to William Zinsser, who taught a class on humor writing at Yale, the limitation of exaggeration is a problem. He recommends that it is better to achieve control — "cutting the extra sentence, for instance, which explains a funny point that is already implicit. It is a hard decision to know how much exaggeration is allowable. It is better to let the humor sneak up."

There are those who feel that exaggeration or overdramatization derives from the performer's attempt to call attention to his story and, thereby, himself. In a study of famous comedians by psychologists Rhoda and Seymour Fisher, the subjects were generally similar in having a troubled adolescence. Most of them were treated inappropriately by parents, especially non-nurturing mothers, who expected too much of their children both psychologically and materially. Their defense was to fight back by painting the whole world as absurd and ridiculous, dedicating themselves to spreading enough chaos so that nothing real can be expected of them.

One way to get immediate acceptance was by creating stories with humorous statements magnified for greater impact. It was then an easier step to move to humor writing and performing, where the successful ones found they could get paid handsomely for being "bathed in love." That's why performers' lives are so up and down. It is a tremendous psychological letdown when they have to go back to their room alone, and so a comedian's claque accompanies him everywhere.

"T" - TENSION

There are many who believe that the release of hostility, anxiety and tension is humor's most valuable asset. Wrote Eric Idle: "Humor puts everything into perspective through satire. It's supposed to take the tension off all unbelievable reality by pointing out how absurd everything is and inviting people to laugh. The measure of freedom in a country is how much comedy they allow."

Freud believed that the paradoxes or conflicts expressed by a joke built up a tension that was instantly relieved by involuntary laughter when the punch line came. Some recent studies indicate that the punchline does not immediately deflate the tension but maintains it for even half a minute longer. Laughter, it seems, does not stop us from thinking about the solution. Some prefer it that way. William Davis once wrote: "The kind of humor I like is the thing that makes me laugh for five seconds and think about for five minutes."

Being successful in the stock market requires two wise decisions: when to buy in and when to sell out. Being successful in humor writing also requires two major decisions: what subject or problem will create the most tension for any specific audience and what clever turn of phrase will puncture that tension and release laughter, not hot air. Gregory said, "Laughter is a response to pain rather than pleasure." It is understandable why a playwrite builds tension into a scene. A humor writer does the same thing, but because a joke is the smallest unit of comedy writing, he must be able to complete the assignment in a few words.

One of the worst ways to build tension is to announce to your audience, "I've got a very funny story to tell you." Invariably, some heckler will shout back, "Just tell us a story. We'll decide if it's funny."

Start the tension by framing the humor with a common and pressing hostility. You can hit the bullseye by making the joke as realistic as possible, using real names known personally to all members of the audience. If that is not wise, you might use celebrity names and localize the rest of it.

> *I just saw a commercial on Dan Rather's news which claims you can send a letter from (our town) to Washington for $7.50 that promises next day delivery. The Post Office calls it Express Mail. I remember when it used to cost 3¢ and was called U.S. Mail.*

The opening sentence of your joke is second in importance only to the last few words. The "set-up" must be carefully constructed to establish the conflict as quickly as possible. At best, it may be from one to five words:

> *Don't knock the rich. When was the last time you were hired by somebody poor.*

> ★ ★ ★

> *Yesterday was so hot a dog was chasing a cat — and they were both walking.*

At the most, it's a short sentence or two:

> *They say our kids don't know the value of a dollar. They certainly do. That's why they ask us for five.*

A common technique used by beginning stand-up comics to infuse tension is to ask the audience, "How many here have ever. . .?" I am not sure why so many continue to do this so often. Perhaps, originally, it was a clever method for bringing an audience into your frame, but now it is so overdone, the take-offs are more fun:

> *How many here went to grade school?*

> ★ ★ ★

> *How many here paid to get in?*

> ★ ★ ★

> *How many here know what sex is?*

There are better techniques. For example, there is something mystical about the number three. It appears often in a joke:

> *OUTLAW: "If we're goin' have a shootout, Sheriff, let's make it fair. When I count three, you turn and fire . . . O.K.? . . . One! . . . two!" (bang!)*
> *DYING SHERIFF: "Hey, I thought you said fire on three."*
> *OUTLAW: "That was your number. My number was two."*

There is also the "triple," a series of three examples or three alternative solutions which are offered consecutively in anecdotes, such as the familiar minister, priest and rabbi stories.

In guidelines for joke construction, three is the number most often recommended: no less than three examples in a story, no more than three stories on any one subject in a sequence, and no more than three minutes on any one major theme. To sustain a "roll," you must build one "topper" on another — with a minimum of three.

> *I teach a class in public relations. Last quarter's college bulletin had a misprint. It came out as* pubic *relations. (pause) . . . The registration was one thousand, five hundred. (pause) . . . and those were only faculty wives.*

Triples can have numerous forms. Here's the most common — three examples and a surprise ending:

> *"You're a lowdown, worthless, ignorant skunk." "Well, nobody's perfect!"*
>
> ★ ★ ★
>
> *My wife's family consisted of three brothers and a dog: Tom, Dick, Harry and Rover. Harry was the dog.*
>
> ★ ★ ★
>
> *I had everything — money, a beautiful apartment, and a sexy, wealthy woman. Then, bang, one morning my wife walked in.*

Here's an example of how the old joke ("My wife is an angel." "Gee," said the friend, "you're lucky. Mine is still alive!") might be done as a triple:

> *My wife's an angel. She's constantly up in the air, continually harping on something and never has a thing to wear.*

The triple can be built up with several adjectives in the series:

> *The bride turned to the marriage broker and said, "Your prospect is old and ugly, his eyes squint and are cross-eyed, and he has bleeding gums and no teeth." The broker replied, "You don't need to whisper. He's deaf, too!"*

The triple is a guideline on how to provide tension, not an unbreakable rule. Sometimes it is necessary to extend it to make a more emphatic impression. Neil Simon wrote this about Goldie Hawn: "She's funny, sexy, beautiful, talented, intelligent, warm and consistently sunny. Outside of that, she doesn't impress me very much."

Woody Allen is another who extends the series, but it is still the same technique:

> *Illicit activities engaged in by the Cosa Nostra included gambling, narcotics, prostitution, hijacking and the transportation of a large whitefish across state lines for immoral purposes.*

The triple can also be the climax of the story:

> *A little, old couple came to a sex therapist's office. "We wish you could watch us make love," said the elderly man, "and give us any advice on how we can improve." "Of course," said the doctor. "Go into the next room. I have a one-way mirror and this way I can observe without disturbing you." After a half hour, the couple came back to the doctor's office. "You were terrific," the doctor said. "You certainly need no improvement. If anything, I'm envious of your enthusiasm and hope I'll have the same vitality when I'm your age." The couple paid him and left.*
> *A week later, they were back. "Could you watch us again?" the little old man asked. "Look," said the doctor, "you don't need my advice. Now, come on, tell me the truth. Why are you coming to see me?" "Well," said the old man. "There are three reasons: first, we're not married, so we can't go to each other's home, second, your fee is less than a motel, and third, we get the cost back thru Medicare."*

To maintain tension, you must keep building the story toward its resolution. Never slow it down. One simple error many amateurs make in telling a story is to split a quoted phrase, which is acceptable in literature, but artificial in verbal humor:

> Wrong
> *"Well then," I said, "You should be very happy about your promotion. . . ."*

> Right
> *I said, "Well, then, you should be very happy about your promotion. . . .*

Another way to build tension is the improvisational technique. There are any number of variations. One is called "working the audience," used by Don Rickles and his protege, Pudgy. Each walks out into the audience and insults what appears to be randomly selected members. Steve Allen is famous for his "questions from the audience" interviews, which are — of course — very carefully plotted.

There is no such thing from a professional as an "ad lib"; it's just instantaneous recall.

Similar is the interview perfected by Mel Brooks and Carl Reiner in their "2,000 Year Old Man" album. Reiner acted as a reporter questioning Brooks, playing an old man who claimed to be a first hand observer of history over the past 2,000 years. The performance seemed so extemporaneous, the tension was contagious. Brooks loved it. He claims the best time for humor is the first time it's performed. "There's something in the voice, the excitement, the fighting for your life when somebody challenges you." Reiner claimed that he always tried to ask Brooks outlandish questions that would force him into a panic "because a brilliant mind in panic is a wonderful thing to see."

"S" - SURPRISE

If laughter is the electricity that makes a comedy writer's blood start pumping, then surprise is the power generator.

It is the most common element in the anatomy of comedy. Without it, clever, pithy remarks may be audacious commentary, but they are not comedy. Some writers consider surprise an absolute "must." "We only laugh because we are surprised," wrote Garson Kanin. Agnes Repplier agreed: "The essence of humor is that it should be unexpected, that is, should embody an element of surprise that should startle us out of that reasonable gravity which, after all, must be our habitual frame of mind."

According to Abe Burrows, the best way to define the construction of surprise in humor is to use baseball terms: a joke is a curve — the ball starts out to the plate and then bends at the last instant and fools the batter. You throw a perfectly straight line at the audience, and then right at the end, you curve it. Good jokes do that.

· *He may not be able to sing, but he sure can't dance.*

Charlie Chaplin defined surprise in terms of a film scene: the villain is walking down the street, on the sidewalk is a banana peel. The scene cuts swiftly back and forth from the banana peel to the approaching "fall guy." At the last second, the heavy sees the banana peel and jumps over it — and falls into an open manhole.

It is easy to tell if your surprise works, because laughter is instant judgement — the most honest emotions. It's hard to fake. You can give a bad speech or perform a bad play and the audience will still applaud — if only politely. But if you perform bad humor, the jury's icy silence is its death verdict.

No matter how it's written, some jokes do not come off in performance because the comedian gets too anxious and telegraphs the surprise.

Many performers, on the way to a funny line, tip it off. They lick their lips, their eyes gleam, they hold up their hand and stop the audience from laughing all out at a previous line — so the audience is primed for that big topper. But then there's no surprise and so there's little laughter. This has a domino reaction: the performer starts to lose confidence in the material. He starts to press and then he loses other laughs, because the audience has a sixth sense about "flop sweat," which you can feel when a performer is anxious and trying too hard.

Surprise comes in two packages; the first clearly lays out the resolution for the audience:

> *She was a widow, and he had recently lost his wife. They hadn't seen each other in 35 years since they were graduated from high school, where they had known each other casually. Now, at their high school reunion, they renewed their acquaintance and, as they chatted, discovered that they had a lot in common. They detested each other.*

The second, encourages the audience to use their own imagination to complete the thought:

> *The three best things in life are a shower before and a nap afterward.*

Audiences like the second style from time to time because it compliments their own intellectual stature, but they do not like it all the time. They just do not like to work hard continuously.

In addition, it is easy to bomb if the performer has misjudged the sophistication of the audience. An ending which takes even two seconds to decipher may discourage those who have gotten the point immediately from laughing too loudly. Laughter is a social exercise and you are encouraged to laugh when you hear others laughing. He who laughs last may be too stupid to get the joke first, but because of his shallowness, he is probably the one who laughs the loudest. They say you should never trust a man who laughs too loudly. Well, we may not want to do business with him, but we certainly want him in the audience.

For some reason, surprise seems to be the hardest component of humor for students to put into practice. "Yes," they say convincingly, "of course we understand it. It's so obvious." Then, you search their assignments and are hard pressed to fine it.

"Where's the joke?" I ask. "There's no surprise ending. Yes, the situation has comedic possibilities, but you didn't carry it through." Their most frequent answer: "Oh, the audience will get it!"

I attribute their attitude to abysmal communication skills which permit our younger generation to grunt instead of trying to speak in complete sentences: "Well, you know . . ." "that's the way it is, man!", "Oh-wow," "O.K. O.K." "Yah, you know what I mean," "Hey, that's cool," "Alll right!", and "Well, it's like. . . ."

Too many youths today are unwilling to take responsible action, let alone engage in responsible conversation:

> *"I don't know why I have to send Grandpa a thank you note whenever he sends me money," the teenager said. "Isn't his cancelled check a good enough receipt?"*

Coming up with a surprise ending to a story or joke takes a good deal of thought, trial and error testing and, finally, rewriting — the toughest part of humor writing.

Here's an example. You're writing for an audience of retired men about the crowded conditions on their beach. Your first attempt is a straight line:

> *The beach was so crowded everyone was on top of each other.*

That's sexy, perhaps, but not for the geriatrics, who think that sex is sensational — especially the one in the winter. So you try another version:

> *Everyone on the beach was so close that the sun could only tan their heads.*

Not yet funny. Try again.

> *The beach was so crowded the rays of the sun only reached the baldheaded men.*

Close, but let's work on the wording now and put a lot more surprise into it:

> *The beach was so crowded the only ones who got sunburned were the baldheaded men.*

That's for the old folks, but for the youth market, the joke has to be dramatically changed:

> *The beach was so crowded that the only thing higher than the pile of bodies was the grass.*

Let's try an example of surprise ending for different audiences. Which ending would you select?

> *(1) He was complimented when the professor called his work sophomoric because he had flunked out of college in his freshman year, or*
> *(2) He had flunked out of college in his freshman year, so he was complimented when I called his work sophomoric.*

The next question is who best tells this joke?: a professor (A) to an audience of students, (B) to an audience of other professors, (C) to an audience of parents and adults, or (D) written in the first person and told by one student to an audience of other students. The right selection would be 2-D: it keeps the punchword "sophomoric" until the very end, and permits the audience to feel superior to the performer playing a "drip" student.

CONCLUSION

Dismembering the works of a joke is like taking a watch apart. It must be done skillfully. Now, let's take apart the following contemporary story and see how the HEARTS theory works:

> *An elderly truck driver was eating his lunch at a roadside diner when three shaggy young men, sporting black leather jackets garishly decorated with swastikas and skulls, parked their motorcycles and came inside. They spotted the truck driver and proceeded to take his food away, they pushed him, insulted him and laughed at his venerability. He said nothing but finally got up, paid his bill and walked out.*
> *One of the cyclists, unhappy that they hadn't provoked a fight, said to the waitress, "Boy, he sure wasn't much of a man, was he?" "Well," replied the waitress, as the truck pulled away, "he's not much of a truck driver either. He just backed over three motorcycles!"*

Hostility: The story obviously takes into account the public anger against the escalating growth of juvenile crime. Note the careful description of the youths — "black leather jackets garishly decorated with swastikas and skulls" — intended to create specific hostility. The truck driver is purposely not macho, but "elderly" and "venerable."

Aggression: The young hoodlums are actively aggressive, taking food, pushing and laughing. This kind of aggression calls for counter-aggression. Since we're law-abiding citizens and too frightened to get personally involved, we'd like to see somebody else "give it to them."

Realism: The main story could happen; the characters, including the elderly truck driver, the smart-alec waitress and the tyranny of the three black-jacketed hoods, are all logical.

Exaggeration: The ending of the story is just too good to be true!

Tension: There's plenty of it here, growing with intensity with each sentence. We care, so we get deeply involved.

Surprise: A glorious ending. Without it, it wouldn't be a comedy, it would be a tragedy.

At the beginning of the chapter, we wrote that the HEARTS elements appear in practically all humor, even in Henny Youngman's four-word classic: "Take my wife, please!" Let's see:

Hostility: You should know by now how common Henny's anger is at the confinements of marriage.

Aggression: All wrapped up in the word "take."

Realism: Using your wife as an example of some action is very acceptable.

Exaggeration: Suggesting that somebody, anybody "take" his wife is a perfect example of a double entendre.

Tension: Not much time for it, but it's there, particularly in the pause between "wife" and "please."

Surprise: The word "please" is the bellringer. Changes the whole meaning of the sentence and suddenly focuses on the hostility and aggressiveness of the problem.

Because America has become more self-conscious and educated, humor writers must have an unprecedented literacy. Our humor has become more verbal and less physical, and, because conditions are changing so rapidly, a humor writer must be uncannily in touch with the things that are on the minds of a vast majority of his contemporaries. Civilized wit is rare.

The HEARTS theory is the skeleton of the body of humor. What we need to examine now is the techniques necessary to put meat and finally smooth skin on our creations.

3

Sick Humor and the Function of Comedy

by Jesse Bier

Condensed From *The Humanist*

The scene is the stage of a vaudeville house. Suddenly one of the performers turns toward the audience. "Is there a doctor in the house?" In the sudden hushed significance of the moment, some medical eminence identifies himself, whereupon the comedian shouts back, "Hiya Doc, how do you like the show?"

Analyzing this hoary example of humor is the deadliest thing to do, but in this case we may be exhuming rather than killing something.

In the quick perfunctory nonchalance of the "Hiya Doc" retort, more is involved, critically, than a shift of mood, surprise or the mere incongruity of the situation, or, in America particularly, the contrast and triumph of colloquial style. All these things are true.

But they are, of themselves, insufficient. I believe that the basic thing that occurs is an instantaneous comic leveling. The doctor has been "set up," even physically and conspicuously stood on his feet, only to be unceremoniously deflated. I wish to call attention to a crucial nuance in the comic process — to what we may call the reactive or secondary nature of deflation. That is, the comic effect generally comes into being by reducing or annihilating a prior inflation.

Comedy, then, represents a deflation of assumed or actual superiority, of a tacit or vaunted imposition of any kind. This fundamentally deflationary process of comedy — a term I use interchangeably with humor — functions to liberate us, with varying degrees of force and finesse, from any social limitation and intimidation whatsoever and, furthermore, from any and all limitations of perceived reality.

In the largest philosophical view there is always the subtle possibility, of course, that our superiority complex is itself secondary and not primary. Our inflated human importance may be a protective psychic phenomenon, arising as a desperate and sometimes valiant psycholgial motive. Very likely the basic human emotion is fear. In any case, the reflex of self-assertion, and, soon after, superiority, was so strong and essential that the assertiveness appeared as elemental. But these are metaphysical depths we need not plumb. Let us assume a ruling human egocentricism, often even egomania, to which comedy is the secondary or tertiary reaction — a redressment necessary for our whole equilibrium.

There has been another side to us, a skeptical, unaspiring, leveling, explosive, threatening, compensatory side that must also be accounted for. With equal and opposite force, the anarchical comic spirit resisted the excesses of psychic unification — all those closures of mind and tyrannies of majority feeling that served nationhood itself. Our larger humanity perversely depended on it, to say nothing of our grasp of reality. That is why, up until recently, we have always been a very funny, as well as idealistic and sometimes fanatic, people — a contradiction, or paradox, vital at a deep level to our whole mental health.

Such a perspective explains, for example, the otherwise surprising amount of verbal humor - punning, comic wordplay, wisecracking, and so on — in Americans, who are not among the most expressive people in the world. The insurgent psyche had to save itself, so to speak, through comic articulation.

To pun, after all, is to give an unexpected other meaning. Never mind how outrageous and merely phonological the device (Groucho Marx's Captain Spaulding finds the ivory trade easier in Alabama "because the Tuscaloosa"), or if it entails sophisticated wit (a snobbish acquaintance of Dorothy Parker injured herself in England trying "to slide down a barrister").

Aggression, often in wild and murderous extremes, is an essential function of comedy. But I see the aggressive effect as a reactive one, of a vengeful or secondary nature, occurring only after a set-up pretension or previously imposed constraint.

We are vengefully glad to laugh at the whole class of overinflated professionals. Nobody is above comic criticism, and least of all ourselves. Perhaps the deepest reason we have for laughing at ourselves, too — as victims of riddles, and so on — is that we know that all self-esteem or authority, even our own, is in some measure either imposture or illusion.

Skeptical, resistant comedy works upon all sorts of subjects. It not only touches on comparatively innocent and safe topics, like restaurants and writers, but in America it particularly reacts to the sacrosanctities of God, country, commerce, class and racism, children and women.

Perhaps then the simplest thing to say about sick humor is that it is utterly mindless. But in view of its selected targets and concentrated morbidity, that is not quite true. Sick humor is not mindless. It functions, as does normal or "gray" humor, in a similar service of resistance and anti-recruitment, especially in the United States. Here is one of our latest examples:

> Q. "What is black and yellow and full of little Crispy Critters?"
> A. "A burnt school bus."

This appears so vile to some and so perplexingly sadistic to others that, perhaps, it ought not to be held steady for any consideration whatever. And yet, repelled as we are by the savage, even cannibalistic, excess, there is something of note inside the virulence.

Think of our aggressively induced allegiances to children, on one side, and to breakfast cereals, on the other, forged by cynical advertising and marketing services: Are they not the fittest targets for counterattack? The desire or need to turn back such massive and remorseless sentimentality and commercialism is, in itself, a healthy reflex of comic feeling.

The trouble is that, as sanctimony and hypocrisy increase, so does the satiric reaction. At a cultural extreme, sick jokes appear — which they are beginning to do again.

"Sick" humor deals, after all, with sickness, crippling deformity, or death — including cannibalism — for the most part. These will be especially prevalent in a country dedicated so mercilessly to the "pursuit of happiness." We may observe, incidentally, that, while matricide is a prevalent subject, incest almost never occurs — proving that it is not the forbidden as such that sick humor treats but only the overt sentimentalities and dignifications insisted upon by the prevailing culture.

> There won't be any Easter this year — they've found the body.

The class-racial motif, also mixed with the economic.

> "You know why Puerto Ricans wear pointed shoes?"
> "Why?"
> "To get the cockroaches in the corner."

Anti-childism, a recent stand-up version:

> Sorry I'm late. Ran into something on the way over. Oh, it was a kid.

Misogyny and anti-Momism combined:

> "Where's Mama, Daddy?"
> "Drink your tomato juice."
> "But where's Mama?"
> "I said, drink your tomato juice before it coagulates."

But if nothing is beyond the pale, still there are penalties for going that far. Cocteau's witticism in defining tact as knowing how far we may go in going too far is germane. Sick humor is not only tactlessly morbid but clearly sadistic in its enjoyment of pain and death and, very often, in its excessive post-mortem satisfactions.

Sick humor pays the penalty of indulging its own kind of monolithism, equal and opposite to what is attacking. It adopts, at last, a totalitarianism of outlook exactly corresponding to original cultural tyrannies. At some point it entails a loss of contact with reality and comes closer to pure or primary aggression than does the enforcing social mechanisms it had designed itself to oppose and cancel.

Phylogenetically speaking, the handshake represents fear and hostility overcome. The clapping of hands in applause is likewise a transmutation of loud threats or defensive clamor. Can we not say also that our smile represents what Ludovici first suggested — the lifted lip and bared fangs of repulsion or anger transmuted to greeting?

If handshaking and smiling bring us together, applause and laughter help to keep us together. Comedy operates when we are neither overcome by primary aggression nor consumed by secondary aggression and when we transmute both into healthy human criticism and self-criticism.

The humorist's supreme challenge is to make fun of even the most sanctified matter, like religion and God, but not to do so revoltingly.

Some planted wag in an audience stands up suddenly. "Is there a Christian Scientist in the house?"
A hesitant "Yes-s?" from somebody rising slowly.
"Will you change seats with me, please — there's a draft over here."

I permit myself that joke, having been at least reared as a Christian Scientist, to show that our principal resistance must be to our own subjectivity, upon which the rest of our fanatic closures and indiscriminations depend.

We want a harder-working comic mentality, liberated from its own subjective indulgences as well as from sanctimoniousness in general.

We must never abandon ourselves to our defensive aggressions, but transmute them into as continuous and vital a comic response as possible. In the widest contexts, that relentless human struggle between still-evolving gestures and ascendancies, on the one side, and terrible self-punishing regressions on the other, goes on and on.

4.

Saturday Night Live: Nihilism or Ethical Absolutism?
by Robert B. Pielke
Condensed from *American Humor: An Interdisciplinary Newsletter*

I

Everyone seems to be aware that something outrageous is happening on Saturday nights and that its "players" are indeed not ready for prime time. Some watch it for this reason, while others avoid it for the very same reason. What I'd like to do is to examine what it is that attracts some and repels others.

What attracts some and repels others is *SNL*'s apparent nihilism, the rejection of any and all values whatsoever.

Contrary to the initial nihilistic impression, *SNL* not only asserts the reality of value per se but goes on to affirm the ultimate value of the human individual.

Nihilism in ethics is simply the denial that the moral terms "good," "bad," "right," and "wrong" (and their equivalents) have anything other than an arbitrary, subjective meaning. Values are thought to be culturally relative (descriptive relativism) and only supportable by appealing to basic cultural norms which often differ and conflict. Further, since there's no way to choose between these basic cultural norms, logically there can be no ultimate evaluative standards at all (metaethical relativism). Hence, the very same value can be "valid" and "invalid" at the same time (normative relativism). This means that evaluations are simply expressions of personal opinion, and that makes them literally meaningless.

Does *SNL* express this kind of all-pervasive relativism or nihilism? There are some pretty persuasive examples which suggest that it does. Humor which is distasteful and offensive to virtually everyone would provide considerable support, and there is some evidence of this kind. After all, if *SNL* rejects all evaluative positions, it must therefore affirm nothing. What else would be implied, then, but nihilism? Offensiveness to all would seem to indicate that nothing is being affirmed and that ethical nihilism is indeed the case.

One of the most notorious examples occurred when *SNL* did a parody of the Claudine Longet killing of her lover, "Spider" Sabich. The segment was called "The Claudine Longet Men's Open Invitational Ski Tournament." It was comprised of film clips of several falling skiers attempting the high jump, and over-dubbed with the sounds of rifle shots and satirical commentary ("Oops, Claudine has just accidently shot another skier"). It should be noted that this show occurred prior to her trial. Hence, the legal and moral norm of "innocent until proven guilty" was quite consciously rejected, and this rejection expressed the views of hardly anyone. (*SNL* was forced to broadcast a retraction the following week due to the insistence of Longet's lawyers.) Almost everyone thought it a violation of "good taste," at the very least.

Chevy Chase, who has since left the show, mercilessly satirized the then President Ford, a person almost universally supported in the wake of the Nixon disaster. A bit of satire is acceptable, but in this case the parody was extensive, thorough going and continuous. His accidental tumbling scene became clumsiness and then, finally, incompetence and stupidity. It was a scream, of course, but it destroyed Ford. When a public figure becomes such a frequent object of satire, bordering on ridicule, at the very least it points to that person's downfall, and might even help cause it. *SNL*, I think, must accept some responsibility for the latter (along with Johnny Carson). The "debate" between Chase's Ford and Dan Aykroyd's Carter was absolutely devastating for Ford. After their treatment of him, who could take him seriously as a president?

One of the finest examples of "sick" humor (which seems to be the epitome of nihilism) was one of Chevy Chase's pseudo, public-service commercials. In the form similar to a typical plea for contributions for cancer or muscular dystrophy, Chevy Chase was shown soliciting funds for I.D.S., a ravaging disease which allegedly afflicts millions of Americans without the publicity of other more famous maladies. Just as he began to drool over his chin, we learned that I.D.S. meant "Involuntary Displacement of Saliva"; I.D.S. sufferers were "droolers." To toy with the severely or terminally ill is a bit hard to take, but *SNL* has apparently done it with no apparent guilt. A recent "Kill the Illiterates" campaign would seem to indicate this rather clearly.

Occasionally, Michael O'Donnohue has had more than a writer's role, and, as perhaps the "sickest" writer on the staff, his material is quintessentially offensive. Even the *SNL* people have a hard trouble accepting it. In one episode, he visited Garrett Morris' Uncle Remus to tell a new version of "Brer Rabbit." In this version, the unfortunate rabbit did not craftily escape from the tar baby trap. Instead, he was skinned alive and eaten. Perhaps his most infamous contribution to the show was one too sick to be shown. It had to do with birthday presents for Karen Anne Quinlan, one of which was moss for her north side. One of his accepted skits differed little in its degree of tastelessness; it was his impression of Tony Orlando and Dawn having their eyes put out with red-hot pokers. It's hard to imagine a more universally offensive writer, a fact in which he has taken considerable joy.

Several times *SNL* has had guest hosts from *Monty Python's Flying Circus,* a seeming affirmation of nihilism in itself. If ever absurdity were favored in contrast to reason, *MPFC* did it in spades. Including them on *SNL* could only imply some kind of agreement. *MPFC's* frequent parody of homosexuality (and heterosexuality, for that matter) was carried over to *SNL* as well, and even commented on in the show as possibly "inappropriate" for American audiences. (The sequence involved a "drag" race.) "Inappropriate," in this instance, meant "it might not get a laugh," not that it was "wrong!"

Aykroyd's portrayal of Carter and Nixon has, on occasion, been far beyond what most people can accept. Even public figures have customarily been granted some degree of privacy, but *SNL* apparently doesn't recognize this. With reference to Carter's Playboy interview, Aykroyd's version exaggerated his having admittedly "lusted" after innumerable women, and then connected his confession to the lyrics of the Beach Boys' "California Girls." In Aykroyd's impression of Nixon, there were some absolutely devastating lines about his sex life as well — or lack thereof.

Gilda Radner's characterizations have challenged a variety of widely accepted values. Rosanne Roseannadanna has confronted our propriety via our stomach (commenting, for example, on that "stoff" between our teeth), Emily Litella has spoken out against presidential "erections," and Baba Wawa has offended our concern for those with speech impediments (and handicaps in general). More than etiquette is being rejected here; respect for a person's privacy and dignity is seemingly the target. Her continuing sketches with Bill Murray about two high school "nerds" is tasteless in the extreme, perhaps because they are so well done.

Loraine Newman and Jane Curtin have satirized things which are far too important and serious to make fun of; yet they do it anyway. Patty Hearst and "Squeaky" Fromme are two notorious examples, for the S.L.A. and Charles Manson are just not acceptable objects of laughter. Jane Curtin's anchor-woman persona, because she affects the demeanor so well (as did Chevy Chase) and because the "Update" sequence deals with real news, seemingly not only parodies truth but the quest for it as well. More important, significant events are put on a level with, and mixed with, foolishness. As a result, life and death events are cheapened, especially with "sponsors" such as "Bleu Ball" cheese and "Colonel Lingus, Lickin' Finger Good!"

As the sole black member of the semi-permanent troupe, Garret Morris has not only satirized racism but also anti-racism. Playing a saxophonist with Chevy Chase portraying a white Barry White (who constantly told Morris to "take it, Boy!"), they enacted a situation no longer acceptable to blacks or whites. On their "Summer Vacation" show, he recounted his summer job as a "black-boy" lawn decoration. Again, a matter of great importance to many people was seemingly cheapened.

After the critical and popular success of *Animal House,* it's hard to remember John Belushi as just another member of the *SNL* crew. Most frequently remembered in the guise of classical Samurai warrior, whose presence in a variety of absurdly non-Samurai roles was the vehicle of satire, Belushi was always humorous and often in violation of accepted moral conventions. Once, as "Samurai Tailor," it was discovered, much to his and his customer's chagrin, that he had mistakenly omitted the fly from the pants that the customer was then wearing. The scene was frozen just as Belushi was correcting the error with a swift downward slice of his sword into the problem area. (Most males and not a few females winced at that!) Another time, as a "Samurai Divorce Lawyer," he was settling a child custody issue with a similar downward slice when, again, the action froze. (The parody on Solomon could hardly be avoided.) Further, his "commentaries" on "Update" have taken legitimate, serious issues and have utterly destroyed them with exaggeration and irreverance. After this one, one has to wonder if anything at all is important to him and *SNL*.

One commerical skit that involved nearly everyone in the cast dealt with the anomaly between the unlikely brand name "Fluckers" and its allegedly superior jelly. Working with the imputed principle that the grosser the name, the better the quality, such "brand names" as "nose hair," "dog vomit" and "painful rectal itch" were suggested. Grossness seemed to be the skit's avowed intention.

Several commercial put-ons and sketches have involved illegal drugs, especially marijuana, which is semi-acceptable, but occasionally coke and "speed" as well. While not literally encouraging their use, the effect of their parodies was hardly in conformity with the views expressed by most people. Viewing *SNL* in an "altered" state is a common practice (as it is for *Reefer Madness*), but this is a violation of the law.

Still other skits and "commercials" have frequently crossed the boundaries of universally accepted mores: Nazi skit close to Yom Kippur, the "Hard of Hearing" sequence in Weekend Update, Squeaky Fromme selling human-hair potholders, "Autumn Fizz" vaginal deodorant, "Bleu Ball" cheese, Susan Ford with a Bicentennial dog collar and Nazi tatoos, the "Nixon Final Days" sketch (a classic!), Freud with his daughter and very little left to the imagination, blindness jokes played on host Ray Charles, the Mr. Bill films with dismemberment and maiming presented in a humorous context, and others too numerous to mention.

Finally, offensiveness and negation have been explicitly intended by a variety of guest hosts and musicians. Richard Pryor's interview with Chevy Chase, in which all the black-white epithets were used, stretched the boundaries of propriety. Randy Newman's defense of his controversial song, "Short People," was a razz, while Devo's mechanical non-music strained our patience. Steve Martin and Dan Aykroyd as the Czech brothers have tastelessly pointed out the bulges in their tight pants to "American foxes." And, last but hardly least, Mick Jagger's typical antics (along with his tongue-action of fellow performers) were seemingly calculated to offend everyone — and probably succeeded. (An attempt was even made to have the Sex Pistols on the show, but it fell through. Elvis Costello, a far more talented "new wave" musician, was substituted.)

How can this show not be nihilistic? Its almost universal offensiveness is perhaps underscored by the fact that, despite this, we still laugh (thus pointing out the absurdity of any and all value positions)! But as I've already said, this is an initial impression; often however, there is the accompanying suspicion that even this apparent rejection embodies something positive.

II

The rejection of nihilism, all-pervasive relativism, is simply the assertion that one or more values have ultimate validity, thus giving values, as such, meaning. These ultimate values then function as the norms or standards according to which all subordinate values are measured. In other words, the claims are made that value judgments can be shown to be true or false and that this alleged distinction between true and false value judgments can be justified in some final sense. This position is called ethical absolutism, the exact contradictory of ethical nihilism. Nihilists can not make this kind of distinction; for them all value judgments have the same cognitive status: they're all meaningless, with no logical pretensions to being either true or false. Only absolutists can affirm some kind of meaning for values (and moral terms in general). It's important to keep in mind, however, that ethical absolutists need not support their evaluations to everyone's satisfaction — only their own (otherwise, this position would be empirically impossible).

Whether absolutism or nihilism is true is another question, and one not at issue here. (The criteria for such a determination are, themselves, a matter of considerable dispute, and the dispute hinges largely on what value and moral terms, as such, mean.) What I'm concerned with is whether or not *SNL* is essentially nihilistic as is frequently charged, and I don't think it is. This, of course, means that I regard the show as exemplifying an absolutist point of view. To be absolutely clear about this, I'm not arguing that *SNL* presents a defense of ethical absolutism, but only that they are ethical absolutists. It matters not whether they can offer conclusive proof for their value judgments as being true; what matters is that they make the claim.

As I mentioned earlier, this claim might not be (and need not be) entirely conscious. The crucial thing is how we interpret what's presented to us, and I'm assuming that a careful and thoughtful interpretation on our part would yield an accurate picture of their (possibly unconscious) ethical position.

What appears first is a remarkable degree of consistency in *SNL's* evaluations. Consistency is a key indicator of absolutism, although it's hardly incontrovertible proof. By itself, all it shows is a reliance on a single basic norm or set of norms. To allege that this is no mere coincidence would not be a convincing counter-charge, since, even if true, it would simply indicate an unconscious reliance, which I've already admitted to be possible. What I've got to do, in addition to showing that basic norms are involved, is to show that *SNL* feels them to be ultimately valid or true. This is more difficult to establish, for they might simply (and somewhat illogically) feel them to be valid only for our own culture or society (hence, not ultimately valid).

The assertion (explicit or implicit) of ultimate validity can be established by showing that *SNL* universalizes its evaluations; that its judgments are not thought valid merely for our own culture, but for all people everywhere. The reality that this is indeed the case is the second thing that appears. Not only are there basic norms expressed by *SNL,* but these norms are also felt to be universally, and therefore ultimately, valid. Ethical absolutism is not at all a denial of descriptive relativism (such would merely be the assertion that all people everywhere do, in fact, accept the same basic norms and values; but logically, it might still be immoral for them to do so). Rather, it's a denial of metaethical relativism (such is the assertion that all people everywhere ought to have the same basic norms and values, whether or not they in fact do).

Taking these two appearances in turn, *SNL's* satire has been consistently directed against institutions — including the laws, conventions, customs, morality and people that support them — but not against the people themselves. In those instances when an individual alone has been singled out for critique, it has been because he or she has become a symbol of the institution or has become identified with it.

Governmental institutions, of course, have been prime targets, and their leaders have become the frequent focal points of *SNL's* attacks (Nixon, Ford, Carter, Bert Lance and Earl Butz among others). Government policies and judicial pronouncements have born much of the wit in "Weekend Update" (drug laws, for example).

"Update" itself has been an effective parody of the entire 4th Estate, and it has included virtually every dimension of the news media. When Ron Nessen was the guest host, because of his role as Ford's press secretary, both the government and the news institutions were satirized together.

Institutionalized religion has felt its share of jabs too. Belushi's portrayal of a priest, who is surprisingly and illegitimately confronted both with personal tax problems as well as with a confessed tax-dodger, is the introduction for an "H and R Block" pseudo-commercial. Reason #17 for using their tax consultant service was they they solve moral dilemmas (not the church)! As with the news industry, governmental influence over religious institutions was clearly and negatively pointed out.

The entertainment establishment has been burned in a variety of ways (especially for its greed). The sacrosanct Beatles have been come under fire as a highly visible symbol of this industry. During a period of particularly intense reunion rumors (not the most recent ones) with $3,000,000 inducements mentioned, Lorne Michaels (the producer of *SNL*) announced that NBC was willing to offer the foursome the incredible sum of $3000 (!) if they would only appear on *SNL*. The following week the offer was upped to $3400! Belushi's and

Aykroyd's quite serious and well done "Blues Brothers" routines were an implicit critique of the way the music industry succeeds in dictating our tastes. A sketch on the cancellation of *Star Trek* was an extremely effective and poignant commentary on the networks' worship of the Nielson figures (and hence, the dollar). They've even satirized NBC itself for trying to follow ABC's mindless "T and A" formula for success.

Other institutions have been handled in a similar way. Every pseudo-commercial knocks "business," and a few have knocked "labor" too (with "union label" and "united Marijuana Growers of America" ads). With the addition of the military, medicine, and education, the list becomes virtually all-inclusive.

Aside from indicating their greed, hypocrisy and pretentiousness, the point of this anti-institutional satire is to proclaim the immorality of some people holding power over others. For in these kinds of relationships, the worth of the individual is denied. Just as slavery corrupts the masters as much as it does the slaves, so any inequality in authority destroys human dignity. The ultimate worth of each individual is morally unalienable (in fact, of course, it is easily lost or violated). Not even the individual can rightfully relinquish his or her worth by voluntarily submitting to another's power (although again, in fact, this is all too possible). Such an act would not be truly voluntary or free; it could only arise from a misunderstanding of what it means to be authentically human. Only acts and decisions based on an accurate understanding of authentic human existence can be free and moral. Their understanding of human existence, then, is the source or basis of *SNL's* moral critique. Respect for the human individual as the absolute and sole end is their ultimate moral norm. In short, they are anarchists.

There are, of course, metaphysical, epistemological and logical problems with this kind of metaethical position, but they aren't at issue here. What's important is the fact that *SNL's* satire is consistently anarchist. Never are individuals evil (or selfish) because of their own natures; their evil (and it can be considerable) is caused by the social and cultural institutions in which they find themselves. The removal of these causes would then permit man's true goodness to emerge. (Peter Kropotkin would have made a great guest host, and of course he, too, would have been satirized!) Evil people as well as good people are both victims of inhuman (i.e., institutional) forces.

That *SNL* takes such a position is implicit in the fact that uncooperativeness and selfishness are attributed to institutional causes. The Beatles were made greedy; Babe Ruth, in a parody of his famous home run for a hospitalized child, was a victim of an image imposed on him; Nelson Rockefeller's true humanity showed through when the protective institutional trappings which made him so pretentious were stripped away. (During a speech in which he was severely heckled, he "broke free" and gave his hecklers "the finger" — for which he was cheered. And this latter fact was stressed on an "Update" report of the event.) Whenever human goodness is shown, it's revealed through opposition to some institutionalized authority. Thus, in the Star Trek cancellation, NBC (the institution) was the cause of the injustice, while NBC officials were merely victimized lackeys following orders. The crew members of the Enterprise were totally opposed to the cancellation, because their identity was at stake. (The cast had become their roles.) As they gradually succumbed to the inevitable, they correspondingly lost their identity, their true humanity. Belushi ended the scene with a poignant rephrasing of the Star Trek introduction, recounting how ignorance and greed have ended their mission to explore strange new worlds where everywhere they were welcomed — except at NBC.

The second appearance, that *SNL* univeralizes its evaluative stance, is evident from the fact that the objects of their satire are not restricted to our culture alone. Sadat, Begin, the PLO, Franco and Idi Amin have all been devastatingly parodied. The absurdity of a situation wherein governments find it easier to make war than to make peace was played upon when Aykroyd's Carter mediated between Belushi's Lennon and Bill Murray's McCartney. Institutions destroy everything everywhere; they are incapable of good. For quite a while on "Update" Franco's continued death was reported (despite alleged fears to the contrary); *SNL* has not taken kindly to dictators. The epitome of institutional corruption has, of course, been Idi Amin, who saw himself as embodying the entire institution: absolute power corrupts absolutely. But he, too, was a victim — a victim of the myths about authority (that it implies superiority).

PART II
HUMOR TECHNIQUE

5

Fourteen Varieties of Humor

by Roy Paul Nelson
Condensed from *Articles and Features*

Humor, over the years, has drawn the serious attention of scholars, who have attempted to analyze and categorize it. A study of the categories cannot make a humorous writer out of one who is deadly serious, but it can remind the writer with an inclination to humor of the several approaches possible.

The best jokes and wittiest replies seem to combine several of the following categories:

1. *Irony* Niebuhr in *The Irony of American History* said that pathos elicits pity if there is no reason for the condition depicted and no guilt; tragedy, if it involves a choice of evil for the sake of good, elicits pity and admiration.

Irony, in contrast to pathos and tragedy, elicits laughter and understanding. When you use irony, your words mean one thing to the uninitiated, something quite different to the person in the know. You create an intimacy between you and your more intelligent or sophisticated readers. Early writers used irony to get dangerous doctrine past the censors.

Pretending to praise a person when, in reality, you condemn him, is a form of irony.

One of the lower forms of irony is sarcasm. It isn't so much another meaning the writer conveys as the opposite meaning.

In one of its forms, irony involves a circumstance that is the opposite of what should be expected or one that is highly inappropriate: an oddity of fate. An American Cancer Society executive dies of — lung cancer. A doctor saves a patient's life, and — gets sued for malpractice. A fire breaks out at — the fire station.

2. *Satire* Satire makes use of irony, including sarcasm, to expose foolishness, cupidity, and pretension. It also makes use of exaggeration and incongruity.

Perhaps the most celebrated satirist in the English language was Jonathan Swift. His *Gulliver's Travels* so smoothly and subtly satirized the politics and science of his day that it became an accepted book for children.

The satirist may write to right a wrong or simply to hold something up to ridicule. When the humor becomes so bitter that it offers no hope, it becomes known as "black humor." (The term does not refer to the humor of any race or ethnic group.)

Woody Allen, in *The New Yorker,* satirizes inspirational biography with his tribute to the Earl of Sandwich, inventor of the sandwich. We take a slice out of the middle: "1745: After four years of frenzied labor, he is convinced he is on the threshold of success. He exhibits before his peers two slices of turkey with a slice of bread in the middle. His work is rejected by all but David Hume, who senses the imminence of something great and encourages him."

Using satire, you always risk some reader misunderstanding. Readers may take you literally.

3. *Parody* No one is likely to mistake the parodist as a comic genius. The parodist mimics rather than invents. Even so, parody can be high art.

Some of the happiest moments in journalism come when one magazine parodies the style of another. *Mad,* the *Harvard Lampoon,* and the *National Lampoon* have devoted articles and whole issues to the affectations and peculiarities of the *Reader's Digest, Playboy, Cosmopolitan,* the newsmagazines, and others.

As unnamed AP writer, on the announcement in 1975 that Howard

Cosell was to host an ABC variety show, came up with an imaginary interview with the ebullient sportscaster. A sample question:

"It is well known that from a humble Brooklyn beginning you have achieved a state of salubrious success as a caster of sports with a pronounced propensity for telling it like it is, as it were. Why, then, one must ask, are you entering this new area as a common hawker of stars, song, and the dance?"

The secret of good parody is to make it as interesting — or nearly as interesting — to persons who may not be familiar with the work being parodied as to persons who are.

4. *Understatement* Arthur Schlesinger, Jr., says, "my enthusiasm for Mr. Nixon has always been well under control. . . ." Bob and Ray, in one of their skits, refer to the United States mint as "one of the nation's leading producers of authentic new money."

These are examples of understatement, a delightful, subtle variety of humor often associated with the British. A disaster of some kind becomes "a bit of a nuisance."

Using understatement you have to be careful that your reader understands you are holding back.

5. *Exaggeration* The opposite of understatement is exaggeration, a form of humor not likely to be misunderstood, provided the exaggeration is extreme. A story comes to mind about a man shouting a greeting to a friend across the Volga River. It was so cold that before the words could get across they froze. They were not heard until the next spring, when the thaw released them.

Nobody objects to a little fictionalizing or exaggeration provided it is obvious what the writer is doing. Hendrik Willem Van Loon said, "I like the Unitarian Church, because the only time the name Jesus Christ is uttered is when the janitor falls downstairs."

6. *Puns* That potential political appointee over there. The one with long hair. He is to replace a bald-headed incumbent. When you refer to him as the "hair apparent" you manufacture a pun. Likely you get groans rather than laughs for your trouble.

A pun is a play upon words that sound the same — or nearly the same. Its occasional use in an article or feature can be excused if not applauded. Like alliteration, a little punning goes a long way.

Sir Walter Scott is said to have written "Please return this book: I find that though many of my friends are poor arithmeticians, they are nearly all good bookkeepers."

7. *Tom Swifties* Perhaps you will want to try using a verb or adverb that relates itself through punning to a chunk of conversation. Such a device is called a Tom Swifty.

"I dropped my toothpaste," said Tom, crestfallen.
"That makes 144," he said grossly.
"I drove from Maine to California," he stated.
"Give it to me on the level," he said flatly.

8. *The Double Entendre* Closely related to the pun is the double entendre, a term with two meanings, one of them risque. What little humor there is comes from the feeling of superiority in figuring out the risque meaning. In a more innocent age, song writers thought they were being daring when they ended a line with ". . . to make you" and waited until the next line to add a "mine."

9. *Manufactured Words* You can also achieve a humor of sorts by manufacturing words. A too familiar example is "couth," coming from the elimination of "un." A fresher example comes from John Simon in his review of *The Return of the Pink Panther*. After a barrage of gags, he says, the viewer becomes "totally slap-unhappy."

10. *The Malapropism* Richard Brinsley Sheridan's play, *The Rivals,* brought to life a delightful character named Mrs. Malaprop, a woman given to hilarious misuse of words, producing grotesque effects. Her misuse came about because of a lack of appreciation of word meanings and a confusion in sounds. Edwin O'Connor's Ditto in *The Last Hurrah* was cut from the same cloth. So is Archie Bunker on tv.

Usually the users of malaprops — malapropisms — don't realize they're being funny.

"Why Congressman, your speech was superfluous, just superfluous." The Congressman thanked her, and said: "I'm thinking of having it published posthumously." "Oh, wonderful," the woman said, "and the sooner the better."

Here you'll find a good selection of malaprops:

> His severe of influence,
> He requested a court-appointed attorney because he was indignant.
> A sale that was coming at the end of our physical year.
> Cutting off your nose despite your face.
> Food sprayed with various and Sunday poisons.
> In 1957, Eugene O'Neill won a pullet surprise.
> The doctor said to take some milk of amnesia.
> Moses went up to Mt. Cyanide.
> A paradox is a lovely place to go when you die.

11. *The Spoonerism* Closely related to the malaprop is the spoon-

erism, named for the Rev. William A. Spooner. A spoonerism is an unintentional interchange of the initial sounds in words.

> *It is kistomary to cuss the bride.*
> *Does your husband wake up mornings dill and lustless?*

Spoonerisms are more a speech than a writing problem; they don't play much of a role in articles, unless you want to count the transpositions that sometimes show up in typing.

12. *The Practical Joke* Reporting practical jokes perpetrated by characters in your story is another way of adding humor.

In one of Peter DeVries' novels, a father and son, under cover of night, added gas to the VW belonging to a neighbor who bragged about the mileage he was getting, and then reversed the process and siphoned gas out of the neighbor's tank.

13. *Incongruity* Using words to draw a picture of the impossible can also add some humor. Arthur "Bugs" Baer wrote: "An empty cab drove up, and Sarah Bernhardt got out."

14. *Getting it All Wrong* One of Robert Benchley's benchmarks was his posing as an authority — and getting it all wrong. It is a device less useful to the article writer than to the fiction writer, but because it can help the writer satirize, it deserves at least passing mention.

When some Americans objected to the length of time institutions kept their flags lowered following the death of Martin Luther King, Bill Landers worked up a formula "to achieve national grieving without overdoing it or underdoing it." The flag would be lowered to various heights and for various lengths of time depending on the worth of the individual. A "blue ribbon commission" would assign ratings.

Landers saw some difficulties in his scheme. "Since it is unquestionably going to crowd the pole when a number of important people pass on at about the same time, a pole schedule will have to be established.

Getting sentences in the wrong order can also do the job. Wrote Marc Connelly in a letter to Frank Sullivan: "Guess who I just had a drink with at the bar. Corey Ford. Give up?"

6

An Outline of Satire
by Dylan Williams

Satire, from the classical Greek and Roman literature of Aristophanes, up to the present with writers like John Barth, Sinclair Lewis, and Joseph Heller, has helped to draw attention to the improvements needed in human institutions and humanity in general. Satire, which means literally "a dish filled with mixed fruits," has undergone many different changes, though its aim has always been the same — to inspire a reconstruction of the institutions set up by men to make them stronger and better.
 As Holman's *Handbook to Literature* explains, "If the critics simply abuse, they are writing invective; if they are personal and splenetic, they are writing sarcasm; if they are sad and morose over the state of society they are writing irony or a jeremiad." Satire, then, is a literary form which mixes humor, wit, and a critical attitude in order to improve society.
 There are two types of satire. (1) Formal or Direct Satire, in which the voice of satire speaks, usually in first person, to either a character

in the satire or directly to the reader. Formal Satire is of two styles: Horatian satire which is gentle, half-kidding, smiling (the style popular in *The New Yorker*), and the Juvenalian satire which is angry, biting, and contemptful. (2) *Indirect Satire,* in which a narrative is used with satiric characters acting satirically within themselves and their situation, allegorically and indirectly delivering the writer's message.

THEORY

According to Hodgart, "true satire demands a high degree both of commitment to and involvement with the painful problems of the world, and simultaneously a high degree of abstraction from the world." Good satire is something that both presents a situation of tragedy and at the same time by its very nature allows for a type of escape. One can recognize true satire, then, by the way the writer subtly blends the painful issues of real life with the abstract and pleasureable medium of the printed word. This special combination of realism and fantasy is what Hodgart calls, "the keynote of true satire."

The "keynote" appears in two literary traditions that are part of satire. The first is the lampoon, or personal attack; the other is the travesty, or fantastic vision of the world transformed. The first form, or lampoon form, is interesting because it was one of the earliest forms of satire.

The second of the literary traditions, the travesty or fantastic vision of the world transformed, also has its roots in the primitive world. The earliest form of the fantastic vision is of course the myth. Using the myth idea for a comprehensible reality is what led to the folk or fairy tale, and Aesop's fables, which relate some tidy moral message at the end of each story.

The link between the lampoon, the travesty, and art is important to the development and theory of satire. The lampoon, used merely as a curse or ridicule, is not satire. The travesty, used merely as an abstraction for the world, is not satire either. The development of satire stems from combining these two literary forms.

"My business," said Mencken, "is diagnosis, not therapeutics." Satirists are not people who reform and provide alternatives for the subjects they satirize.

Through satire there is always the hope that indirectly or directly it is causing social change, but the purpose, at least in theory, is only to point out problems.

However, most writers of satire feel that it is only their duty to recognize problems and then shout them out to the public in an agreeable fashion. It is enough for them to rise above the social malaise and become aware of problems.

Satire is pleasureable because it is a fresh way to look at old problems. The satirist creates a new perspective which makes the reader feel an awareness of truth. He appeals to the intellect by making up a system of logic based on a distorted view of his subject. He purposely exaggerates and distorts his subjects so as to prove how illogical it is. Satire is, as Leonard Feinberg says, "a playfully critical distortion of the familiar."

Another reason satire is so pleasing is because it appeals so much to the ego of the audience. A good piece of satire makes the audience feel superior to the subject and at the same time provides them with a socially acceptable way of releasing aggression. Satire does not place the burden of the problem on the listener, except in the most roundabout way since he is a member of the society in which the object of satire is contained. Rather it asks only that he enjoys the piece and become aware of the writer's posture. He shares in the attack of the subject without having to bother considering the morality of an alternative position. The satirist needs only to present a strong attack that appeals to his audience. The only stand then that the writer needs to take is against his subject.

"Without humor, satire is invective; without literary form, it is mere clownish jeering." says Garnett.

TECHNIQUE

It is important to establish the boundaries of satire. The first is humorless attack, ridicule without the addition of wit. Many people enjoy reading ridicule simply because it places them, like the writer, in a superior position. However, though the ridicule may work by itself, it is not true satire. The other boundary is at the other extreme. Namely, humor without ridicule. It tends to fantasy with no real social implications.

A useful technique is utilizing obscenity. Obscenity is reductive, which is one of the main goals of satire. As Hodgart says, "The satirist's aim is to strip men bare, and apart from physique one naked man is much like another. By using obscenity, the satirist can go even further, reducing man from nakedness to the condition of an animal, in which any claim to social or even divine distinction must appear even more ridiculous."

Unmasking and degrading people of high positions, and the parody and travesty that destroy the unity between the characters as they present themselves to us, are essentially the goals of satire.

Holding the reader's interest is the first problem of the writer. The satirist appeals to the mind, so he must keep the mind active. He does this by using "playful distortion" as Feinberg calls it. The writer should use all his comic devices and not get too bogged down in dramatic narrative. The satire is usually broken down into many short satire units that should come across like short punches from different angles, eventually expressing the entire theme. Another problem is offending the reader, though Swift observed that men see others being satirized, but rarely themselves. There are two ways in which the writer can avoid this conflict. The first is to show the victim as ridiculous instead of wicked. The second is to imply that the satirist's own position is just and proper. The satirist must be technically perfect in his wit. When using exaggeration, it must be brought in naturally and seriously.

The four general techniques are also a very important part of a satiric work. The first is distortion, in which exaggeration and overstatement are used to attract attention to the subject. The second is indirection or the amount of humor subtly used in expressing the ridicule of the subject. This varies from a blunt, humorous put-down to a less direct, quietly ironic form. The third is externality. The satirist is not concerned with the psychology of individuals who commit an act. He is concerned only with the act. The fourth is brevity. Don't be wordy. Be brief and to the point. The final technique is variety of technique. This has to do with writing in different modes, such as realistic, romantic, naturalistic, expressionistic, etc. These four techniques serve as a type of framework for the satiric piece to rest on.

Feinberg examines four specific techniques and their subheadings in a detailed context.

1. Incongruity
   Exaggeration
   Invective Writing
   Reductio Ad Absurdum
   Understatement
   Contrast
      Disparaging Comparison
      Epigram
      Paradox
2. Surprise
   Unexpected Honesty
   Unexpected Logic
   Unexpected Event
3. Pretense
   Verbal Irony
   Parody
   Deception
   Mask Persona
   Symbol
   Allegory
4. Superiority
   Small Misfortunes
   Unmasking
   Banality
   Insult

Incongruity, that perception of the difference between concept and object when the concept is supposed to represent the object. The object is distorted so as to fit the concept. The recognition of the distortion is what evokes laughter.

Exaggeration is part of incongruity. All satire contains exaggeration, intensifying or emphasizing one point while de-emphasizing others. *Invective writing* is very close to outright abuse, although there is no real formula for distinguishing between the two. Exaggeration and invective are the two main sub-techniques under incongruity.

Reductio ad absurdum is the extreme of exaggeration, almost to the point of absurdity. This technique is used especially in satiric utopias, in which the writer appears to agree with an idea, and then applies it to an actual situation, exaggerating the effects so as to belittle the idea.

Understatement may be defined as "exaggeration in reverse," says Feinberg. The emphasis, the magnification of the nonchalant gives understatement its power, as when the detached head of a dueler in a Thurber cartoon says calmly, "Touche."

Contrast, really a part of all humorous writing, is usually defined in terms of the relationship between the subject and the tone in which the author presents his work. Swift's *A Modest Proposal* is very reserved and formal, whereas the subject matter deals with the grotesque idea of eating children.

Under the contrast, there are three minor styles involved.

The first is *disparaging comparison,* a style which employs metaphors and analaogies to contrast the subject. For example, Mencken writes, "A professor must have a theory, as a dog must have fleas."

The second style is the epigram. An epigram is a cliche that has been altered for an effect, such as the reconstruction of a popular proverb in this manner: "Poverty is not a sin, it's a great deal worse."

The last style is the paradox, a statement seemingly self-contradictory in which the two "opposite" parts are interdependent. Paradox produces an odd emotional effect that confuses and at the same time delights the logic-oriented mind of the reader, as in Stendahl's, "God's only excuse is that he does not exist."

The *incongruity* technique is one basically concerned with exaggeration, invective, and contrast. It is important because it gives the satiric piece the "twist" that makes the work uniquely satirical, as opposed to some other literary style.

The second technique is one of . . . surprise! There is a sudden change in the flow of things that releases the tension brought on by that flow. A laugh is really nothing more than a scream without the fear. But the idea of tension buildup and the sudden release is parallel in both reactions.

Unexpected honesty is a part of surprise. As Feinberg says, "It is not truth that is homorous; it is only truth at a socially inappropriate, or inconvenient, or embarrassing moment that is humorous." So honesty can come forth in the form of humor when it goes against the grain of social mores, like an admission of cowardice or greed.

Another part of surprise is *unexpected logic,* which uses the same reasoning as the everyday world only with a surprise or ironic twist. Swift in *A Modest Proposal* logically proposes that unemployment and famine can be eased by eating children.

The *unexpected event* or dramatic irony is the last technique under the surprise heading. More than just words, this technique uses the events in a story to add the twist and surprise the reader. A good example of this is in Guy de Maupassant's *The Necklace,* in which two people slave away for fifteen years to replace a necklace, which proves to have been worthless.

Surprise plays an important part in satire. Surprise keeps the piece alive and unpredictable, always building up tension and then twisting the flow of words in a satiric way.

The third major technique is the technique of pretense, called "censor-evasion" by Freud. Censors are the inhibitions of man which appear to come from "out there." In olden days, the court jester served as a release from the censor on the pretense that what he was talking about really was something other than what it appeared to mean. Today, hostile jokes against authority are a popular form of censor-evading.

One form of pretense is *verbal irony.* Verbal irony is a gentle form of sarcasm. It is a type of "sham praise," as Feinberg puts it. An example of this comes from a returning hunting party when the leader says to his wife at the house, "Our guests shot beautifully, but heaven was very merciful to the birds."

Parody is another technique. Parody is a mimic or imitation of something serious that uses exaggeration or contrast to create a humorous effect. The better the imitation, comments Huxley, the better the humor.

Disguise and *deception,* the familiar man-dressed-as-a-woman routine, is also part of pretense. The imposter, the mistaken identity, and misrepresentations are all part of this technique. Closely related to disguise and deception is the *mask-persona* technique. The mask-persona style, the satirist pretending to be someone else, speaking through an alter-ego, gives the writer a greater freedom in his speech and protection from possible attack.

Symbol is the fifth technique under pretense. As Feinberg states, "The poet uses symbols to represent things; the satirist uses symbols sometimes to misrepresent things." Symbols are often uses as distorting devices, changing satirically the thing it is to represent. For example, a donkey can represent the Democratic Party, but if a satirist has that donkey put its tail between its legs, that says something satirically about the Democratic Party. Closely related to symbol is the last of the techniques under pretense, *allegory*. Allegory represents something abstract, like an idea or concept.

Pretense, then, is deception. Pretense never directly attacks but rather underhandedly ridicules, always leaving itself with an escape route and safe hiding place. Pretense is guerrilla satire.

Superiority is the last of the major techniques. As Hobbes says, "Laughter is nothing else but a sudden glory arising from a sudden concept of some eminency in ourselves, by comparison with the infirmity of others, or with our own formerly." Satire by its very nature of ridiculing one thing allows another to feel superior. Cobb says, "nearly all humor is founded on the idea of embarrassment or ridicule or suffering for somebody else."

Small misfortunes are the first part of the superiority technique. Small misfortunes come in two categories, according to Feinberg. First is the practical joke, which usually in some way relates to a misfunction of the body or "mechanical elasticity." The second is the revelation of ignorance or social inadequacy. Both categories allow the observer to feel superior to the victim.

Another is to unmask, in which the common foibles of the person are brought out, degrading his dignity and any false airs.

Making a person seem banal is another way to lower him. The feeling of banality is achieved mainly through the use of clichés and trite expressions in conversation, thus wiping out the victim's personality and individuality. This leads to the insult, the most outright aggressive form of humor. Its aim is to degrade a person in any possible way, thus placing the aggressor in a superior position.

Incongruity, surprise, pretense, catering to the superiority of the audience are the legs on which the table of satire stands and gets it strength.

THE SATIRIST

The satirist is a man who has in him a lot of undesirable characteristics as far as society is concerned. He is not the average man on the street. He is a man superconscious of his own being, and the rest of the world is this great negative force that constantly prods his mind. So he strikes back in the form of satire, attacking the world's injustices before they can close in on him.

Panneborg attempts to classify satirists by personality types. The most popular satirists and their lifestyles were studied throughout history and then classified by Dr. Panneborg into one of three groups according to their common personality traits.

First, The "Schizothymic Satirists," which includes such writers as Byron, Erasmus, Gogol, Ibsen, Pope, and Strindberg, have certain characteristics in common. "They are very egotistic. Their intense emotionalism has these results: excessive reactions, a personal emphasis in satire, a 'narrowing of the mind' which make them ignore extenuating circumstances. Schizothymic satirists are vain, ambitious, proud, and haughty misanthropes. . . . They like the positions of leadership. They are thrifty, avaricious, and lack character. They go through periods of apathy. Their characteristic qualities are violence, irritability, intolerance, somberness, fluctuation of mood, and melancholia. . . . They are not very social, detest large groups of people where they are not the center of attention. They eventually withdraw into their own psychic and spiritual lives. They are likely to die as a result of licentious behavior (one-third of those in their group died of either venereal disease or alcholoism). They are hypochondriacs and travel extensively in their restlessness. . . ."

Group Two, the "Sanguine Satirists," includes the likes of Defoe, Holberg, Montesquieu, Machiavelli, and Voltaire. "Like the members of the first group, they are egotistical in character, but in their temperament a 'sanguine' element replaces the nervousness of the schizothymes. They are very active, strongly aggressive personalities. Contempt for others is present but not as preponderantly as in the satirists of the first group. Uncharitableness and a lack of a sustaining moral background express themselves in skepticism and cynicism, and account for the callousness they sometimes exhibit. The 'sanguines' tend to attack groups and situations rather than individuals, and are likely to use irony in their derision."

The similarities present in both groups are: "impulsiveness, use of superlatives, immoderateness, inconsistency, jerky development, good observation, snap-judgment, good memory, concrete fantasy, imperiousness, and aversion to contemplation."

The third group consists of two writers, Hugo and Vondel. They are put into the category of writers motivated by "noble indignation" because they do not fit into either of the other groups.

SATIRIC SUBJECTS

Anything is a possible subject for satire: hypocrisy, pretense, double standards, greed, immorality, and other such negative influences inflect individuals and society. The three main areas of life that serve as the outward subjects of satire are the individual, the society, and the cosmos.

The individual can be a source of satire because we so often rationalize, sublimate, and repress our true selves that we become dishonest with ourselves and pretend we are something we are not. When dishonesty is a source of satire the writer must decide whether he wants to deal with a specific individual or the general character flaw. In the first case, he would bring out the flaw in the character and exaggerate it to the point of ridicule. In the second case, he would create characters that would sharply accent the flaw by indirect satire.

Society is the second area of satire: religion, business, and politics. Attacking society's institutions a writer is often charged with immorality simple because he dares to use the systems created by society as subjected matter.

The last area is the abstract world of the cosmos. The apparent illogic of events in this life makes the cosmos seem hypocritical. The feeling that gods play with the lives of men makes the writer feel the injustices in the universe, just as in society.

THE RESULT

The cosmos will never change because of satire. Institutions rarely fall because of it. If the satirist is to really have an effect, it is usually on the individual. By working on the individual, however, especially a prominent person who is linked intimately with an institution, the satirist can have a say in the direction of society.

7

Switching: Clichés, Synonyms and Truisms

In railroading, a switch is used to alter a train's direction by switching the engine from one track to another. In comedic writing, switching is defined as the technique of changing the direction of the audience's mind.

To be an effective switch (i.e. evoke a laugh or at least a smile) it must meet the following criteria:

It must be a realistic or logical change of direction.

> *My mother liked me best*
> *Because I was an only child*

It must be a surprise; therefore the switch is frequently the last word or phrase in a sentence.

> *"You're hopeless," said the professor to the dunce.*
> *"You haven't read one book in four years of college."*

"I remember one book from my freshman year."
"Really, what was it?"
"Green."

The new direction must have a target that is of interest to the majority of the audience.

> You know they just took away the license of one of our doctors. Yeh, they claimed he was having sex with his patients. And that's too bad, 'cause he's the best veterinarian in town.

The new target must elicit a hostility shared by a majority of the audience so that they feel comfortable laughing out loud in a group. Group laughter functions as a mechanism for promoting group solidarity and individuals feel uncomfortable laughing alone.

It must be "clever." Unfortunately like "taste" and "love," *cleverness* is one of the most personal of evaluations. Each member of the audience must discover the new direction by his own intellectual process. Humor loses its cleverness ("Aw, that's kid's stuff") when the performer telegraphs the punchline and the switch is so obvious it can be anticipated.

Here's an example. Godfrey Cambridge performed this edited piece of stock material, called "Why, Lord?" in 1974. Only his acting ability overcame the switch telegraphed in this story:

> "This colored fella is standing on the corner. And he looks up and says, "Lord! Lord! Why did you make me so dark?"
> And the Lord says, "The reason I made you so dark Is that when you're running through the jungle, The sun won't give you a sunstroke.
> And then he asks, "Lord! Why did you make my hair so coarse?"
> And the Lord says, "That's so when you're running through the jungle, your hair won't get caught in the brambles."
> And then he asks, "Lord! Why did you make my legs so long?"
> And the Lord says, "That's so when you're running through the jungle in quest of wild beast, you could run very fast and swiftly."
> "Now my son," asks the Lord, "do you have any other questions?
> And he said, "Yeah Lord! What the hell am I doing in Cleveland?"

To the erudite, the more the intellect is challenged, the more the phrasing is appreciated as "clever." I call it *dimensional humor,* and it ranges from first dimensional humor (the most simple, such as slapstick) to fourth dimensional humor (the most complex, such as the sophisticated patter of Tom Stoppard which requires knowledge of several languages and Freudian psycho-therapy). It's like a chess move. The novice makes a move without much thought as to what his opponent's counter move will be. As chess players become more proficient, they anticipate their opponent's counter moves, sometimes four and five steps ahead of their next decision.

It's the same way with humor:

first dimension

> *My sister, Lola, was very mature when she was in high school. Of the 26 boys in the class, she was the first to shave.*

second dimension

> *"I got thrown out of my college because I pissed in the pool outside my dorm."*
> *"Come on, lot's of students do that!"*
> *"From the 14th floor?"*

third dimension

> *I got thrown out of college because they caught me cheating on my metaphysics exam. I looked into the soul of the boy sitting next to me. (Woody Allen)*

fourth dimension

> *Jewish guys first gotta smell everything they eat: "Hey, when didja get this, Thursday?"*
> *That's why they make such lousy lovers. (David Brenner)*

In this fourth dimension example, the sudden twist of direction toward an alternate meaning first causes surprised embarrassment (which ignites the laugh) and then, secondly, acceptance of a shared hostility through a clever claim of superiority (which really gets it rolling). It can be compared to the crowd reaction to a surprise forward pass which comes at the end of a double reverse in football. In this play, the quarterback hands the ball on a reverse to his back, who starts on what appears to be a standard end run. Surprise one, the back hands the ball to a wide receiver going in the opposite direction, and he starts for the other side of the field. Surprise two, suddenly the end stops running, fades back and to the surprise of the defense who have come up to stop a run lofts a long pass downfield. It doesn't work all the time, but when it does it's a terrific crowd pleaser, and that's why there's always a lot of laughter mixed in with the cheering.

The most common sources for switch material are:

clichés — a classification covering not only clichés but its descendants — bromides, metaphors, titles and slogan.

word play — a classification for synonyms, antonyms and homonyms.

truisms — a classification covering facts of life, current events and acknowledged personal characteristics.

The classifications each have two common denominators: familiarity to a numerically large group of people and instantaneous comprehension of their significance.

CLICHÉS

We speak in clichés. They are part of every conversation. If we tried to eradicate them from our vocabulary, we would take three times as long to communicate our thoughts. Yet academics disdainfully dismiss them as shortcuts to verbal communication, literary crutches or stereotyped ammunition of the mentally bankrupt. But to a hungry humorist, they are his dinner's *pièce de rèsistance* (now, there's a cliché!). Since the cliché is a hackneyed phrase so overused that it has lost is original semantic impact, the audience is accustomed to accepting the current colloquial meaning of the cliché rather than its original and perhaps literal intention. (If this were really *a dog's world,* being called a *son of a bitch* would be a compliment.) With the use of clichés lies the easiest opportunity to switch the thought direction from the routine expected result to an unexpected ending. While the new direction contains a logical or realistic premise, it must still be unexpected. It is this surprise, plus the "sudden glory" recognition of Hobbes' theory, that produces the laughter of embarrassment (that we were fooled) and delight (that we recognized a shared hostility within an immediate social context).

There are four main methods for converting clichés, metaphors, titles, etc. to surprise endings:

1. the simple truth
2. the reverse
3. the take-off
4. the added twist

The first is the *simple truth* — switch an important word (be it noun, verb, adjective, adverb or pronoun) and reconceive its basic, literal meaning. Then complete the statement or answer a question as might a simpleton (thus, the *simple* truth) who did not understand the deeper meaning of the cliché.

> "Call me a taxi."
> "O.K., you're a taxi."

> ★ ★ ★

> "Who's dead?"
> "The one in the box!"

> ★ ★ ★

> "What do you call a dog who has no legs?"
> "I dunno? What?"
> "It don't make any difference. He won't come anyway."

> ★ ★ ★

> "I was going' tell you a joke," said the humor writer to his hospitalized friend, "but I can see you're in stitches already."

> ★ ★ ★

> If a single dolphin has as many as 2,000 babies, can you imagine how many she'd have if she were married.

> ★ ★ ★

> "What would you say to a martini?"
> "Depends on what the martini said to me first."

> ★ ★ ★

> "Did you take a bath Saturday night?"
> "Why, no. Is one missing?"

The *simple truth* is obviously an example of *first dimension* humor, as easily understood by a five year old as by every adult. To scale it up to a *second dimension* grade, let's look at this example:

First dimension, using simple truth:

> The forest ranger approached the Indian riding his horse up the steep canyon trail, his aged squaw trudging along slowly behind him.
> "Chief, I've been noticing for months now that you always ride up the trail and your wife always walks. How come?"
> "Because," the Indian said solemnly, "she no gottum horse."

Second dimension, using the added twist:

> The GI approached the Tunisian Arab riding his donkey along the military highway, his aged wife trudging ahead of him.
> "Hey, Abdul, I've been noticing for months that you always ride along the highway and your wife always walks. How come?"
> "Because," replied the Arab, "she no got donkey."
> "But why does she always walk ahead of you? Old Arab custom?"
> "No. Land Mines."

The second method is *the reverse* — switching the key word to the direct opposite meaning. Again, there must be some basis for realism, proven or not, and even sick humor contains contrasting nouns and accepted truth.

> "Leave my house," said the tyrannical father to his wayward daughter, "and never darken my bathtub again."

★ ★ ★

> During the height of her homosexual notoriety, Billie Jean King was referred to as Billie Jean Queen."

★ ★ ★

> Every once in a while, they send an innocent man to Congress.

The third method is *the take-off* — switching the meaning of a major word in the cliché, bromide, title, etc. by adding or eliminating one or two letters, the fewer the better. This technique is the springboard for thousands of puns, malaprops and spoonerisms:

> "Having a wonderful time," wrote the husband to his wife, "wish you were her!"

★ ★ ★

> "The party was a great success," said the swinger, "while I lasted."

★ ★ ★

> The wife described her crotchety husband as "one who gets up at the crank of dawn."

Again, to be successful (comedic), the new meaning must not only be original and a surprise, it must also be realistic. Note how the following story loses its punch because it carried the scenario past the point of realism, or believability:

> *I bought one of those new talking cars. You know the kind that tells you when you're going too fast or reminds you to fasten your seatbelt. Unfortunately, it's not working properly and has to go back for repairs. The last time I got a ticket, the car not only didn't say a word to the cop, it testified against me in traffic court.*

The realism must also share a hostility between performer and audience. Thus, it is easy to see why this method is so commonly used for name calling and insults, just by changing one or two letters:

> *Opponents of Prime Minister Margaret Thatcher called her "Atilla the Hen."*

★ ★ ★

> *Familiarity breeds attempt.*

★ ★ ★

> *He's a ragged individual.*

★ ★ ★

> *Said the fork to the spoon, "Who was that ladle I saw you out with last night?" "That was no ladle," said the spoon, "that was my knife."*

★ ★ ★

> *Headline on a new tire ad: "We skid you not."*

★ ★ ★

> *And finally, of course, wouldn't it be nice if this book became a jest seller!*

The fourth switch is the *added twist* — adding to the cliché a second statement which twists the meaning of the opening segment into a new train of thought (damn it, there's another cliché).

The procedure is very simple. First write a straightforward cliché (i.e. bromide, title, slogan). Example: "I'm an atheist." Then add the switch, in this case a twist which takes, often, a 190-degree turn. What's the opposite of an atheist: a believer. So now we have this:

> *"I'm an atheist — thank God!"*

Easy. O.K., let's try a few more examples:

> *My father was wiped out in a crash. A truck backed into his pushcart.*
>
> * * *
>
> *I told that joke before President Roosevelt — was elected.*
>
> * * *
>
> *"I have three children," says Rodney Dangerfield. "One of each."*
>
> * * *
>
> *It was suggested that Werner Von Braun's autobiography be entitled:* I Aimed for the Stars — But Sometimes I Hit London.
>
> * * *
>
> *"I couldn't wait for success," says Jonathan Winters, "so I went ahead without it."*

What is fascinating is that every cliché can be used as a humor springboard. It's just a matter of waiting for the time when the switch has value to the right audience.

The humor writer has two choices in attacking an assignment. He can take a file full of jokes and string them together (we're full of clichés), hoping there will be some common theme, plot or personal connection. Far better, however, is to first write the material for the occasion in a straight, direct manner (unwittingly!), being careful to make all the points to fulfill the purpose of the speech, or article or scene. Then, rewrite to make use of a number of appropriate clichés, metaphors and titles which can be switched and substituted for the original, "straight" copy.

This is done by association, listing as many ideas associated with the occasion, then analyzing each one to see where the humor may be naturally inserted.

For example, let's take a roast for a retiring professor.

The speech was written first as a simple tribute, listing many of the characteristics of the retiree, but paying particular attention to his idosyncracies, reputation (deserved or not), and fantasies.

Then, the first draft was dissected. Each line or two was examined for cliché switches which could provide a humorous opportunity. Examples:

> *"We honor tonight Horace Richardson, Ph.D., MA, BS, LL.D.— oh, what the hell, you all know how to spell Richardson.*
>
> *A man so erudite that even freshmen are honored when he calls their work sophomoric. A man who tried to get the*

college to build a halfway house for coeds who don't want to go all the way."

For a roast of a retiree, notice how many clichés can be shuffled in. And using the four switch methods on the preceding pages take a crack at adding your own humor.

> Overstepping his authority
> But first a word from our sponsor
> It's the first dollar he ever earned
> It was a slip of the tongue
> He took the words right out of my mouth
> He had the last word
> To put it in a nutshell
> He always keeps two feet on the ground
> Time and tide wait for no man
> He sold him a bill of goods
> He has money to burn
> He's rolling in wealth
> He's a chip off the ol' block
> His son is following in his footsteps
> He fell head over heels in love
> He had a hard day in the office
> Where there's a will there's a way
> He's seen better days
> He's a gentleman of the old school
> He's in the prime of life
> He's turning over a new leaf
> Out of sight, out of mind
> He lives by his wits
> Shake well before using
> We all have to go sometime
> It costs more to live nowadays
> Visiting hours are over
> He cut off his children without a cent
> He'd give you the shirt off his back
> He'll try anything once
> Once over lightly
> Relax dear, I can explain everything
> Darling, there's no one in the world but you
> Stop me if you heard this one
> He's as clean as a whistle
> He's under the weather today
> Oh, I can't complain
> How about one for the road
> He carries his office in his hat

Have you read any good books lately
You men are all alike
He's quite a homebody
He's pouring his heart out
He hasn't got a thing to wear
Travel is broadening
He's in the driver's seat
What are you going to be when you grow up
He just stepped out for a minute
I simply can't go on living without him
It's nice for a man to have a hobby

SYNONYMS, ANTONYMS AND HOMONYMS

Every professional humor writer has a copy of *Webster's Treasury of Synonyms, Antonyms and Homonyms* at his deskside because — after clichés, etc. — these are the second most common resource of humor catalysts for switching.

In humor writing, synonyms are words or ideas having the same meaning!

> "When I went to college," said the father, "a girl got pinned. Today, she gets nailed."

★ ★ ★

> "My boss," said the complaining employee, is frugal, parsimonious, and niggardly."
> "Not only that," said his dumb wife, "he's cheap, too!"

Antonyms are words or ideas having opposite meaning:

> "If you fall off that mountain and break a leg," warned the mother to her adventurous son, "don't come running to me."

Homonyms are words or ideas that sound alike but are spelled differently and have different meanings:

> "I was abroad myself for two years," one actor said to another, "but a psychiatrist fixed me up."

★ ★ ★

> Then, there's the tale of the cow who went dry — a case of udder failure.

Homonyms are used more often in speeches and particularly

broadcast and theatrical material where the communication is totally oral. Synonyms appear more often in written material.

Homonyms are, of course, the inventory of punsters, a form of humor that is contemptible, unless you happen to think of the pun first — a famous quote credited to Oscar Lavant. But Groucho Marx is best remembered for his homonym humor, which was combined with his reputation for caustic sarcasm.

> *In my opinion, women should be obscene and not heard.*
>
> ★ ★ ★
>
> *CHICO: "Hey boss, he wantsa meet for lunch."*
> *GROUCHO: "I don't know if I want meat for lunch."*
>
> ★ ★ ★
>
> *CHICO: "The lady in 304 wants ice water."*
> *GROUCHO: "Send her up an onion. That'll make her eyes water."*

Groucho also effectively used antonyms:

> *Groucho to hotel guest: "You can only have a room in this hotel if you'll agree to make up your own bed. O.K.? Well, good, here's a hammer, nails and some wood."*

Not very contemporary humor, and certainly it's not very sophisticated. But perfect for neophytes to warm up on. Like athletes and musicians, comedy writers need warm-up drills. Trying out 20-25 of the clichés or the group of synonyms for a half hour each day is standard comedic calisthenics.

TRUISMS

There is no etymological connection between the words pun and pundit, but they are closely allied in the technique of humor writing.

While pun is a humor switch on a common word, the humor pundit derives his material by a switch on a common truism.

Let's follow this simple procedure for creating humor from truisms. Subject: work. You don't like it and you avoid it whenever possible. That's a truism. It is obvious you can create innumerable humor opportunities from this base, so let's structure it by applying the HEARTS theory. Since most people dislike work, too, you now have a shared hostility. But just saying, "I dislike work. I try not to do any," gets very few laughs — a few nods of the head, maybe, but very few laughs.

We can increase the tension a bit by exaggeration — changing the word dislike to hate. But there's still no surprise, so forget about hate and prepare the switch by starting out in the opposite direction, "I love work." What has this done? The common hostility against work is still there; you've just added an example of aggressiveness because now the audience also has an obvious target — you. You've twisted them into becoming suspicious and that's helped make them even more attentive. You've increased the tension while, at the same time, kept your options open for any surprise you might be clever enough to think of.

That's the comedic logic of it, but we're still only at this point: "I love work. I just try not to do any." You might get a few smiles out of that — from friends, good friends. And admittedly, Woody Allen got mileage for years from the line, "I've got nothing against dying. I just don't want to be there when it happens."

Since more exaggeration will increase tension, let's double our salute to work. "I not only love work, it fascinates me." Now — "fascinates" — here's the key word to switch the truism. What do we do when something fascinates us? Most likely, we watch it, study it and sometimes actually get involved with it. But that normally wouldn't be true of hard work. Instead of quickly getting involved with it, we postpone the work for as long as possible. Minutes (that's too short a period). Hours (that sounds more realistic). Days (funnier, but not as credible), so reluctantly we settle for "hours." And finally, instead of postpone, we add "sit and look at." Now what do we have? "I love work. It fascinates me. I can sit and look at it for hours" (Jerome K. Jerome). A modern humor writer? No, Jerome wrote that over a 100 years ago. It's one of our most quoted witticisms.

Chico Marx was a notorious gambler. When the famous gangster Bugsy Seigel was shot dead, police found in his wallet a large check from Chico. Groucho used to say that was lucky for Chico, because if Seigel had tried to cash the check, the check would have bounced and then Seigel would have shot Chico.

Chico used this hostility against his bad gambling luck in one of his most quoted interviews, in the *London Express,* a good example of a switch on a truism.

"I guess I lost around two million dollars gambling . . . The first crap game I played I lost $47,000 in one night. But I learned as I went along. In time, I was able to lose a lot more than that."

As a final example, here's another truism switch, based upon human characteristics. Put a pencil mark at the point in this story where you've figured it out. In New York City, cab drivers are fearful to take passengers into Harlem late at night because of muggings, so they are reluctant to pick up black passengers. David Brenner tells the story about himself and a black friend who would go slumming all night. When the time came to hail a cab home, Brenner would stand in the street while his black friend hid in the doorway. When the cab stopped, they would both jump in. If the driver grumbled, Brenner would yell, "First stop is 69th Street and Third and then go to 125th and Lenox." When they would get to the ritzy East Side address, the switch was on. What switch? You guessed it. His black friend would jump out and Brenner would shout, "Now, mothah, take me to 125th and Lenox."

And since you probably did guess the switch, you now know how to write 50% of all humor. The rest is a little bit harder.

8

Ask the Pros
Professional Advice on Humor

Humor is a language, not unlike English or French or Spanish, except that it's called funny, *talking funny*. First you learn to see things funny, then you start to think funny, and finally, with courage and encouragement, you start to talk funny. If you are good at it you may soon become known as a wit. If you're only half funny, you may soon get to be known as a half-wit.

Before we get into the details of the language, let's get an overall flavor by sitting in on a free-for-all discussion about contemporary humor with some of the most famous comedy writers today. They include such writer/performers as Woody Allen, Mel Brooks, Steve Allen, Steve Martin, Bill Dana and Johnny Carson, plus more than fifty comedy writers from all phases of commercial humor . . . print, broadcast, theater and cinema.

This "ask the pros" roundtable, of course, never took place — but how every neophyte writer wishes he could attend one just like it. This compilation came from hundreds of books, magazine and newspaper interviews and personal interviews. Readers are highly recommended to three invaluable sources: *How the Great Comedy Writers Create Laughter,* by Larry Wilde (Nelson-Hall, Chicago, Ill., 1976); *Gene Perret's Roundtable,* a monthly newsletter for comedy writers, edited by Ed Hercer (P.O. Box 13, King of Prussia, Pa., 19406); and *Make 'em Laugh: Life Studies of Comedy Writers* by William Fry, Jr. and Melanie Allen (Science & Behavior Books, Palo Alto, Calif.).

WHAT ADVICE DO YOU HAVE FOR A BEGINNING COMEDY WRITER?

HAL KANTER: We will always be in the need for new writers, new performers, new directors. If somebody really wants to write comedy, or to provide laughter in some way, nothing is going to stop him.

CHARLES SHOWS: See the world through twinkling eyes. If you are naturally funny, you can learn how to write comedy and you eventually will learn how to sell it. Don't let anyone keep you from giving your valuable humor to your unfortunate fellow man (or woman, even).

MEL BROOKS: Don't use a typewriter. Somehow, when you use a typewriter you fall in love with everything you write. It just looks so good you don't want to tear it up. I use a pencil. You can see how scrawly and how stupid-looking it is, and you can always erase it.

GENE PERRET: You must make an effort to sell yourself. How can you market a product if you don't let buyers know that you're around. It takes confidence to expose yourself to auditions and reviews. Perseverance is definitely a factor because rejection is a fact of life. You simply have to follow the musical refrain, ". . . pick yourself up, dust yourself off, and start all over again."

RICHARD ARMOUR: Humor can be taken only in small doses. It comes off best in epigrams, anecdotes, sketches of a few hundred words.

STEVE MARTIN: Have a lot of confidence in your ability. In show business, if you don't think you're great, you haven't got a chance. Because if you're doing something different you have to bomb for three years before they start to get it.

MARTY KLEIN: Right! Uniqueness is the most important thing. Someone who has the courage to be different — in attitude, presence and, of course, material.

MARION LITTLE: Write humor without laughing, as though what you say is deadly serious. It works better if what you are telling is outrageous.

ROBERT ORBEN: First get out and watch as much live comedy as possible. Go to your local improvisation club, like a Comedy Store in L.A. or the Comedy Factory Outlet in Philadelphia. Don't learn just by watching tv and listening to laugh tracks. A whole generation of comedy writers grew up with a laugh track dictating to them what was funny. You've got to get the reality of audience reaction and you can't get it from tv. When I grew up, I'd go to vaudeville shows — three, maybe four shows a day. I'd just sit there, learning right along with the performer. You'd see the comedian deliver the line differently each show. The audience, in turn, reacted differently with each reading and I learned what worked and what didn't.

BILL DANA: It's a god-damn shame, but it has to depend so much on luck.

WHAT ARE SOME COMMON CHARACTERISTICS OF HUMOR WRITERS?

DEE HOLMBERG: Chances are you're very serious, almost solemn. Yet, you keep coming up with remarks that makes your friends laugh. Why not get paid for it?

HAL KANTER: The importance of having a good ear. One could develop an ear by listening and by observing. A performer is what the general public assumes him to be rather than what he really is. Therefore, by being an intelligent listener, one becomes a much more intelligent writer.

JACK DOUGLAS: You have to be observant. You watch people. Remember incidents and how they developed. Doing comedy is great training for straight writing (Herman Wouk was one of Fred Allen's writers) and straight acting. I don't think it's the other way around.

CARL REINER: Most people do not say exactly what they feel, but the comedian says exactly what he feels . . . what everybody was already thinking and he enhances his statements with comic techniques.

GENE PERRET: You don't need a college education, but I never met a stupid comedy writer. To write comedy you have to be alert to what's going on all over the world. Most of all, we watch people. Study them. Humor stems from human weaknesses or frailties. A funny character will lead to laughs no matter what he says or does.

ART BUCHWALD: Most comedy writers had an unhappy childhood. I did, and it makes you go into fantasy early in life.

MAX EASTMAN: Humor is derived from pain. A humor writer is masochistic and enjoys pain in many forms and the audience likes to suffer vicariously.

WOODY ALLEN: Off stage I'm very serious. I'm not a joker, but the point is I can't not see the funny side of things. Comedy just occurs to me. By being naturally attuned to the absurdity in everything, humorists have the constant problem of what to believe in wholeheartedly without satirical asides. That shakes people. The real problem is human nature. If there were only two people in the world and they were identical twins, one would find something wrong with the other.

JACK DOUGLAS: You need reading to stimulate your brain. Go a couple of weeks without reading a goddamn thing, you get dumb.

ART BUCHWALD: The problem with reading everybody else is that there isn't a new idea under the sun, that everybody had thought of your idea before you did. So I stopped reading the famous humorists so I wouldn't be inhibited by anything they already wrote.

JACK DOUGLAS: I feel the same way about Max Shulman. I started to read *Rally Round the Flag, Boys* and I said to myself, "This guy's awful close to the way I think and I don't want to copy anything," so I never did finish reading him.

ABE BURROWS: You need an excellent vocabulary. Without words, you're dead. Syntax! Comedy requires a knowledge of natural conversation, of real conversation. If you've never read Shakespeare, you can't satirize the balcony scene from *Romeo and Juliet*. You're always adapting, and the more you know, the more you can adapt. It's a writer's tool.

IS THERE SUCH A THING AS A NATURAL COMEDY WRITER?

CARL REINER: I think it's both natural AND developed. You start with it naturally, and then you develop it. As you get applauded for something you do instinctively, you keep doing it and it develops by usage. It's just like swimming; the more you swim, the better you are at it. But talent has to be there to begin with.

PAUL PUMPIAN: Lots of people say funny things now and then, but to be a professional you must be able to create a new joke on a moment's notice — or at least a related joke that will fit the occasion. Having a mind like this is a gift that one is born with and then nurtures over the years.

WOODY ALLEN: It's an ambivalent and internal thing. You can't study it. It's like jazz. If you listen a lot, it starts seeping in by osmosis. A comedy writer is frequently solitary, endlessly driven and endlessly guilty, because nothing one writes ever meets expectation's ideals. I wanted every line to produce a laugh even when the lines were being used to build to a large episode, and I toiled over them until they did. I'm not as normal as I appear.

CAN ANYBODY LEARN COMEDY WRITING?

MEL BROOKS: Yes. Any intelligent person can learn it. Whether he's good at it or not is another question. He can learn it. He can learn some basic rudiments. And the way to learn it is by doing it. But my advice is not to be a comedy writer. It's a very difficult and competitive job and I'd say don't do it. Don't ever do it. I'd say learn a trade.

DANNY SIMON: I teach a three day seminar on "The Craft of Comedy Writing" at universities all over the country. I can't teach anyone to be funny unless they're already funny — but I can guide them so they're five to ten years ahead of where they'd be learning on their own. I teach them how to write better, learning basics like how their humor must contribute to the building of a sitcom's characters or you toss the joke out. Only about five percent of the students actually go on to be professional comedy writers. That's not bad. I'm helping make a lot of people laugh!

ROBERT ORBEN: Beyond talent, the added ingredients are determination and aggressiveness. It's 50% talent and 50% aggressiveness. Once you're in, you're only as good as your last joke. That's one of the things I don't like about being a comedy writer. If you develop a business and make a success, the business goes on. But in writing, except for royalties, when we stop punching that machine, our income stops. We can never coast.

JACK ELINSON: You can't learn to write comedy in college. Oh, you can learn certain fine points and technical things, but I don't think there's a course in the world that can teach a guy how to be funny.

RUTH FLIPPEN: I don't think that's true. If they want to work on the exercises, you can teach them. There are basic rules. For example when you're in trouble and a scene won't work, try writing it backwards. Or take the lines the girl is saying and give them to the boy. Or take an old joke and switch.

HERBIE BAKER: You can learn technique, but you can't learn timing. You're born with it. There are no rules. You get a feeling that the timing is right. When performers start out their sense of timing isn't too sharp. That comes through experience — waiting for a laugh, knowing when to come in. When to start telling the next joke so that the laughs of the last one come down and they'll be ready to listen to the next joke. Neophytes step on their own laughs. They don't wait long enough, or worse, they wait for a laugh to die down completely then have to start building all over again. What you want to do is create a rolling laugh — a roll — and more often you start with verbal routines and then to keep the roll going it becomes physical — it builds.

NAT HIKEN: I wouldn't hire a man unless he felt sure he was the funniest writer in the world. Every guy on my staff thinks he's the funniest, but, of course, they're all deluding themselves — because I am!

WHAT'S THE BEST TRAINING FOR A COMEDY WRITER?

BILL DANA: A writer should be a "scholar of comedy," a term originated by Harold Lloyd. Some people have a joke file — cross indexed — which is a fantastic thing but can lead you down treacherous paths because it can give you a sameness. If I see something funny, I make a note of it. But you must THINK FUNNY.

GENE PERRET: The best training for a writer is actually standing up and delivering lines. Then you really learn what's funny and what's not. You can speak at private parties and before service clubs which are always looking for free speakers. You don't have to get paid. The education will be your reward.

MEL BROOKS: The hardest thing in comedy writing is to remember how people phrase things — to get down the rhythm of human speech. They do not speak in balanced sentences. They sometimes skip words, and they make jumps in their head. They don't always use a verb. Things that look good on paper don't often sound good.

J. MILTON JOSEFBERG: If you want to learn to write jokes, watch Bob Hope. Record one of his monologues. Get it down on paper and then analyze it. Notice how the jokes are constructed, the wording, the topics he uses.

WOODY ALLEN: Like so many other humor writers I am a prisoner of the work ethic. If I'm not creating something funny after half a day goes by, I start to feel guilty. I fit the traditional pattern of the comedy writer — solitary, endlessly driven, endlessly guilty because nothing one writes ever meets expectation's ideal. But salaries are insane. One is very lucky to be paid so much to do one's hobby.

WHERE DO YOUR BEST IDEAS COME FROM?

NORMAN LEAR: Start anywhere. Make notes. Try an outline, but start letting the ideas come out. Ideas, if you don't let them out, are like somebody yelling fire and everybody rushing to a door. If everybody rushes, the door doesn't get open and nothing comes out. If you open the door and let them out one at a time, they might all get out.

JACK ELINSON: This is a business today and it has to be more or less mechanical. We spitball ideas at first — my partner and I — writing down as many ideas as can think of, then we'll zero in on those we think can bear fruit. That'll be about one-third of the ideas. Then we'll work on those, dropping by the wayside those ideas which won't work. We shut ourselves off from everything. Once we get rolling we can write very fast, as much as fifteen pages a day.

MAX WILEY: When you're writing something, never talk about it, never tell anybody about it until you've put it down on paper, because, if you do, it's like giving the performance. You will have received the failure or applause already; then when it comes time to write the stuff, it's like after-the-fact. You will have lost the enthusiasm.

PADDY CHAEFSKY: First I draw on my own experiences, then I draw on the experience of others through observation and research. Research is vital.

RICHARD ARMOUR: Some people reminisce. I find sufficient material in the present. I consider my world — office, colleagues, car, traffic, parking, service station, public library, supermarket, house, garden, neighbors, etc. I try to turn an irritation into a humorous article. When I get paid for a 1,500-word piece, it quickly offsets the initial irritation. Another source of material I have found useful is the newspaper.

GENE PERRET: If you are writing for a special group, learn some of the inside material about them and gear your comedy directly towards that group. But sometimes just an expression starts a whole train of thought. On the *Carol Burnett Show,* one of the writers mentioned that he went to a restaurant and his waitress was constantly following around another waitress. "That's my puppy," she explained, "a waitress in training." The writers thought it was funny, and developed a sketch about a bank teller training another teller. They were held up by a bank robber training another robber. Ultimately, they are foiled by a policeman and, you guessed it, his trainee.

ART BUCHWALD: Big government is a particularly funny subject. The things that people are afraid of are the best things to sock it to. I need something that everybody knows something about so I don't have to devote any of the column to explaining the situation. I only have 600 words.

RUSSELL BAKER: You go into a dark room and close the door, and you're alone inside your head.

RICHARD ARMOUR: One of the rich areas is reminiscence. The idea is to write playfully about events of an earlier day, that seemed serious then but in retrospect have a comic look about them: the misadventures of childhood, the first love affair with the teacher, stealing a smile, pets, camping trips, oddball relatives. It helps to come from a large family and to have plenty of brothers and sisters, aunts and uncles, cousins and grandparents to write about. In such writing, the writer must be willing to make fun of himself.

WOODY ALLEN: I'm envious of Robert Altman. He had a dream, woke up and was so excited about it that he sold it as a movie idea that very day. It was a hit, so now his studio has an option on his next two dreams.

HOW DO YOU MAKE UP A JOKE?

NEIL SIMON: I don't know for sure. It's not just the situation, it has to be the character in the situation.

ROBERT ORBEN: Just as there's a blueprint for building a house, there are blueprints for writing jokes. You just think about the audience, ask yourself what would strike an emotional response. You craft around that. My goal is 25-26 jokes a day. If I get them in two or three hours, I quit. That's my reward. If not, I go until five or six or into the evening.

STEVE ALLEN: Some of the funniest jokes are those in which we expect to hear one thing but we hear another.

MEL BROOKS: Not at all, sometimes comedy is exactly the opposite. Sometimes comedy is wanting to hear something, being tortured into nearly not hearing it and then hearing it. Surprise is basic.

BUT WHAT TECHNIQUES DO YOU HAVE?

DEE HOLMBERG: Some of my best gags materialize at night in bed. I keep a tape recorder handy and talk them down. Most of them turn out — in the morning — to be better forgotten, but occasionally there's a gem. Brevity enhances wit. Drag an idea out and it loses punch. Work with your lines. Twist them, juggle the words around and chop until you have the tightest, funniest arrangement.

NEIL SIMON: I'm never very conscious of comedy techniques, devices or gimmicks. It's there, but I think most of it's instinctive. It's mostly either getting people, forces of opposite desires and opposite personalities, opposite characters, and putting them in contact with each other — and letting the sparks fly in what I like to consider an intolerable situation. A good joke always has an easy flow, and there is a cadence or a rhythm in the language. In a play, it must seem to the audience that the character is making the lines up, that the writer is completely unseen. The minute you sort of see the *sweat* on the word, you are aware of it being a joke.

LLOYD ERIC REEVE: Any humorous effect must be plotted — that's the juxtaposing of two or more serious statements against each other in such a way that the *final* effect becomes, by contrast, ludicrous. Take this example: "There are three things I never forget. One is my name, the second is my address and the third is — well, dammit, I can never remember what the third one is." It's funny because of the plotting, but it would fail as a joke if we had given away the surprise by saying at the start, "I can't remember what the first one is, but the other two are my name and address."

STANLEY RALPH ROSS: Either take an ordinary person and put him in an extraordinary circumstance (like a priest who wanders by mistake into a massage parlor), or an extraordinary person in the ordinary circumstance (like an escaped ape who strolls into a PTA meeting). After I get the idea for the sketch, I write a detailed outline of what's going to happen. Then, and only then, do I begin the comedy dialogue.

GOODMAN ACE: Joke construction comes from years of practice. Right now it's a very fine art. You learn to put the right word in the right place so that the rhythm is there, and the joke makes sense. You can tell a joke to a layman and he'll repeat it and tell it all wrong. He'll leave out a word or transpose a word. Each word has to be honed, refined to make it say what it's supposed to say.

MAX SHULMAN: You must write humor that is not threatening to the audience. You want the reader to say, "Hey, I know somebody just like that!" If the reader ever said, "Oh, my god, that's me!" you're dead. You've failed. Humor can never hit target dead-center but must strike obliquely and not allow the reader to feel threatened or to identify himself.

CARL REINER: Yes, there are certain techniques, formulas. For example, if you write a one-line joke, you try to save your key word for the last word. Good writers know that instinctively. They talk that way. In the beginning, teaching writers the cliche is very good: "This is the cliché. You put the straight line here and the joke comes out here and you use the letter 'K' if you have a hard word." I use mystery, surprise, saying the thing that's unexpected or the most expected, either one. When they expect the unexpected, give them the most expected. It's a joke. Like: "I just flew in from Washington, D.C. You know what Washington, D.C. is? It's the capital of the United States." That's a non-joke, but there's something humorous about it because the audience was expecting the unexpected.

MAX SHULMAN: Technique is more important in humor writing than any other. The very positioning of a single word is vital to the successful telling of a joke or story. For example, a character in a Noel Coward play says: "Women should be struck regularly, like gongs." Substitute the word bells for gongs, and it's not funny.

HOW IMPORTANT IS THE PUNCHLINE?

GENE PERRET: A joke is a relationship between two ideas which must be expressed in a way that saves the surprise. A really good joke should "explode" with the punchline, and it is necessary to keep polishing it until you're satisfied with that "explosion."

JACK ELINSON: The punchline is the truth. Each member of the audience suddenly recognizes it as an old acquaintance, a bit of wisdom each has long possessed but had forgotten or hadn't seen before in quite that light.

WILLIAM F. FRY, JR.: Humor is to play as adult is to child. A major difference is that only humor has a punchline. Humor does not exist without a punchline of some sort; even in the most extreme cases of captionless cartoons, the punchline is there — it's just a visual nature. The punchline acts to reveal a hidden truth, accompanied by a strong sense of discovery.

WHAT IS A FORMULA JOKE?

BILL DANA: A repertoire of constructed jokes that already exist. You take the skeleton and put different flesh on it. The "would you believe" joke I wrote for Don Adams is such a formula. Here's the original. The British in India. Leftenant Favershim (Don Adams) is confronting Mohammed Sidney Kahn:

> "Not so fast, Sahib Kahn. You may think you've got me, but I've got you surrounded by the entire Mounted 17th Bengal Lancers!"
> Then Kahn says: "I don't believe that!"
> "Would you believe the 1st Bengal Lancers?"
> "No!"
> "How about Gunga Din on a donkey?"

We used it so extensively, "would you believe" has become a part of the American colloquial language. Another example is the "question man" routine. Steve Allen originated it and Johnny Carson still uses it. The premise of the "question man" is that today everybody knows all the answers, so you find an answer and then create a funny question:

> The answer is "chicken teriyake." And the question is: "Give me the name of the oldest kamikaze pilot."

JACK DOUGLAS: The most common formula is to make a serious or straight statement first. Then follow it with a ludicrous or ridiculous comment, which hopefully comes out as a joke.

SHERWOOD SCHWARTZ: There are usually two key words or phrases in a joke . . . one is in the straight line and the other is in the punch line. These words must be closely associated in the audience's mind. Therefore, the sentences should be phrased so that the key words are as close together as possible. In addition, the key word in the punch line must be placed as near the end of the line as can be managed — because the joke is over as soon as this word is spoken.

JACK BENNY: There are lots of formulas. For instance, put last things first, because the last word is often the most important. People laugh with surprise, so you've got to polish that punch line — you must line up the most effective combination of words. And that takes practice. Practice also helps us learn how to stretch out the story, where to put in pauses, gestures and intonation.

HOW DO YOU "SWITCH" A JOKE?

ABE BURROWS: You change it from a streetcar to a motorcycle. It's also an inverted one-liner.

WOODY ALLEN: I call it the "Big Non Sequitur" — or the old switcheroo. For instance:

> (1) He carried a sword on the street, but in case of attack it turned into a cane so people would feel sorry for him.
> (2) He carried a bullet in his breast pocket. Someone threw a bible at him and the bullet saved his life.

IS THERE A CERTAIN FORMULA ABOUT THE NUMBER OF JOKES IN A SEQUENCE ON THE SAME SUBJECT?

JACK DOUGLAS: Yeah. It's called the series of three: a joke, a topper and a second topper. It's a magic thing. When you get a laugh and you top it and then you top it again, you have a roll going. It makes each successive joke in the sequence easier for the audience to understand and digest because you've gotten them laughing.

MAX BEERBOHM: Laughter becomes extreme only if it's consecutive. There must be no pauses for recovery. The jester must be inexhaustible. Only so can he exhaust us.

WHAT'S A TOPPER?

BOB HOPE: One kind of topper is the supposed ad-lib that comes after a bomb. For example, two duck hunters weren't having too much luck and one says to the other, "Maybe we ought to throw the dog a little higher." If that joke doesn't work, I'm ready with: "Maybe *I* ought to throw the dog a little higher."

STEVE MARTIN: A topper is a real thrill in timing. That's the greatest fun of all. You've got the next line in your head and you're just waiting for that little intimate moment. If you're prepared, you know it's right.

WHAT ARE SAVERS?

GENE PERRET: These are apparent "ad-libs" performers use when their best joke or jokes get nothing but confused stares. The performer gets "flop sweat", a fever of humiliation, and reaches into his memory file for "savers" like "I thought that would be a biggie," then takes out a small file card and tears it up. Others are: "Ladies & gentlemen, that was the comedy portion of my speech," or "That's the last time I''ll buy a joke from . . . (and blames it on the president of the organization). Comedy writers have to prepare their clients with "savers," against hecklers, ("Quick, give me my camera. I always wanted to take a picture of an asshole"), a plane flying overhead ("I hope that's one of ours"), to the lights going out ("Will somebody call Con Edison and tell them the check is in the mail").

HOW DO YOU TEST OUT YOUR HUMOR?

NEIL SIMON: Comedy needs a lot of time. I need four weeks of audience reaction so I can cut and trim.

WOODY ALLEN: Out of 20 jokes, 10 may fail at the mike and you have to work constantly to keep the material fresh.

ROBERT ORBEN: Try it out yourself in front of an audience. Go through the agony and the ecstasy. The agony is the pangs of "flop sweat" when you're telling jokes and the audience isn't laughing. It's similar to mid-life crisis. Hot and cold palms, you're dying. You'll never be inclined to give a performer a weak joke if you go through that.

GENE PERRET: Try it in front of a mirror when you're alone in your room. This is preferable because medical science has now lifted the veil of shame and masturbation is respectable.

MEL HELITZER: I count the number of times the audience not only laughs, but applauds — the ultimate tribute. The final topper in a series should get laughter plus applause, but that's like getting a grand slam home run.

DAVID BRENNER: The comedy club serves the role that a typewriter might otherwise. I write on stage. I just get up with some premises, start to talk, take questions from the audience, and some nights I'll get 15 minutes of new material. You can't practice on the *Tonight* show or in Las Vegas. Comedy clubs are a place you can be bad and that's how you get to be good.

BILLY CRYSTAL: Yeah, a comedy club is like a gymnasium. The way to use it is not to do the same thing every night, try different things and don't be afraid to bomb. Comedy club audiences are a little like the people who go to stock car races. They come in looking for winners, but they've also got their eye out for the accidents, for the bomb.

MARTY KLEIN: The most important spawning grounds are the comedy clubs. The clubs afford the comedian and his writer a chance to continuously work up new material. Television will only hurt the comic who has five minutes and no more.

HOW CAN YOU TELL WHEN SOMETHING FUNNY IS IN GOOD TASTE?

NORMAN LEAR: I've got a mechanism in my belly. My belly says this is funny; my belly says this is good taste, and this is in bad taste; and I don't know of any other definition that I could possibly work with. For example, I ran into trouble on toilet humor. Archie Bunker flushes the toilet in *All in the Family.* A lot of people think that's vulgar. I find nothing vulgar in it. Toilet humor makes me laugh. The very first joke or bit of amusement that passes between a parent and a child is a toilet joke. It has something to do with "doo-doo" or "pee-pee" or something of that nature. And it's perfectly lovely.

MEL BROOKS: Years ago, in my first comedy experience, if I did a joke, other people would laugh but then say, "No, we can't do that! That's in questionable taste." Or, "The audience won't get it." But on the "Show of Shows," whatever made us laugh was the only test. Whatever was funny was in.

GENE PERRET: You can never guarantee against offending someone, but comedy is a powerful force and can cause pain if misused. You draw the line on good taste yourself.

SHECKY GREENE: If a joke runs the risk of offending someone, it may be wise to drop it rather than take a chance. Once I took a few shots at Frank Sinatra. I'm lucky. Frank, God bless him, saved my life. I was getting beat up by a couple of guys, and Frank said: "That's enough."

WHAT ARE THE MOST FREQUENT PROBLEMS OR DANGERS?

BOB MILLS: Becoming discouraged and giving up. No matter how talented you are, it takes time. The one trait that distinguishes writers who have "made it" from those who haven't is *persistence*. The writer who's good loves a challenge.

MAX SHULMAN: One of the most common mistakes is writing for your friends. You find this in so many college humor magazines. It's not what panics you and your friends that is necessarily universal — you must hope to make all readers privy to the joke. On the other hand, there's simply no way of finding the common denominator in humor. I challenge any scholar in humor to deliver a joke — one joke — that will make 100% of the people laugh. It's impossible. And it's damn frustrating.

HAL KANTER: Getting a unanimity of opinion about what really is funny. When you are working in committee you have many points of view and you hear some real horror stories about the amount of re-writing being done for one reason or another.

ANN BANCROFT: One evening, I came home from a difficult rehearsal. Mel (her husband, Mel Brooks) had been working at home all day. I was feeling very sorry for myself, and I wailed, "Acting is so hard." Mel picked up a blank sheet of paper and held it in front of me. "That's what's hard," he said. I've never complained about acting again.

WOODY ALLEN: Comedy is such difficult work. It's hard to make an audience laugh and keep on laughing. Everything has to be spare and quick and precise. You'll see writers on a comedy with long faces, wondering where the laughs will come, how to get them, how to get the rhythm right. It can make for a terrible atmosphere.

STEVE MARTIN: Stand-up comedy is the hardest job in show business. There's no music, you can't sing for three minutes, there's no room for failure. Missing a joke or a mis-timed joke or a failed laugh reduces the audience's confidence in you. That's why it's so difficult, because there's never a chance to fail. They're literally hanging on every word — and you're being hung by every word. But my best advice to young comedians who want to do stand-up is, "Always take your wallet on stage with you."

GENE PERRET: Most novices quit too soon on each gag. They get frustrated if they don't write a lot of professional material in one night. If you can write even one good line in a night's work, you have talent. The buyers want material — they don't care how much you write and throw away. I find my strongest gags are my first and my eighth — the first is often the result of inspiration, and the eighth is the result of hard concentration. Another common fault is excess verbiage — too many words.

HERBIE BAKER: Despite the success of your last effort, all humor writers repeatedly wonder if they can do it again. That's what makes them so insecure, always on the attack, frightened that the whole world is about to find out the awful truth about them. . .that, in fact, they aren't very talented at all.

SIDNEY SMITH: Surprise is so essential an ingredient of wit that humor can't bear repetition — at least the original electrical feeling produced the first time can never be renewed.

IS COMEDY WRITING DONE BETTER ALONE OR WITH COLLABORATORS?

ABE BURROWS: I'm accustomed to working in groups, bouncing things off other people and seeing how they will play. We used to divide up the writing of a variety show: Two of us would do the opening monologue, others would write a sketch. Then we'd all get together, eight of us in one room, and "pitch." You sat there throwing out lines as fast as they came to you, and somebody would write them down. There was a lot of fun but a good deal of tension.

BILL DANA: It's like ping-pong. It's hard to ping unless somebody else pongs. It's good to bounce ideas off somebody. But then, there's the matter of ego. A lot of things I like to write alone. Then, you can say, "Hey, that belongs to me!"

ARNIE ROSEN: In tv personal routine is a luxury that you can't afford. The deadline motivates and stimulates you. That's another reason for working in teams.

ERIC IDLE: Getting six guys to agree on what's funny is easy. We read it aloud. If we laugh, it's in; if we don't, it's out. If four guys thinks something's funny and two guys think it's not, we solve that very simply: we just take the two guys and kill 'em.

STEVE MARTIN: The most fun game in life is exploring your own wit and intelligence and feeding off someone else's. But it's important to choose your friends. If you hang around with slobs, you'll be a slob.

ABE BURROWS: The worst thing that can happen when writers are collaborating is excessive politeness. There comes a moment when someone has to say something real, like "That's lousy," or if that's a bit rough, a gentler equivalent, "I don't think that's quite right." Collaborators must be honest with each other.

MEL BROOKS: You're more unsure writing alone, because there's no immediate laughter. If you describe something in a room with five other comedy writers and you get an immediate, insane response — a big scream — then you know you're home with the joke.

DON CARPENTER: I wrote a book about this called *A Couple of Comedians*. A comedy team is a marvelous paradigm to explain to the anxious set. It is a marriage of needs, a form of bonding that is also a paste-up job and a prison. Think of twins, and then think of ventriloquism. Without the other we are incomplete, jagged, full of holes, pretending a self. We require the other, and the fact that we do so makes us fearful and angry. We aren't free.

GENE PERRET: The reason most weekly shows have so many writers is because of time. Material has to be generated quickly. One particular show could have been written by only two people on the staff. But while they are writing that one show, somebody had to be turning out something funny for next week's show. It takes several groups of writers to stay ahead of schedule.

ARNIE ROSEN: Some writers are better joke writers than others, so they'll write the sketches that clearly call for several jokes loosely linked together. Other guys are better constructionists, so they'll do the sketches with more interplay between the characters. Some writers do pantomime material better than others who are more verbal. That's the good thing about writing in large teams.

JACK ELINSON: Working alone is harder, but probably it's more rewarding. But creating in association with another writer is even more crucial than a marriage because you spend more time with your partner than you do your wife. We have to respect the rejection of the other. There are rejections and acceptances all day long. You have to be able to feed each other without destroying each other.

BOB HENRY: The team thing is very common. Anything you get you have to bounce off somebody right away. It takes the other guy to see if it's any good. Many times one guy is the idea man; the other is the dialogue man.

MORT LACHMAN: Most gag writers work in pairs, hoping that something they say will inspire their partner to a better line. But no procedure could be more deflating to the ego. Suppose you had to make up jokes all day, tell them to a partner and have him greet one after another with a stony silence?

HAL KANTER: Every once in a while, some writer will point out that the really classic comedies of all time were all written by one man — Charlie Chaplin. The answer to that is, "All right, when you're Charlie Chaplin, we'll let you do it alone, too."

CARL REINER: I know why something works and why it doesn't. I can help performers take the jewel — the line — and place it in the setting. Of course, with Steve Martin, I'll mention something and he'll look at me and say, "Carl, how many times do I have to tell you? I've been in this business for six years!"

NORMAN LEAR: George Kaufman once said, "Nothing is written. It's rewritten." We spend months on some scripts. Only a team can afford to do that. For example, the first draft may be written by two writers from the outside. Then, the second draft is done by two writers on the inside, and the third, fourth, fifth and possibly sixth is written by all the guys on the inside. . .and that's how a dozen writers' names may appear on a credit.

GENE PERRET: You don't need a collaborator if you have a good friend in the business that you can call when needed. The other day I was stuck on what sort of jokes to write for Wayne Gretsky, the sensational hockey player. I called my fellow writer, and he suggested attacking it this way. . . . " You knew he was going to be a hockey player when he was a kid, because . . ." That was the breakthrough idea I needed, and I soon polished off 12 new jokes. A few days later I reciprocated. He was writing for a comic who was "working" with a movie star, and was stuck for an angle. I suggested he go through some of her movies and give reasons why he was almost, but not quite, cast to play opposite her. For example, "I was almost in your movie *Picnic* but at the last minute they decided to use real ants."

GIVE SOME EXAMPLES OF "WRITING AND REWRITING"

ROBERT ORBEN: The original joke read: "The sales manager I want reads Jaws and is on the side of the shark." Well one thing to do to improve the tone is change sales manager to bill collector — more audience hostility. We can add a conversational tone by associating the overall idea to a real place. And then add "roots" (a funny word) and cut out four words. Now the joke reads: "I've found the guy to hire as our bill collector. He's sitting out in the reception room reading Jaws — and rooting for the shark."

WOODY ALLEN: You're constantly putting in words, taking out words, rearranging and crossing them out. The flexibility of writing for print is infinitely greater than film — no expensive reshoots, no actors, no long nightmare delay in working it out. In print I can try 15 different endings in one day.

NEIL SIMON: Rewriting is a monumental pain. After a play opens, there are very few authors who don't second-guess themselves, don't wish they'd tightened a scene, changed a line here or there for better impact. Strangely enough, the big chunks that aren't working are often the easiest to fix. It's when you get down to those last few lines, the last few words, that it becomes harder and harder. When we tried out *The Odd Couple* in Boston, Mike Nichols was directing it and the third act was in trouble. So I wrote 15 pages of new dialogue. He read it, laughed his head off and said, "It's the best dialogue you ever wrote." We rehearsed it, put it on stage and didn't get a single laugh. The reason was that the audience didn't like what was happening to the character. So in rewriting, it's not just funnier dialogue, but the characters and the situation that does it, enhanced by the lines.

ABE BURROWS: Sometimes George S. Kaufman, when he was directing one of my Broadway shows, would point to a joke in the script and say, "Abe, that's too easy." It was a gag I had written because it was the first line that came to my mind. I had hurried to put it down because subconsciously I thought we were going on the air tomorrow. And he was right. The joke was too easy. I forgot I had plenty of time to think it over and to rewrite it. The more I worked at it, the better it got.

IS THERE MORE OF A DIFFICULTY BEING A FEMALE COMEDY WRITER?

SELMA DIAMOND: Comedy writers have a natural hostility to each other. I thought it was that they just wouldn't accept me. Men aren't that nice to each other. I don't think I had trouble because I was a woman. I had trouble because I was another writer.

STEVE MARTIN: The problem is that women comedians are emulating men, and it doesn't work that way. The tradition of being a comedian is hard sell — having to really sell your material. And the female tradition is being soft and vulnerable. The two haven't met. Like Gilda Radner who said, "Comedy is having your panties down around your ankles."

KATHY GREEN: There's no problem in most cases. There are a few men who prefer to hire just male buddies, but for the most part I think one's material speaks for itself. Comedy writers have no sex . . . and you can take that any way you want.

WHAT SHOULD BE YOUR FIRST MARKET FOR HUMOR?

RICHARD ARMOUR: I suggest trying the highly specialized magazines. Maybe the editor is a little bored himself and just ripe for a little something with which to lighten his pages.

HARRY GOLDEN: There's no better place than the local newspaper. In fact, there's no better apprenticeship for any writer than working on a newspaper. Not only does reporting and editing sharpen a writer's overall skills, but it also teaches him that what humor he writes is not important tomorrow. And that is the hard truth that all writing geniuses must learn sooner or later.

BOB MILLS: Every town, no matter how small, has a radio station with disc jockeys struggling to fill those moments between records. Writing lines for them has two advantages. It gives the writer a chance to hear his work performed and to hone his skills in tailoring a joke to a specific individual. Second, it gives him a chance to build up a body of material which can be used later to show others what he can do. It's a free testing ground.

GENE PERRET: An excellent place to start is with your local newspaper. Offer them a weekly humor column. If it's good, it will help your newspaper and it can be a big boost to your writing career. Begin by working on your column as if you already had a contract. Get used to the pressures of a deadline. Show the editor that you can be consistent. Offer to have him run it for a limited time at no charge, with a set fee agreed to after the free trial period. You can also trade off for advertising space, offer to have your column sponsored by a local merchant (it's easier on radio) and your compensation may be that your new popularity will lead to paid speaking engagements.

MARTIN LEVIN: Keep sending out your material, regardless of how many rejection slips you get. I've known people on *The New Yorker* and in all media who have been dead wrong, because I have taken their rejects and published them — and they have been republished and collected and are still alive.

JACK DOUGLAS: It's tough for a new guy. Dick Cavett used to hang around NBC. One day he just buttonholed Jack Paar, gave him some material and said, "Please read it!" Doing a thing like that to Paar is like talking to Holy Christ. But somehow he read it and he liked it and that's how Cavett got his first job with Paar. So aside from the ability to write jokes, you must have the initiative and the aggressiveness to go out and sell them.

DEE HOLMBERG: Smother your desire to see your name in a byline. Comics don't recite a list of credits. All of them give the impression that every gag comes right out of their own head. Contrary to what you might think, your best market is with the well-known and established comics. Don't think you must write a whole monologue or that all of your gags must be tied together and become a five-minute bit. Comics use their own style. But never send the same batch of gags to two comics. Besides, if you have tailored them properly, they wouldn't fit anyone else's style. Don't send one or two gags, a batch is six or more. Always keep a copy. Expect a response within three weeks and always include a SASE (self-addressed stamped envelope).

GENE PERRET: Find a banquet or a party that would be glad to have an emcee. Volunteer. If you can't stand in front of an audience, write jokes for the guy who is ham enough to. Either way, you'll get an audience reaction. Another possibility is your home town's most popular comic. If you can't contact him by phone, send a special delivery letter addressed to him at the club. Always mention you're a professional comedy writer and have some great material for him. This is the key that opens the door.

PHYLLIS DILLER: Start right where you are. Offer to do it for nothing at first, but you have to prove yourself. Work banquets, send lines or monologues to your local tv hosts, try to send out material regularly. A trip around the world starts with the first step, and the first step can only be taken where you're standing now.

GENE PERRET: Read Variety. The weekly is a wealth of information: a review of nightclub performers, new acts, comedians looking for fresh material, sit-coms in production and a thousand other important facts in every issue. It's the Bible of the entertainment business.

ROBERT ORBEN: Latch on to a rising comedy star. Most comedians are fairly accessible when they're on the road. If they get to your city for a one-nighter, they may get a little stir-crazy after the show. Sometimes they want to talk to someone. If you knock on their door and say, "Look, I've admired your work. I have a piece of material written especially for you, and I'd appreciate your looking it over." If it's written in his style, you're immediately perceived as something of a pro. If the material works, you're in. All performers have an insatiable need for new material.

HOW MUCH MATERIAL DO YOU SEND OFF AT ONE TIME?

JACK DOUGLAS: It's pitiful. I get stuff in the mail. There'd be one joke on the page. It's like a would-be song writer who writes one song. This is his masterpiece. And he's so shocked that nobody will buy it. It might be a great song — who the hell ever knows — but it's just one song. If you're a professional, you write a lot of material and keep writing until you sell some. Then you know it's worthwhile, so you keep writing more.

GENE PERRET: In writing a monologue, I'd try to do at least 30-35 gags for several reasons. First, by setting a demanding quota, you insure that you won't quit too soon. Second, you are selling to someone else and they will discard at least half your jokes and still have enough left over to make a routine worth putting in their act.

HOW MUCH DO COMICS PAY FOR STAND-UP MATERIAL?

DEE HOLMBERG: The rate for one-liners differs with each comic — $5 to $15 and the rate is negotiable. Not much, you say. I once sold five gags about Las Vegas for $35, all of which were hatched in 15 minutes.

GENE PERRET: Anywhere from $2 to $5 for individual jokes. I've sold material for 5% of the comic's income. I wrote monologues for $100 to $1,500. Don't charge too much at the start. You're mostly interested in getting your material tested and a career started. As your material gets better, you'll be able to command higher prices from better performers who get to know your skill. As a beginning writer you are not selling jokes. You are selling your skill to write more jokes. Comics don't buy jokes, they buy a supply of jokes.

WHAT ARE THE MOST IMPORTANT SUBJECTS FOR HUMOR?

PAT McCORMICK: Ridiculing celebrities. I like to combine inanimate objects with well-known people. For example: I pick up a large, clear, round glass ashtray and guess what it could be used for — a contact lens for the Jolly Green Giant, a bathtub for Mickey Rooney or the Statue of Liberty's diaphragm. They all can't be obvious. They have to be surprises.

BOB HOPE: It helps if you can tell jokes about important people, especially if they're in the room. But you've got to be sure they can "take it." One of my favorite targets is my friend Gerald Ford. I played golf with him the other day and he got a birdie, an eagle, an elk, a moose and a Mason.

JEAN KERR: My favorite is the insult — a witty insult is like a sneeze: you know that it's coming, but it still manages to surprise you. When the insult seems heavy-handed or mean, it's not because of the presence of malice, but because of the absence of genuine wit.

NORMAN LEAR: I learned early that the things that people laughed at the most were the things that they cared about the most. If you want to make people laugh, hit them where they breathe and where they live. It's much easier to get an audience to laugh after they care a lot. They love warm and tender moments, mixed with comedy, mixed with drama. What I look for is a good, solid piece of substance that has something more important to it than just a series of one-line jokes. All the forerunners of *All in the Family* dealt with a lost skate key and roasts that were ruined while the boss was coming to dinner. That's no forum for social comment and points of view. Situation comedy is not a label I accept. That's what it's called, I know, but I consider I'm doing a half hour of theater, and my genre is comedy.

HOW IMPORTANT IS THE AUDIENCE ON DECIDING WHAT MATERIAL TO USE?

GENE PERRET: Above all, the gag writer must remember that he is the servant of the audience and not the other way around.

MORT LACHMAN: You can't make a joke about something that people don't know. For Bob Hope, we use current events because that's what people have in common. You have to know or find out what reference unites an audience — that embarrasses them or things that an audience is upset about. Those are the things that work for comedy.

STEVE MARTIN: Sometimes I get very frustrated over the need for new material. Stand-up is such a tough thing, there's a tendency to leave it the same because it works. I just can't leave it the same, but it's for my own head. On a recent tour, about 75% of my material was new but the audience still think they've heard it before. I knew it would happen. I can't change it. I can't make it 100% different. It's impossible. Besides, you're going to fail 50% of the time anyway.

WHAT'S THE DIFFERENCE BETWEEN WRITING ONE-LINERS AND SKETCH MATERIAL?

ED SIMMONS: One-liners are somewhat akin to a machine gun. Every shot won't hit the target but if there's enough quality in the quantity, you're a winner. When you move into sketch comedy, the lines must be germane to the central idea and you're allowed fewer misses. In sit-com writing, the story is the most important element and you can go four or five minutes without a laugh. Sometimes, this is even done deliberately. The difference between a good sketch and a bad sketch is very personal. Sometimes with my material I have modestly admitted it was great and sometimes I have reluctantly admitted it was just good. A bad sketch is a sketch written by other writers.

GENE PERRET: In writing a sketch, make sure you have a workable premise . . . one that has a beginning, a twist in the middle and an ending. Many sketch ideas are merely places or costumes — the star in a caveman outfit or deep in the Grand Canyon. You must have a well-prepared outline with all the plot points and comedic twists well-defined. It isn't necessary to struggle with lines until the first draft. The purpose of the outline is to allow you to concentrate on just adding "funny."

STEVE MARTIN: Once you write a piece and you think it's funny, you hand it to a producer and he changes it. Then you hand it to the star and he changes it or doesn't rehearse it and fucks it up badly. Then the director shoots it and he misses the joke. Then it goes to postproduction and they sweeten it till there's no spontaneity, no charm. Sometimes the distance from the printed page to what you see on screen is so far that the joke's been homogenized and disappeared.

ROGER EBERT: Dramatic comedy, perhaps more than any other form of entertainment, depends on context. Most often, to know what makes a situation funny we have to know what went on before. And we must be familiar with the comic personalities — their weaknesses, their egos, their tender spots — to understand fully their behavior.

LOU DERMAN: A man who just knows jokes is not going to make it writing for the top comedy series. He has to be a story teller. He should know the elements of play construction. He's basically writing a half-hour play every week which conforms to the rules of playwriting.

WHAT ABOUT THE SUBJECT MATTER FOR TV SITCOMS?

CHARLES SHOWS: The cheap use of sex and violence is in lieu of the ability to write good humor. It is not altogether the fault of the writers. They are not given enough time to write really funny scripts.

JULES FEIFFER: Sitcom material has traditionally been concerned with middle class American trivia: anxieties about walking the dog, finding a parking place and beating a teenager to the last seat on the bus. What really happens is that these petty details are what truly drive us crazy. They have a corrosive effect.

BENJAMIN STEIN: Prior to the mid-70's, all tv might have had the log line: "Bud loses his house keys." Nothing happened to a character outside of getting locked out of his house, spilling oil on his brother's tux or leaving the golf clubs out in the rain. Today, on tv, it's different. On *The Jeffersons* George and Louise shed bitter tears during the preacher's eulogy during a friend's funeral, only to find out that they are in the wrong church at a service for a total stranger. On *Mork & Mindy,* Mork goes to what he thinks is a friendly gathering for ecologists. It turns out to be a meeting of a racist hate group. The anxieties of today's tv characters are fundamental. Some believe tv is reflecting more reality. Others, like Bob Schiller and Bob Weiskopf, believe that because so few writers can write comedy, more and more of them turn to socially gut-wrenching situations and anger. They write soap operas — people in wheelchairs, people getting lynched. One night the healthiest person on tv was the Hunchback of Notre Dame.

CARL REINER: In sitcom you have to like the people, otherwise you won't buy the premise. Lucy was great. Whatever she did was great because they loved her. To get real laughs, the audience has to identify with the hero and his targets. A lot of shows have stayed on, not because they are good, but because the people are so attractive, warm lovely characters.

MADELYN DAVIS & BOB CARROLL: Certain themes are constantly being repeated: greed, envy, jealousy and don't do business with a friend. Humor is basic.

NORMAN LEAR: I look for a good, solid piece of substance, something more important than a series of one-line jokes, like a mentally retarded kid who fell in love with Gloria (in *All in the Family*). That's at once sweet and poignant. Then the comic lines come easier because you're writing a family episode, because your characters have built-in humor.

GARY BELKIN: For a variety show any funny notion you have can be turned into a sketch, a short piece or even a single joke. For sitcoms, you need a story. And you need one that will last for 22 minutes — no more, no less. A sketch should last as long as it's funny.

GOODMAN ACE: It is more important to develop a situation and to build up the characters than to go for big belly laughs. I'll throw away a sure-fire joke any time rather than sacrifice character. Once you develop a good, recognizable character, you get yucks even with soft lines.

WHAT ARE THE ODDS OF SELLING YOUR SITCOM SCRIPT?

GARY BELKIN: Any show that has been on for any length of time has already had a few hundred stories pitched by members of the staff and any number of free-lancers. So a newcomer has to have two good scripts: the first a "spec" one which gets him an invitation to pitch a story for the actual show. Just consider how many stories have been done, or pitched, to *M*A*S*H*.

MARVIN HIMELFARB: Last year, about 2,000 ideas for new sitcoms were submitted to one network from the professionals alone. And out of those 2,000, maybe 70 go to script and about 12 may shoot pilots. Of these 12, only one got on the air last year. One out of 2,000!

GENE PERRET: It's a waste of time to write full scripts for sitcoms as a beginning writer. It would be much better to spend the time and effort in preparing a good presentation rather than a full script. A book called *The Cool Fire,* by Bob Shanks, tells how to write a show presentation and gives several different examples.

WHAT HAPPENS TO UNSOLICITED MANUSCRIPTS FOR SITCOMS?

NORMAN LEAR: They come in by the hundreds, but they can't be read. First of all for legal reasons they can't even be opened. Nine people have the same idea at the same moment, and one of them makes it to air, and you've got eight lawsuits. If I were living anywhere in the country and wanted to write for television, I'd come to California. There is no way you can be in this town working at getting read and not get read.

WHAT ABOUT AGENTS?

CHARLES SHOWS: The agents are a real stumbling block. They put enough pressure on the Writer's Guild to agree that no scripts could be submitted by a writer — only through an agent. If you are a lousy writer, no agent will even talk to you. If you are a "hot" comedy writer, you don't need an agent!

SELMA DIAMOND: You need an agent to get you your first job. Once people know you in the business they will call you, but you need an agent to negotiate the contract. It's a necessary evil in this business.

GENE PERRET: Get an agent who cares about new writers. There aren't too many. Another way is to get your material to an established writer who cares about new writers. Surprisingly, there are more of them than you would imagine. A producer, a director and a performer have a much harder time breaking in. A writer doesn't have to sell himself. His pages speak for him. All you need is the right person to read them.

ABE BURROWS: The William Morris office is, to me, like a family. When I pay them my ten percent, I don't think of it as a commission, I think of it as sending money home to mother.

HOW CAN WRITERS BREAK INTO THE HOLLYWOOD "BUDDY" SYSTEM?

CHARLES SHOWS: I don't know the answer, but I sure as hell see the problem. There should be a "clearing house" to look at all scripts and help writers to break through the iron doors of Hollywood.

BOB MILLS: Submit sitcom scripts and keep submitting them. You have absolutely nothing to lose except the time required to write it and everything to gain if it's good enough to make some producer sit up and take notice. Besides, a good "spec" script for a top show can be a terrific showcase of your talent and could lead to other assignments.

IF YOU HAD TO DO IT ALL OVER AGAIN, WHAT WOULD YOU DO DIFFERENTLY?

ART LINKLETTER: Charge more sooner.

9

Funny Words:
The Sparkplugs of Humor

In the play *The Sunshine Boys,* Neil Simon wrote about funny words. One of his main characters, Willy, says: "Fifty-seven years in this business, you learn a few things. You know what makes an audience laugh. You know what words are funny and which words are not funny. Alka Seltzer is funny. You say 'Alka Seltzer,' you get a laugh . . . Words with 'K' in it are funny. Casey Stengel, that's a funny name. Robert Taylor is not funny. Cupcake is funny. Tomato is not funny. Cookie is funny. Cucumber is funny. Car keys. Cleveland. Cleveland is funny. Maryland is not funny. Then, there's chicken. Chicken is funny. Pickle is funny. . . ."

Mel Brooks agrees. He claims there are phonetic values in certain words that will insure a laugh. "That's part of the craft of comedy writing. Instead of saying salmon, turkey is a funnier sound. It just helps. We naturally go to the 'k' sound — *chicken,* turkey. (It doesn't have to be the first letter.) Like a line I wrote for Sid Caesar. He was playing the part of Jungle Boy, a man who comes out of the jungle.

He's asked, 'What's your greatest enemy?' And Jungle Boy says, 'Buick! Only way to kill Buick, punch in grill. Hard! Buick die!'"

My own opinion is that the "k" sound is a subliminal residue of the most frequently heard words associated with comfort and enjoyment of our infant years. Here are about forty of them:

ca-ca	comb	cute	clean
cat	come	cutie-pie	cling
catch	count	cuddle	climb
call	coo	cup	clothes
candy	cootchie-coo	curls	clown
carpet	cotton	creep	cock-a-doodle
car	cow	crib	cough
carry	cookie	cry (don't)	close
care	cold (don't be)	kiss	cupcake
careful (be)	couch	kiddie	
	kitten		
	kitchen		

Every comedian has his own favorite buzz words, all of them carefully selected to fit his onstage personality and, more importantly, his audience.

Steve Martin is so famous for *"Excuuuuuse me,"* he's frightened that that's what they'll put on his tombstone. He also trills the word crazy like crazy.

Woody Allen, ambivalent about his Jewish heritage ("I'm Jewish — but with an explanation"), uses Jewish names frequently:

> *My parents were too poor to buy me a dog. They got me an ant. I called him Spot. I trained him. I was once coming home and Sheldon Finkelstein tried to bully me, and I had Spot with me, and I said 'Kill.' And Sheldon stepped on my dog.*

★ ★ ★

> *When the other kids learned my name — which was Allen Stewart Konigsberg — they'd beat me up. So I'd tell them my name was Frank, but they'd still beat me up.*

He also uses such words as *feathers, herring, dwarf* and *butter* consistently. They work for him.

Mel Brooks also loves to use heavy Jewish ethnic words and phrases. Most of his characters get Jewish names: *Bernie, Sidney, Morris*. He frequently uses the word *dummy* to refer to his interviewer. And he loves unique food names, like *nectarine*, and packaged goods terms like *Saran Wrap*.

There are hundreds, perhaps thousands, of funny words, and the master humor writers and improvisationists use them frequently as spark plugs to kick over the audience's laugh motor. Unlike key words which come at the end of a sentence for maximum humor effectiveness, funny words can be used anywhere in the body, and frequently several at one time are jingled together like charms on a bracelet.

The funny words listed in this chapter fit the most popular humor categories

AUTHORITY

President *(name)*	boss	IRS agent
The Speaker	foreman	FBI agent
Congress	big budda	Congressman
Senator	head man	Secretary of State
The V.P.	chief honcho	

No person in the world is ridiculed more often than whoever happens to be the President of the United States, and rightly so. But you never use the full title — it sounds too formal and impressive — and you rarely use "The President" for the same reason. What is preferable is the last name of the chief executive as in "Did ya' hear what President Reagan said last night?. . ." encouraging any stereotyping with which each President gets tagged in his first 12 months in office.

> *"Did ya' hear about President Reagan's solution to the minority unemployment problem? He wants to increase the number of teams in the National Basketball Association to 1,500."*

★ ★ ★

> *"Did ya' hear President Reagan's new motto? A pencil in every cup."*

Other titles of authority need to be changed, shortened or disguised to achieve maximum humor impact. The vice-president (after all the jokes about "vice" have been exhausted) becomes more humorous when titled "the veep" or "the vee-pee." The House of Representatives gets extra mileage if identified just as "the House."

> *Crime in this country is up 12% in the home and 25% in the House.*

★ ★ ★

> *There's a burglar in the House and four crooks in the Senate.*

CELEBRITY NAMES

Historical
Religion
God
Christ
Moses
Mohammed
Confucius
The Pope

Military
Napoleon
Hannibal
Julius Caesar
Marc Anthony
Joan of Arc
Charles DeGaulle

Writers/Composers
Shakespeare
George Bernard Shaw
Oscar Wilde
Sigmund Freud
Mark Twain
Bach

Presidents
Washington
Lincoln
Nixon & Agnew
Ford
Carter (& Billy)
Reagan (Nancy)

Government
Henry Kissinger
Alexander Haig
Senator Hayakawa

Actors
Frank Sinatra
Brooke Shields
Dolly Parton

TV
Richard Simmons
Howard Cosell

Authors
Norman Mailer
Truman Capote
Tennessee Williams

Current Headliners
Prime Minister Thatcher
Yasser Arafat
Ayatullah Khomeini

The important prerequisite for using celebrity figures as funny words is that they have or had a unique characteristic — real or fabled. This list is topped by God, runs through every major religion and covers a wide variety of historical names from Bach to Beethoven and Bach again.

Shakespeare was a terrible writer. He had the worst penmanship you ever saw. (Mel Brooks)

One of *The National Lampoon's* sick jokes was a picture of a Volkswagen, which advertised that the car floated. The Lampoon reran a picture of the ad but changed the headline to: "If Ted Kennedy had driven a Volkswagen, he'd be President today."

And when they hand out Academy Awards this year, how about an Oscar for Ted Kennedy for either Goodbye Girl *or* A Bridge Too Far. *(Maureen Murphy)*

DOUBLE ENTENDRES

Defined simply as a word or expression that conveys two or more meanings, one of which is frequently risque, a double entendre is, by far, the most common category of funny words mainly because sex is, by far, the most common category of humor. The expert humor writer tries to use expressions which tempt the listener to complete the meaning himself, thereby accomplishing three major objectives: (1) the humorist is not the one to use the vulgar expression, (2) the listener congratulates himself for his perception in understanding not only what was said, but what was NOT said, yet implied, and (3) since

122   COMEDY TECHNIQUES

the double entendre is sexually oriented, the odds of hitting an appreciative audience are considerably enhanced.

Double entendres fall into the following three groups:

(1) Words ending in "uck."

buck	luck	suck	tuck
duck	puck	schmuck	yuk
muck			

(2) Words ending in "er."

feeler	catcher	spreader	sucker
Fokker	layer	runner	snatcher
kisser	liquor	rubber	

The purpose, obviously, is to associate the word with some contraction of ". . . .her," so that J.D. Salinger's famous novel becomes "R" rated as "Catch Her in the Rye." Another example: "She's one girl who prefers men to liquor."

(3) Articles -

What advertising copywriter on an airline account hasn't dreamed of writing, "and when your TWA plane lands in Honolulu, our beautiful Hawaiian hostesses throw a lei around your neck."

Whenever you can substitute *gongs* for bells or *jackass* for donkey, you know your humor response ratio will go up.

> *Teddy Roosevelt told the story of how one of his children tried to sneak one of his pet ponies into the White House to cheer up a sick brother. Two Supreme Court Justices were visiting in the lobby just as the pony trotted by. "I don't believe there's ever been a pony in The White House before, said one. "No," said the other, "but several jackasses."*

Words like *button* (can I kiss your button?), *tit* (tit for tat), and *balls* have a wide variety of humor uses.

> *Why do policemen have bigger balls than fireman? . . . Because they sell more tickets.*

NOUNS

bang	pits	boobs	tail
dingy	feces	marbles	wha-zoo
piece	hole	breast	lei
pussy	organ	bat & ball	heart
knockers	organ grinder	screw	dates
trick	guts	bongos	piece
fly	headlights	belt	head
ballroom	rod	ping-pong	tip

VERBS

clap	blow	fly	finger
stroke	eat	knock	enter
screw	come	bang	feel
love	swish	suck	boos

ADJECTIVES

quickie	cocksure	pinned	nailed
upper crust	popped	sectional	hard

CLICHÉS

pop your cork   going down

SONG TITLES

"I wonder who's kissing her now?" (Where's her *now?*)

BOOK TITLES

Moby Dick

MOVIE TITLES

The Secret Policeman's Other Ball

EXAMPLES

Guys do funny things in bed. They yell "I'm coming. I'm coming." Sometimes I think I'm not there as a partner, but as a witness. (Lily Tomlin)

★ ★ ★

At his age, the biggest thrill he gets is when his nurse blows into his hearing aid.

★ ★ ★

The most interesting sight he saw in Saudi Arabia was two Arabs sitting under a palm tree eating their dates.

★ ★ ★

I'm a statistician. That's a guy who figures out that the average man's penis is 6½ inches long and the average vagina is 9 inches deep. That means that there are 156,798 miles of unused pussy in the U.S.

★ ★ ★

Many an old man likes to sit and dream of the dames gone by.

A woman walked into a furniture store and asked for a sexual couch. "You mean sectional," said the salesman with a smile. "No," said the woman, "I mean sexual. I need an occasional piece in my living room."

★ ★ ★

"This party is dull," he said, "let's blow the joint." She looked at him for a second and then asked, "Everybody?"

★ ★ ★

"That's a mail plane flying overhead," he said to the freshman co-ed. "Gee," she asked, "From this distance how can you tell?"

★ ★ ★

I sure would love to see your dingy.

★ ★ ★

A man and woman get on a self-service elevator and the man says, "Ballroom, please." and the woman says, "Oh, am I crowding you?"

FOODS

Many funny food categories also are double entendres:

whopper	pea	ham
peanut	frankfurter	egg
nuts	all day sucker	pumpkin
cheery	lollipop	jelly bean
fruit	prune	salami
fruitcake	pig	

A large group have Yiddish (or German) origins:

| kosher | matzo balls | lotkes |
| seltzer | streudel | lox |

Many just sound kookie. The funniest word in foods is *Twinkie*, which Archie Bunker used ad nauseam, because it sounds a lot better than "Hostess Cupcakes."

tootie fruity	applesauce	Tootsie Roll
sarsaparilla	coconut	nectarine
banana	doughnut	fortune cookie
popsicle	shrimp	fried foods
mozzarella	kumquats	garlic
pizza	Jell-O	onions
meatball	lemon	pepper
hot dog	noodles	turkey
popcorn	root beer	chicken
haddock		

Chicken soup is a favorite of Jewish comedians. Allan King calls it *Jewish penicillin* and Woody Allen calls it *mythological panacea.*

> *Sign on a street vendor of hot chestnuts: "I don't want to set the world on fire, I just want to keep my nuts warm."*

★ ★ ★

> *If you can't fight City Hall, you can always feed the pigeons prune juice.*

★ ★ ★

> *When you're a hit, they egg you on. And when you're a flop, they egg you off.*

★ ★ ★

> *If they opened a bar with a mechanical pig, they could call it "Bucking Ham Palace."*

EXCLAMATIONS

These sound a lot funnier than "Oh, my!"

wow	gee-whizz	oye (gevalt)	zoowie
wham	lalapaluzza	whoa	sic
bang-band	yuch	zonk	voom
gee	ugg		

Sid Caesar, as a restaurant patron, and Carl Reiner, as a waiter, have this dialogue:

> *Caesar: What have you got to eat?*
> *Reiner: Klochomoloppi. We also have lich lock, slop lom, stock-lock, rishkosh, and flocklish.*
> *Caesar: Yuck!*
> *Reiner: We have "yuch," too. Boiled or braised?*

SEXUAL ACTS & PRODUCTS

There's no need to belabor the popularity of sex as a comic theme. All we need do is categorize it for different subjects and audiences:

SOFTCORE

oral sex	phallic symbol	stud
menage a trois	Oedipus complex	nympho
bisexual	soul kiss	voluptuous
homosexual	scrotum	sexy
climax	testicles	erotic
obscenity	condoms	throbbing
sin	macho	orgy
pregnant	sperm	mate
vibrator		

A Jewish guy's idea of oral sex is talking about himself.

★ ★ ★

My daughter's Little League team has the only father who flashes instructions from third base with obscene signals.

★ ★ ★

Do you handle condoms?" asked the young man of the drug store clerk. "Yes, I do," the clerk answered proudly. "Well, wash your hands, I want a ham sandwich."

HARDCORE

piss	come	crap
fuck	cock	blow-job
shit	cocksucker	cunt
bullshit	mother fucker	pussy
prick	suck	snatch
ass	screw	sonuvabitch
dick	lick	bastard
jerk-off		

    George Carlin, particularly, became famous for his dissection of hardcore words and their use in comedy. His "seven dirty words" monologue, which has several variations, is part of his most popular record albums. In one of them, he indicates over 50 different uses for the word *shit,* such as the Indian who didn't know shit from Shinola — you ought to see his moccasins.
    He also analyzed the word *prick* and noted that in society you can prick your finger but you can't do it the other way around.
    Richard Pryor uses *motherfucker* so often in his conversation that his youngest boy was 14 before he found out it was two words. Pryor uses *fuckin'* as his most common adjective. While eating with him, he just doesn't ask you to pass the butter, he describes it.
    Lenny Bruce, the father of publicly performed scatoglogical humor, was arrested for using the word *cocksucker* in his nightclub act. When threatened by a judge for public obscenity, he said: "Look, your honor, I just say it in public, I don't do it."
    The public acceptance of hardcore words grows each year. There was a national hullaballo in the late 1930's when Clark Gable in *Gone With the Wind* said, "Frankly, my dear, I don't give a *damn.*" The salty language of the GIs in World War Two made previously taboo words like *fuck, Jap bastard, pussy, screwed, snafued,* among dozens of others, acceptable in films, newspaper and magazine copy and speeches.
    Today, the word *bullshit* is used without hysterical protest in political campaigns (a recent tv commercial for a political candidate

started out with the word *bullshit* in describing an opponent's claims and record). A common bit of irony in normal conversation is to describe certain sentimentality as "Very sweet. Bullshit, but very sweet!"

Among comics and their writers, their final exam — no matter how successful they have been financially in show business — is an appearance at one of the famed celebrity roasts of the New York Friars Club, a dinner in honor of some celebrity during which his friends show their adoration by insulting him with material so scathing it can rarely be used in other places:

> *Milton Berle, in roasting Howard Cosell, described him as someone who hadn't had a blow job in so long, he forgot what it tastes like.*

> ★ ★ ★

> *George Burns said of Georgie Jessel that if we are what we eat, Jessel was the biggest cunt in town.*

These stag roasts, which draw more than a thousand members to each charity dinner, are so celebrated that secret tape recordings have been made and sold on the black market as "party" entertainment. The net effect, moreover, is the permissive encouragement of obscenity in public. "If Johnny Carson and Art Linkletter can say it, why can't I?"

Steve Martin discussed the problem of hardcore language in a recent magazine interview:

> You go on *The Tonight Show* and you don't say "fuck." Then the parents say, "He's great for little Billy, 'cause he doesn't say 'fuck,'" and they buy your album, and it says "fuck." The only thing I apologize for is that it doesn't say on the jacket: "By the way, this says 'fuck' on it." That's fair. Tell them what they're buying. But you don't change it. That's censorship. It's not like I suddenly went on stage and said "fuck." I've been saying it in my act since I was 19. It used to be worse.

In truth, using a hardcore word is one of the easiest ways to get a laugh. Depending on the makeup of the audience, the words can provoke the nervous, tension-relieving laughter that comes from a public exhibition of a taboo language. Young comedy writers, in particular, resort to hardcore humor when the going gets tough. "Reach out," I told one class, "for the satirical wit of George Bernard Shaw, the ironic word play of Oscar Wilde, the gentleness of a Jack Benny and the twinkle of a George Burns. In other words," I told them, "up your standards." And they yelled back, "Up yours!"

128   COMEDY TECHNIQUES

But the use of hardcore language in humor is also an art — if you're willing to even consider it.

Mark Twain was an inveterate user of swear words. His wife repeatedly tried to cure him, but made little progress. One day he cut himself while shaving and proceeded to use every cuss word in his vocabulary. When he had finished, his wife repeated every word she had heard. Twain listened silently, then said, "My dear, you have the right words, but you don't know the tune."

BEDPAN HUMOR

hernia	herpes	feces	lousy
dysentery	loaded	plastered	fat
body functions	urination	pee	drunk
diarrhea	zipper	ca-ca	prostate
enema	vasectomy	stink	coma
fart	gynecologist	small	puberty
falsies	hemorrhoids	stool	stethoscope
guts	latrine	toilet	navel
circumcision	tonsils	diapers	constipation
specimen	tongue	pit	belly
dirty	proctologist	dung	bug-eyed
smut	stick it	toupee	rear end
chamber pot	shove it	throwing up	stacked
giggle	small (size)		

Body functions and malfunctions are a favorite source of humor that is enhanced by the judicious use of certain words — and harmed by the poor choice of others. For example, *puke* and *throwing up* work more effectively than *vomit* (although *vomit* was memorably used in *The Man Who Came to Dinner*).

> *One feeling keeps running through me — I feel like throwing up.*

The word *diarrhea* obviously permits a more general use than some of the hardcore words listed previously. Another common bedpan expression is fart. When somebody asks Steve Martin, "Mind if I smoke?", he loves to answer, "Not at all. Mind if I fart?" Of all the bedpan words, *enema* is the most popular.

> *If they ever give this country an enema — Newark is where they'd stick the pipe.*

Allan King has an oft-quoted monologue called "Enema Was Mother's Love":

> *ALAN KING:* One day I called my mother in Florida. She asked me how I was feeling. I said, "Not so good." My mother said, "Take an enema." I swear, as long as there's a

God above, I took an enema . . . two days later, I felt better. I know young people, this is amusing to you, an enema. It's funny isn't it. It's a funny word. Enema. Enema. Just say it, it invokes a laugh. An enema. But an enema . . . let me tell you about an enema . . . An enema was love. An enema was a family affair. When you came from a large family. When you saw that enema bag coming . . . and you knew you weren't the recipient . . . "Yeahhhhh! Give 'em an enema!" It was your mother's hand . . . you had to get well. Because, what do the doctors tell you now .. give yourself a Fleet. What the hell is a Fleet? A disposable. I don't understand it. Did ya' ever see one of those things. You go . . . keeeeet! You can't clean out a chicken with a Fleet. I showed it to my mother. She says, "It must be a mouthwash." My mother had a bone that went from the tip of my finger all the way to my elbow. That was just the bone. When she inserted it, it cleared out your nostrils, the sinuses, the wax from your ear . . . I always remember my father standing on the dresser holding the porcelain pot. You remember the porcelain pot? And my mother always hollering, "Higher, Bernie, higher." And I was laying there, yelling, "All right, all right. That's enough. That's enough" . . . But you got well. We had the best attendance record at school. Get up in the morning, "I don't feel good, ma." "Bernie, get the enema." "Look out, ma . . . I feel great. That's it. I'm going right to school." It didn't make any difference how you turned. She's made a new hole . . . in your head. . . ."

Other examples:

A navel destroyer is a hula hoop with a nail in it.

★ ★ ★

A circumcised penis looks like Telly Sevalas in a turtleneck.

★ ★ ★

The doctor bent over the old man looked up at the doctor as he put on his stethoscope. "Just my luck to get a doctor who's hard of hearing."

★ ★ ★

My wife and I have been married for 50 years, and in all those years we've never had one fight — because of my physical disability. No guts!

★ ★ ★

Puberty is when your offspring quit asking where they came from and refuse to tell you where they're going.

NUMBERS

zero	eleven	seventy-five	vote results
zip	thirteen	a hundred & one	sports scores
one	twenty	one thousand five hundred	nickel
three	forty	two thousand	dime
seven	fifty	a million	million dollars
nine	sixty-nine	a zillion	
ten			

Numbers convey humor through acceptable exaggeration ("I've got a *million* of them," said Jimmy Durante). Others because of their association with sex (*sixty-nine*), and still others because they just sound funny (*zip, zillion, zee-row*).

Other numbers have something mystical about them: most of all, the number *three*. It is the most important number in comedy: triples build tension, help to describe the parameters of subject matter and the successful sequence of three jokes in a row on one topic not only is part of a roll, but generally the acceptable limit of material to be used on one subject.

The use of selected numbers in scores or vote tallies is common:

> *The rabbi knew he was in trouble when he went to the hospital for a minor operation and the board of directors, by a vote of thirteen to ten, wished him a speedy recovery.*

* * *

> *Notre Dame played our school in football last fall and won 75 to zip, but the game wasn't as close as the score indicated.*

* * *

> *Two caterpillars were crawling along the ground when a butterfly flew over them. One turned to the other and said, "You couldn't get me up in one of those for a million dollars."*

* * *

> *A repairman was in bed with a woman when suddenly there was the sound of the front door being opened. "My god," said the woman, "it's my husband. Quick, jump out the window or he'll kill us both." "I can't," the man said, "we're on the thirteenth floor." "For Christ's sake, jump," said the woman, "This is no time to be superstitious."*

* * *

> *A woman with ten children in the car went through a red light. "Don't you know when to stop?" an angry pedestrian shouted. "They're not all mine," she yelled back.*

> Carl Reiner, as the interviewer in his famous "Two Thousand Year Old Man" record with Mel Brooks asks: "How many children do you have?" Brooks: "I have over forty-two thousand . . . and not one comes to visit me."

According to Robert Orben, numbers have to be easily understood and NOT command too much attention. "Like you would never mention a 19-mile-per-hour speed limit. If the original joke is: 'I got an eight percent loan yesterday — eight percent of what I asked for,' the word eight is more difficult to understand than the number three. So the joke just sounds better if it's rewritten: 'I don't like to brag but I got a three percent loan today — three percent of what I asked for.'"

PLACES

Newark	Jersey City	The Bronx
Brooklyn	Miami Beach	Burbank
Van Nyes	Sausalito	Paducah
Oshkosh	Philadelphia	New Jersey
Vesuvius	Mt. St. Helens	Baltimore
Washington	New York	L.A.
Harlem	Las Vegas	Peoria
Cannes	"— Motel"	Uranus
The LA Freeway	Sunset Boulevard	

There is no limit to the number of cities, small towns, volcanoes, street names, local restaurants, bars, hotels, resorts, schools, hospitals, mental institutions and old age homes which can be used as humor fuses. Regardless of where you live, there is some nearby town, suburb or locale which is common fodder for ridicule.

Sometimes the name alone permits humor from mispronunciation:

> "You know how Van Nyes got its name?" asks Joey Bishop. Well, one day, my little old mother was visiting me and I took her to the top of the Hollywood Hills and had her view the valley below just at sunset. Well, ma, what do you call that?" She said, "Ver nize."

Each comedian has his own pet targets: Johnny Carson attacks *Burbank,* Bob Hope frequently joked about *Hollywood and Vine,* Robin Williams takes on *Sausalito* (where "Long Live the Queen" takes on a new meaning).

No state and its cities get as much abuse as *New Jersey.* "Isn't it a shame," said one comedian, "that the light at the end of the tunnel is New Jersey." "I'm from *Jersey City,*" says Robert Whol, "but I have a summer home in *Newark.*"

> They call the mountains around Sausalito, the swish Alps. (Martin Mull)

I'm from Miami Beach, and the main form of transportation there is by stretcher. (Rita Rudner)

★ ★ ★

Two Las Vegas chorus girls met in the MGM Grand powder room. "I'm sure we've met before in Cannes," one said. "Was it in this one," asked the other, "or the john in Caesar's Palace?"

★ ★ ★

Bob Hope was being honored for 25 years with the National Broadcasting Company. "It's been great," said Hope, "in all those years I've been rewarded with money, adulation, respect and encouragement. And to think I owe it all to the morning I saw General Sarnoff coming out of the Dixie Motel."

Cities like *Washington, New York* and *L.A.* (better not to pronounce it Los Angeles) provoke humor interest almost automatically because of their stereotyped occupational activity. As a locale gets momentary notoriety from some newsworthy public event, humorists get added mileage by including reference to it in their standard material. *Mt. St. Helens* is one example. *Slippery Rock Teacher's College* is another.

NAMES

Jewish	*English*	*Italian*
Mendel	Peter	Guido
Sidney	Charles	Tony
Bernie	Reginald	Two-Ton Tony
Irving	Victor	Giuseppe
Shirley		Hortense
Mrs. Cohen		John
Sadie		Humphrey
Sam		Percy
Becky		

American	*Chicano*	*French*
George	Jose	Lucky Pierre
Gladys	Speedy Gonzales	
Pop	Pablo	
Doc		
Dick		
Chuck		
Phil		

Every national origin has its own set of names, some of which seem more humorous than others.

A grasshopper walked into a bar and ordered a drink. "My god," said the bartender, "a drinking grasshopper.

You know, we have a drink named after you." The grasshopper said, "Irving?"

YIDDISH EXPRESSIONS

kosher	delicatessen	Goldstein	tzuris
bar mitzvah	klutz	Fagenbaum	fagalah
megillah	Lefkowitz	nebbish	shamus
lotkes	Bernstein	kvetch	rabbi
bubbe	Cohen	gevalt	meshugana
chutzpah	Shapiro	schmuck	

ALSO

Being Jewish   Being Israeli

The birthplace of contemporary American humor was New York City and its godfathers were second generation Jewish writers and performers whose parents, from many Eastern European countries, spoke Yiddish as a common language. The impact of this Yiddish culture became so strong an influence in New York that, as Bill Adler wrote, "even the goyim are Jewish."

Yiddish is a language (with a strong German base) overflowing with expressions of ridicule with the same guttural sounds used by a person about to expectorate. Its colorful expressions and inflections quickly enriched the venacular of New Yorkese — answers that sounded like questions, oaths that sounded like blessings, and words that sounded like English. Such Yiddish expressions as kosher, kibitzer, shtick, schmaltz, matzos, bagels, lox, gefilte fish, pisher, schiksa, schvartza, gonnif, gelt, schmateh, magilla, etc. are so assimilated into English that linguistic scholars and authors now rarely put them in italics. Groups of people, like the Indian tribe called the "schmo-hawks," get Yiddishized. The advice "dress British — think Yiddish" is popular in the theater, finance and communications industries.

Jokes in which the rabbi outsmarts the minister and priest are legion. While the origin of each could have come from a Jewish writer with an inferiority complex, more likely it is because the Jewish outlook based upon practicality, opportunism, and self-deprecation is more comedic.

CHARACTER LABELS

fag	gay	albino
queer	broad	frog
queen	hustler	nigger
dyke	hooker	spic
AC-DC	chick	greaseball
lesbian	whore	kike
homo	hood	chink
stud	wop	commie

These are derogatory terms which are funny to bigots and secular groups — and therefore must be even more carefully chosen for the audience (if you believe it is necessary to use them at all).

ANIMALS/FISH/INSECTS

beast	mouse	rabbit
chimp	duck	sheep
chickie	doggie	ox
elephant	kitten	shark
gorilla	pussy	whale
ewe	herring	pirrhana
dog	cockroach	elk
fly	moose	

The word beast *is the only term used by woman to both insult and praise a man.*

★ ★ ★

Know what the farmer called his loving sheep? An embraceable ewe!

The most popular of all animals, of course, are dogs. They are not only man's best friend, they are a comedy writer's, too. As the most numerous of household pets, people think of them as a member of the family, endowed with human characteristics. For some reason, they are particularly related with children's retorts.

A little girl and her mother came to my office to visit. At the same time in came a dog. "Does your dog bite?" I asked the girl. She shook her head — no! I bent down to pet the dog and he sunk his teeth deep into my arm. I yelled, "You said your dog doesn't bite," I yelled. "This one ain't mine," said the girl.

★ ★ ★

The college senior came into the county health office. "I'd like to buy 10,000 cockroaches. I promised my landlord I'd leave his apartment just the way I found it."

★ ★ ★

The comedy team had so many clones they called them Rabbit and Costello.

★ ★ ★

I don't know if my girl's pregnant or not, but the rabbit's in a coma. (Andy Huggins)

★ ★ ★

They call the play Inherit the Wind *gorilla warfare.*

OCCUPATIONAL DESIGNATIONS

analyst
psychoanalyst
monk
Christian Scientist
kamikaze
beggar

layman
Mafia
burglar
fence
pawnbroker

stockbroker
politician
cop
butcher
judge

PHYSICAL PHENOMENONS

volcanic eruption
earthquake
brushfire
tornado
flood
fire
blizzard
hurricane

MISCELLANEOUS

freckle
sophomoric

ACCIDENTS

tailspin
crash
wipe-out
massacre

You think you've got problems. I just found out my doctor is a Christian Scientist.

★ ★ ★

"My son is so thoughtful," one woman bragged to another. "He sends me flowers every week." "My son always remembers me too," said the other. "Every week when he goes to his analyst, I'm the only thing he talks about."

PRODUCTS

This category is broken down into two classifications: (1) generic names and (2) brand names, which frequently relate to advertising slogans.

(1) GENERIC NAMES

zipper
yo-yo
bubble bath
bubble gum
kimono
cuckoo clock

piccolo
bass fiddle
umbrella
harp
rocks

spray deodorant
auto recalls
pothole
dingy
rock music

She called the car's handbrake a kimono because she was told to put it on quickly in case of an emergency.

★ ★ ★

I'm so thin that when I spray a deodorant on, I get windburned. (Andy Huggins)

★ ★ ★

You know times are getting better when the auto industry starts recalling workers instead of cars.

My wife is so fastidious she puts newspaper under the cuckoo clock.

(2) BRAND NAMES

Ex-Lax	Hartz Mt. Foods	Fab
Serutan	Dr. Pepper	Sanka
Chock Full of Nuts	Macadamia nuts	Barbie Doll
Gucci	Frisbee	Kotex
Tidy Bowl	Saran Wrap	Pinto
Buick	Winnebago	Tide
Time Magazine	Ben Gay	Scotch Tape
Crazy Glue	Ivory	McDonald's
Perrier water	Tums	

The conductor asked for requests from the audience, and someone shouted back, "How about the second movement by Ex-Lax."

★ ★ ★

The people who make Serutan — you know, that's "natures" spelled backward — have just introduced a new mouthwash called SIP.

★ ★ ★

I understand the Tidy Bowl man comes from Flushing, N.Y.

★ ★ ★

"We break into this program to bring you a special news announcement: the Russians have hit New York with hydrogen bombs. We'll be back with further details after this important announcement from Hartz Mt. Birdseed."

★ ★ ★

"Dr. Pepper. Dr. Pepper. Please report to the diabetes ward at once."

★ ★ ★

"I wouldn't say that Nancy Reagan is designer conscious, but the first words out of her mouth when she was a baby were "Gucci. Gucci. Gucci."

★ ★ ★

The film The Ten Commandments *is chock full of nots.*

★ ★ ★

They call the Pinto the world's most expensive cigarette lighter.

Letter to CBS-TV 60 Minutes, . . . *"After seeing Harry Reasoner's report on the killing of elephants for their precious ivory, I realized I'm as guilty as all the rest. I have decided to change soaps."*

HERE'S HOW IT WORKS

Mel Brooks has been called "a mesmeric power for vocal improvisation" and he knows how funny words, placed in the unexpected places, bring maximum comedic results. In this bit, taken from his "Two Thousand Year Old Man" routine, note how he uses the following five terms: *Israeli, small, soul kiss, Greek* and *garlic*.

> *Reiner: Sir, you're the Israeli wrestling champion of the world, yet you're extremely small. How do you manage to defeat all those enormous opponents?*
>
> *Brooks: I give them a soul kiss, and they're so shocked they collapse. Sometimes I hate doing it, like when it's a Greek wrestler, because they have garlic breath.*

Brooks was discovered at a show business party when he and Mel Tolkin, a writer friend, performed this extemporaneous skit in honor of Moss Hart, the evening's guest of honor. Note the inclusion of at least 14 funny words: *psychoanalyst, Freud, number One, nickel, little, couch, smut, dirty, puke, Oedipus complex, mother, Jewish,* and *Greek*.

> Q. (TOLKIN) I gather, sir, that you are a famous psychoanalyst?
> A. (BROOKS) That is correct.
> Q. May I ask where you studied psychiatry?
> A. At The Vienna School of Good Luck.
> Q. Who analyzed you?
> A. I was analyzed by number one himself.
> Q. You mean the great Sigmund Freud.
> A. In person. Took me during lunchtime, charged me a nickel.
> Q. What kind of a man was he?
> A. Lovely little fellow. I shall never forget the hours we spent together, me lying on the couch, him sitting right there beside me, wearing a nice off-the-shoulder-dress.
> Q. Is it true, sir, that Moss Hart is one of your patients?
> A. That is also correct.
> Q. Could you tell us, sir, what Mr. Hart talks about during your analytic sessions?
> A. He talks smut. He talks dirty, he talks filth, he talks pure, unadulterated smut. It makes me want to puke.

Q. How do you cope with this?
A. I give him a good slap on the wrist. I wash his mouth out with soap. I tell him, "Don't talk dirty. Don't say those things."
Q. What are Mr. Hart's major problems? Does he have an Oedipus complex?
A. What is that?
Q. You're an analyst, sir, and you never heard of an Oedipus complex?
A. Never in my life.
Q. Well, sir, it's a man who has a passionate desire to make love to his own mother.
A. (long pause) That's the dirtiest thing I ever heard. Where do you get that filth?
Q. It comes from a famous play by Sophocles.
A. Was he Jewish?
Q. No, sir, he was Greek.
A. With a Greek, who knows? But, with a Jew, you don't do a thing like that even to your wife, let alone your mother.

Examples of "funny words" appear most often in the monologues of topical comedians like Hope and Carson whose humor is necessarily very national. Whether it's network tv or state fairs, their subject matter must be of the most general nature and triggered by today's headlines and fads.

For example, this actual Carson monologue, recorded on August 11, 1982, uses over 40 funny words (italicized) and 13 references to well-known names, including President Reagan four times, famous locales in the Los Angeles area, a dig at a small town, and a wide assortment of hostile arrows directed at authority figures from NBC vice-presidents to the Beverly Hills Fire Department and the celebrity sperm bank.

McMAHON: . . . and heerrrrrre's Johnny!

CARSON: (lengthy applause) Well, I suppose you want to be entertained now. A little *cheap* applause and "Entertain Us." . . . What an enthusiastic group . . . Your hopes are only exceeded by my fears . . . I just saw a *little old lady* selling maps of the stars' erogenous zones . . . Hi, Tom (bandleader). I'm fine . . . He's a great musician, a great arranger, but not an electric personality. Tommy's idea of an exciting day is to buy a hamburger at *McDonald's,* then go outside and watch the sign change from *24 billion* to *24 billion and one* . . . I shouldn't kid him because Tommy had a deprived childhood. Yes, it's true. He couldn't afford a *yo-yo* as a child, true, he just had a

FUNNY WORDS 139

yo . . . it *went down* but it never *came up* . . . How many of you took the *NBC* tour today? What do they get for it now. Three bucks, remember when we first came out here, it was a dollar and a quarter. *Inflation!* What did they show you for that. Nothing? NBC is not so dumb are they? Did they take you by the *NBC executive offices?* Well, that's fun. We set very high standards here for our *vice-presidents*. To be hired and become a *vice-president of NBC*, you have to be able to complete the *TV Guide* crossword puzzle. Didja ever see that? That's really a devastating mind boggler. They have to fill in two little blanks and one says "Minutes" and it asks "Name of a top show?" and you have to figure that out . . . *Sixty, sixty,* that's the answer . . . How many of you felt the earthquake yesterday? We had an *earthquake* out here. One guy? Where were you when it hit? (On the *Freeway!*) In your car? No, just on the *Freeway!* How could you tell if there was an *earthquake* if you were on the Freeway? (I got rear-ended!) That's not an earthquake, that's getting rear-ended . . . They actually had one which registered 4.5 on the Richter scale. That's a pretty hefty jolt. When it was over, the girls on *Sunset Boulevard* were on horseback chasing the cops . . . We are in what is called the brushfire season out here, in California. We have not had any rain since — a long time. So don't throw your cigarettes out of your car, or do dumb things like that. Now the *Beverly Hills Fire Department* is very good, but probably the most exclusive fire department in the world. They use giant helicopters and they drop *Perrier* water and they use the blades to chop up the *limes* . . . If you're going to be out here for a while, one of the local stations, Channel Five or Nine is having a local *Ronald Reagan* week. They're showing all of the famous *Ronald Reagan* films. What's the one in Montana? See you know, *Cattle Queen of Montana,* but next week one of the stations is holding a *Freddie DeCordava* retrospective — our producer here — including only two commercial interruptions, Fred's 1952 film classic *Francis the Talking Mule Irrigates the Kettle Farm.* . . . Good picture . . . Fred's movies were actually the first in-flight movie, did you know that? They used them during the war to instigate paratroopers to bail out . . . How many of you out here are familiar with the grunion? They're little silver fish, about so big, and they have what they call "the grunion run." You go out to the beaches, at night, the grunion come in from the ocean very quickly. They *mate* in the sand and they disappear. For about how long are they on shore, do you know? People used to think it was a joke, but the grunion are now running, but they have not yet shown up on the California beaches and scientists say that they're a little reluctant to *spawn* this year, they're a little *paranoid* over the *herpes*. That's no laughing matter 'cause it's changed the *mating* habits of the grunion. They're really looking for a long term relationship instead of one of those one night *spawns* . . . But if you go out there you'll see some weird sights on the beach. The other night I saw a *herring* in a raincoat. *Herring* in a raincoat, little weird. O.K. I knew it was not going to get anything! . . . Ya wanna talk about our baseball team, the *Dodgers* are in first place. I'll tell you they came from ten and a half games behind to take first place. *Reagan* called *Manager Tom LaSorda,* congratulated him on this miracle and said, "Well, now how about one for the *Gipper?*" Remember when he played *George Gipps?* Obviously not! . . . *Fernando Valenzuela* pitched the *Dodgers* to first place. And to show their appreciation for this, the *Dodger management* told *Fernando* that he no longer had to report to *Peter O'Mally's* backyard for the picking season . . . There was a late report from the news room. *General Alexander Haig* just donated his sperm to that genius *sperm bank*. He's donated that to see if they can come up with the first baby who can take charge . . . Speaking of *President Reagan,* and I was just a couple of moments ago, he is out on the country taking his case, his tax cut, to the people. He's out in *Billings, Montana,* the pulse of the nation. When he spoke out there, he only spoke to *twelve* people and a *puma* . . . Can I go with you wherever you're going? . . . We have a good show for you tonight. This is no indication . . . We'll take a break here and — never come back!

10
A Philosophy for Beginning Comedy Writers
by Gene Perret
Condensed from *The Roundtable*

With young comedy writers certain recurring problems become evident.

One I call "send the limo" syndrome. Writers will send a few pages of material and sit home complacently and wait for you to send a chauffeured limousine to whisk them off to Hollywood.

It is just not going to happen and you do yourself a disservice in expecting it because your disappointment could be fatal to your enthusiasm. Many young writers abandon their career when their first inquiries don't bring Dramatic results.

You can't get those kind of results for two reasons. First of all, the person you send your material to has seen great material before, so he's not going to be knocked off his feet even if your stuff is way above average.

Secondly, most of the people you would send your material to really don't know good stuff when they see it.

If you're a good writer, you'll know it. Your mission now is to get other people, preferably influential people, to agree with you. But don't allow any negativism you meet with to shake your confidence.

Recognize going in the reality of the situation. You not only have to be good ... you have to be better than the talent that is already there. Why? Because the buyer knows what the proven talent can deliver. In his mind, you are still a question mark. Can you continue to write as well as you have? Are you fast? Can you work under pressure? Can you accept editorial comments? Until you are proven and as long as you are just "as good as" the other guy he'll opt for the other guy. You have to be better than your competition. And you have to continue to be better until someone finally recognizes your skills and then you become the proven talent.

A second problem beginners have is in asking for too much money too soon. There is nothing wrong with making lots of money as a writer. Samuel Johnson once said that no man except a blockhead would write for anything except money. However, asking for too much money before you actually deserve it kills more potential careers than it benefits.

A novice writer will read in a paper that so and so makes $1000 a page for his monologue material. (First of all, you should at least divide that number by two.) Now that writer asks that kind of salary from a comic who plays the local club on weekends for $50 a night. The novice may never write again.

The beginner doesn't need top dollar at this stage of his career, he needs experience.

The first thing a novice wants to do is get his career started. Here are four steps:

1. Write
2. Get Into Circulation
3. Sell
4. Publicize

Write: Some author once said there are only three ways to learn to write ... write, write, and write. That author is right, right, right. Every time you put something on paper, whether it sells or not, in fact, whether it's any good or not, you educate yourself. The poet Hugh Prather said, "If the desire to write is not accompanied by actual writing, then the desire is not to write."

Set a quota of weekly writing for yourself. Make it a comfortable goal, because one that is too exacting may also be too demoralizing.

Get into circulation: Get your material to an audience. Getting feedback from an audience on your material will help your writing immeasureably.

The absolute best training for a humorist or a writer is to deliver his own material. You learn the agony and ecstasy of hearing the audience react. When you write for someone else, a certain amount of detachment is unavoidable, but when you are up there living or dying by the material, you learn quickly what works and what doesn't

However, if you're too shy to deliver your own material, give it away. Write for those who will stand up and speak.

Sell: Obviously, you'll have trouble eking out a living when you constantly give your material away. The object is to sell it.

Get it out to magazines that buy fillers and short anecdotes. Pick up a writer's market list from a bookstore and maybe a book from a writer's magazine that teaches you how to sell this type of writing.

Try to sell to comics appearing in the local clubs. Get their names and where they're appearing from the newspapers, and then contact them at the club. Some disc jockeys may buy material and you can reach them at the station. *Weekly Variety* has a listing and review of comics appearing at nightclubs all over the country. Read about what kind of topics they're working on, and send a letter to the nightclub. Most working comics are on the lookout for a new source of material, and they will at least read it.

Comics who appear regularly on tv can be contacted by mailing an inquiry to the network. Obviously, they are a tougher sale, but many of them will look at new material and may buy from beginning writers.

One warning, though. You will get rejected. Go in knowing that so that you don't become discouraged.

Publicity: Let people know what you're writing and speaking. It's the best way to get more writing and speaking assignments. First of all, tell people. They'll tell other people. Then you'll become a humorist.

Also, contact the newspapers and the radio and tv stations with your successes. They're constantly on the lookout for interviewees. And once your career is validated by appearing in print or over the airwaves, more and more people will come to you.

Allow your career and your talents to grow slowly. As Arnold Glascow said, "The key to everything is patience." You get the chicken by hatching the egg . . . not by smashing it.

So you've hit a mental block with your writing. You have so much to do, you're keeping such a blistering pace, you don't know where to start first.

1. *Relaxation* As long as you're worried about all your problems, that worry will choke out your thinking processes.

You can shake that feeling by doing anything that's a diversion for you. Read a book, watch tv, do exercises, whatever relaxes you.

2. *Planning* All big jobs are nothing but a bunch of small jobs tied together in a common package. A little time spent in planning your work will save you quite a bit of time in executing it.

3. *Concentration* You have had to devote your energies thinking about the problem at hand. If you can't, then it's time for that relaxation. Take a break, clear your mind, and then come back . . . and concentrate.

Planning helps you concentrate. Spending time planning help you to pinpoint your concentration. When you concentrate on too large an area (like trying to solve a crossword puzzle all at once), your mind can't contain it and it wanders. So planning and concentrating actually complement one another.

4. *Remembering* Believe you can get done what you want to get done in order to get it done. Do this by remembering that you did the same thing in the past.

5. *Stealing Time* Do a little bit of your work when you're busy doing nothing. Then when it comes time to do the work, it's already started.

Your most creative work is often done when you think about a problem lightly and then consciously forget it. That's when your subconscious works on it diligently.

Doing what you want to do is fun. Relaxing, planning, concentrating, remembering and stealing time — they're five secrets that can stave off the snapping alligators for many writers.

Bob Hope has kidded his good friend, Ronald Reagan, by saying: "Our new President doesn't lie, steal or cheat. He's always had an agent to do that for him." It's a serious concern to the beginning writer, though.

It is more important for the novice to get material before an audience than it is to demand top dollar for the writing.

One's career will build on its successes. Each assignment, if well executed, should lead to a bigger and better sale. Initially you will sell your services for less than you deserve and you most likely will be taken advantage of. However, this is not a loss. It is an investment in yourself.

There are a couple of things to remember about comedy writing. First of all, you as a writer are not selling jokes. The jokes you have written are not the valuable commodity that you possess. Your skill is in your ability to write more jokes. If, for example, the jokes you have already on paper are the only ones you'll ever write in your life, then, by all means, demand top dollar for them. It's the last dollar you'll make. If you know you can come up with other jokes that are just as funny as those already on paper, then no one can steal or gyp you out of that ability. Jokes may be taken from you for little or no recompense, but your value does not diminish at all.

Secondly, good comics don't buy jokes . . . they buy a supply of jokes. No single joke or comedy routine is really going to make or break an entertainer. A steady supply of humor, though, just might. Actually, gags are of very little use to Bob Hope because he keeps his act so topical that once he uses a funny line, it is practically worthless to him again. What he prizes highly are writers who can come up with new funny material on the news events that break that day.

Suppose you have a comic who likes your stuff and you want to arrive at a fair price. How do you go about it? Again, there is as much creativity involved in this as there is in the gag writing itself.

My first sales were to magazines. That price is definitely established before you ever send out any material. You simply write your gags, ship them off, and the magazine selects and buys what they want at the established price.

A national comedian liked my material and we settled on a percentage payment. I would supply lines to him constantly for his act. In return I would be paid 15% of his contracted price for nightclub engagements.

I used this same idea for a local comic. I wrote the same quantity of jokes, but his contract price was considerably lower, so I made much less. However, it's important to note that with the local comic, I could travel with him to most engagements and see how the material went over with the audiences. Perhaps I got more value with the second contract.

I also signed a deal with a much better-known local comedian. In this contract I agreed to provide a certain amount of original material each week for which I was paid a flat weekly fee.

I contacted Phyllis Diller and sent her several routines that I thought she could use. She bought many of the jokes and responded with a check. After that I would send Phyllis about 60 jokes each week and she would buy roughly half at $5 per joke.

Eventually, Phyllis Diller decided that she would simply pay me a weekly stipend and would not bother to mark and return the jokes that I sent.

From selling one-liners to the guy who works the local nightclub on weekends to selling a tv pilot to a major producer, the same principle applies . . . they want to pay less and you want to make more. It's always negotiable.

When I talk money with my agent (and I always want more) he asks me the ultimate question . . . "Are you prepared to lose it?" If you don't want the job then you can ask any fee. But if you really want this one, you must be prepared to bend a bit.

Beginners must be more flexible. In bending to the buyer's demands, remember that you are building a career. There will come a time when this comic won't be able to afford you.

PART III
HUMOR MARKETS

11

Speechwriting

Confessions of a Speechwriter
by Daniel Lynch
Condensed from *Dun's Review*

Why do so many executives make dull speeches? To put it another way, why does an executive so often find himself facing an audience with a speech that either is not at all what he wants to say, repeats what too many other executives have said already or, worse still, does not even sound like him?

At least part of the reason is his misuse, or nonuse, of a speechwriter. Far too often, the speechwriter is the lowest of corporate underlings. Although he may be indirectly contributing more to corporate sales and well-being than some vice president, his best work often fails even to reach the desk of the man for whom he is writing. His ideas languish in a sea of corporate cliches, while his more persuasive insights and keener strokes of humor disappear completely.

And — the crowning blow — the public relations director "forgets" to introduce him to the man whose public personality he is supposedly communicating.

If only the speechwriters suffered, it could perhaps be argued that we were receiving our "just desserts." Unfortunately, this is not the case. For the real sufferer is the speaker who must stammer through twelve pages of dull prose and the audience that must politely listen. How many times have you idly toyed with your dessert fork while listening to:

"My subject today is the role of profits in the increasingly competitive world of free enterprise, and in the light of increasing competition from abroad."

"The largest enemy to profits is labor — big labor, supported by a bureaucratic big government."

"We must be diligent in the face of the creeping inroads of socialism into American life."

We hear that it is not a businessman's job to speak his mind on subjects other than those directly related to sales and profits. In my opinion, this attitude only serves to promote the public image of a businessman with half a head, and less heart. Saying nothing is no way to say something.

I am most frequently asked two questions: "Why are there so few good speechwriters?" and "What makes a good speechwriter, where are they, and how cheaply can I hire them?"

Few good speechwriters are available for business speeches because most good writers who have tried writing for businessmen have run into the problems just discussed. So they write for the men who know and respect good speeches: politicians.

A good speechwriter is not a newswriter, feature writer or policy writer. While these three are all verbally oriented, only the speechwriter is aurally oriented.

Where do you find a good speechwriter? The best way is to ask the man who owns one.

Besides a personal recommendation from a businesswoman you trust, you might run an ad in The *Washington Post*. Offer a salary so high that some good political speechwriter will not be able to resist compromising "principle" for "principal."

Why does the top executive need a speechwriter in the first place? Obviously, because he does not have time to write the many speeches that he must deliver over a period of time. A well-researched, well-written speech takes at least a week to compose.

Speechwriting as a craft has come out of the shadows. The hidden persuaders are not nearly as hidden as they used to be. You might even hear a top executive bragging at his club about the new speechwriter he has just hired.

The emergence of the "ghostwriter" into a position of respectability also helps to explain the writer's antipathy to public relations directors and others who would interfere in his relationship with the person for whom he is writing. Speechwriting has become exceedingly important in a world distinguished by the most marvelous means of technical communication. Yet we are woefully short of persons with personal communicating skills. We may be speaking more, but our audiences are enjoying it less.

Which brings up a most important question: How does an executive give a good speech?

First of all, he develops his speech with the aid of a professional speechwriter, one who knows the subtleties of oral persuasion, who is not afraid to tell him that his ideas are lousy, and who insists that the speech bear the clear stamp of one voice — the speaker's — not a chorus of discordant notes and sounds.

This is not to suggest that the speaker should take only the writer's opinion about his speech. On the contrary, I always recommend to my clients that they show a completed script to several friends.

A good speech should be a creative achievement but we humble mortals must admit that a genuinely new idea is rare; therefore, it is often the way a speaker says things rather than what he says that is significant. In other words, a good speech must have tone: the order and consistency of texture found in a work of art. Nothing in a speech is more important for success or failure than appropriate tone — what we writers call "felicity of phrasing."

It is in planning speech strategy, by the way, that your public relations director can be most useful to you. After all, he worries about that sort of thing all the time. Moreover, he is in touch with all the currents and crosscurrents of political thought and opinion in your company. Fair return is fair play, however. So while you let your public relations director plan the strategy, you should let your writer do the writing.

How to Spice Up Those Dull Speeches

by Robert Orben

Condensed from *Enterprise*

I begin my humor workshops for corporate speakers and communicators by saying that a lot of show business terms will be used.

The minute they stand up in front of an audience, they have crossed the line. They are in show business and the further they are from that awareness, the less effective they will be.

Humor has often been the key that unlocks an audience's receptivity. The apt, well-timed and confidently executed opening immediately puts listeners at their ease. They realize they are in secure hands and can look forward to hearing a professional communicator.

"Apt" is the operative word. Some top-level executives shy away from humor because they feel it may be undignified. The distinction between a jokester and an accomplished raconteur lies in the choice of material. To get laughs, the jokester relies on one-liners and stories, some old, some new, but usually irrelevant to the purpose of the event. The raconteur never loses sight of his or her reason for being there. The laughs are supportive or illustrative of the occasion, the audience or the speaker.

Where does such "apt" material come from? Obviously, it can be custom-written by a specialist in the field. The problem with such special material is the expense. It may only be a page or two of double-spaced items — three or four jokes — but the right three or four jokes may have taken up to a week to research and create. Consequently, the professionals in this area charge from $500 to a few thousand dollars to do it.

There is an alternative to custom-written humor and it has the down-to-earth title of "do-it-yourself." Creating humor is an art form that relatively few writers have mastered and only after years of trial and error.

The good news is, there are hundreds of sure-fire laugh lines that are just perfect for you. They are in the many humor books and services readily available to public speakers. The bad news is, to get them you will have to go through tens of thousands of jokes that you can't use.

You can't read a jokebook as you would a novel. You have to proceed as if you were eating marzipan. One or two pieces are delicious

— 20 or 30 pieces, sickening. So restrict your reading of any jokebook or humor service to no more than 15 minutes, two or three times a day.

What are you looking for? First, is the item funny? Two, would you feel comfortable saying it? Three, is it performable humor?

The reason for the first question is self-evident: If the joke doesn't strike you as funny, that's it. If you are concerned about a piece of material, follow the old adage: "When in doubt, cut it out!"

The second question also involves a critical decision: Would you feel comfortable telling the joke? An inappropriate anecdote dragged in by the heels will invariably make you look like a candidate for the *Gong Show*. "To thine own self be true" — in all things — even humor.

The third question is just as important: Is it performable humor? If someone tells you a joke, the chances are it is constructed in such a way that it "plays."

Good performable humor sometimes looks rather drab on the printed page. If you read one of the great comedy routines like *Who's On First?*, you may be somewhat disappointed in it. But when you heard it performed by Abbott and Costello, it was hilarious. It often takes a practiced eye to spot the performing values of a joke. You get this practiced eye by going out and doing material in front of an audience. The jokes that work give you the warm feeling of success. The jokes that die eventually give you the practiced eye.

The next step is to have the selected jokes and stories transcribed onto 3 x 5 cards and then classified according to possible use and subject matter. Cross-index liberally.

The last step in the process is the use of the file itself. When you accept a speaking engagement, make a list of all possible aspects of the occasion — the subject of your talk, the location of the hall (city and state), the audience, who will be introducing you, other head table guests, etc. Turn to your file and look up the categories your list would suggest as relevant and then pull all of the items in those classifications.

Lay the cards out on a large table and, in many cases, a natural continuity, linking a few of the jokes, will suggest itself. Keep in mind that in humor, less is always more. One, two or three laughs at most should be the maximum used before a serious speech. And please keep the whole speech to 20 minutes.

Even though you're chairman of the board of the multi-billion dollar John Doe Corp., don't be afraid to adopt a somewhat playful attitude when you go up to the podium: "As I look out over this assembly, I realize that we represent the finest minds and talent our industry has to offer — so before we begin, I'd like to ask Reverend Jones to say a short prayer for our country."

To a speaker, the current use of humor is invaluable.

Humor can drive home a point, illustrate a problem, humanize the speaker and the company he represents, build rapport with others, win over an audience, or defuse a tense situation.

Humor is a social lubricant. That's its principal value to the businessman. It helps put him on the same plane as the people he is speaking to.

If you can, tell a story on yourself that pokes fun gently. The reaction you're striving for is to have the audience nudging each other in the ribs and saying: "Hey, he's a regular guy."

If you can come up with that kind of material, you're home free.

Your manner is as important as your material.

If you are the main speaker, sitting at the head table, you are not the Invisible Man.

Whenever there's an idle moment, everyone in the room will have his eyes on the head table. If you are well known, the audience will be looking you over pretty carefully.

Yet sometimes a businessman seems totally oblivious of this.

During the program he may bury his head in the speech he's going to make. Or he may simply sit like a bump on a log, looking bored, tense, or grim, and not uttering a word to anyone on either side of him.

Then he's introduced. He bounds to his feet, and suddenly he's Mr. Charm.

Unfortunately, if he didn't look the part before, the audience won't buy that. Even humor won't turn on an audience already turned off by the speaker's actions. What you do on stage — and the speaker is always on stage — is part of the image you convey to your audience.

A speaker has to lead his listeners on until, suddenly, a trapdoor opens and their mental processes drop right through the floor — in another direction. That's the essence of humor.

There's a classic example from my book, *The Encyclopedia of One-Liner Comedy*. It goes something like this:

Three people are sitting around trying to define fame.

One says: "Fame is being invited to the White House for a talk with the President."

The second says: "No. Fame is being invited to the White House for a talk with the President, and the hot line rings and interrupts your conversation, but he doesn't answer it."

The third says, "You're both wrong. Fame is being invited to the White House for a talk with the President, and the hot line rings. The President answers it, listens for a moment and then says: 'Here, it's for you.'"

This illustrates what I call the rule of three. One remark tops another, until you reach the climax that triggers the laugh.

Many speakers make a common mistake. They think a twice-told story is stale.

Nonprofessionals are often very self-conscious about repeating a story, but if a funny story works, no speaker should be intimidated by the fact that he has used it many times.

A professional performer will never be. In fact, the professional will give his right arm for this kind of sure-fire material. He will prize it.

The only old joke I know of is one told by the previous speaker.

If an audience laughed the first time, chances are they'll laugh again.

Oft-used, successful stories are like hit tunes that are perennial favorites. The record industry calls such tunes evergreens.

PITFALLS TO AVOID

There are don'ts as well as do's for successfully using humor in public speaking.

Avoid humor when speaking out-of-doors.

Even a very funny movie, playing to an almost empty house, won't get many laughs. Playing to a packed house, it will.

The out-of-doors is something like the almost empty theater. The audience is spread out and often distracted. In that setting, even big laughs sound feeble. They won't catch on and run through the crowd.

Shun puns.

It is a temptation to think of puns as performable humor. In most cases, they are not. By the very nature of its construction, a pun has the speaker saying: "Look how smart I am."

That is a challenge to your listeners. You don't want to challenge them. What you want is to have fun together with them.

On some television shows writers have not been allowed to use a pun unless they have a tremendous "saver." That is a one-liner which has fun with your audience's reaction — almost invariably a groan.

Audiences are conditioned to groan at the cleverest of puns.

So your saver might be: "I just threw that in. I should have thrown it out."

How many times have you heard someone like Johnny Carson use that type of saver?

Don't step on your lines.

Storytellers who lack confidence are prone to this mistake. They don't have the courage to wait out a laugh. They pause for a split second. Then, if the audience doesn't instantly react, they plunge ahead. They step on their lines. So you have to stop, smile, and wait after telling your funny story.

If you are scared, the time between telling a story and hearing the audience react seems like an eternity. But crowding a laugh is the surest way to ruin humor.

Don't be afraid to lay an egg.

Inevitably, sometimes a joke will die on you. If so, don't just squirm a little and go on as if nothing happened. It is good technique to acknowledge the fact that your story bombed.

Every professional, every monologist in show business has a dozen savers memorized to cover a situation like that. Build up a collection of your own. It will take the terror out of storytelling.

Never speak at length if you are at the end of a long program.

Make a quiet exit. Say something like: "I've been up here so long, the spotlight has faded my suit."

And then: "Now I'll race you to the door."

How to Tell a Joke
by Fred Ebel
Condensed from *Better Communication*

Laughter at the start of a speech will "hook" the listeners who are waiting for the next joke.

While it's true that some people are naturally gifted in joke telling, it's also true that joke telling can be learned. Following are seven techniques used by many professional speakers:

1. *Make a Point* Unless a joke makes a point, the speech will stop progressing — just as a swimmer who treads water makes no progress.

2. *Avoid Adverbs* Don't use adverbs to describe things you could express with the tone of your voice. Adverbs are required to explain written humor, but used in speech they can kill a joke.

For example, suppose this joke were exactly as written: "A woman turned to her husband and said complainingly, 'The way I have to dress, people would think I was the cook.' The husband called back sarcastically, 'Not if they stayed for dinner.'"

Both "complainingly" and "sarcastically" are unnecessary. Instead of using these words, you should make your voice sound complaining and sarcastic.

3. *Punch the Punch Line* All too often, speakers lose steam toward the end of their jokes. Everything is loud and clear — up to the end. Then the punch line is delivered in a voice that trails off so that only those in the front rows can hear.

If you should emphasize anything, it's the punchline. Also, be sure to deliver it accurately. Paraphrasing the punchline can lead to disaster. Make sure you memorize it!

4. *Personalize* Use the "I" approach. Tell the story as though it happened to you. This is the popular, "A funny thing happened to me on the way to the club" style used by professional stand-up comedians. By making the joke sound like something that happened to you, you impart a degree of believability.

5. *Make it Timely* If the joke is from another era, bring it up to date (unless this period of history has a bearing on the joke). Timeliness can be achieved through phrases such as, "just the other day," "last Saturday," or "last week."

6. *Know Your Audience* It helps to know the educational and social background of your audience. A nontechnical audience, for ex-

ample, won't understand the technical jargon used in a joke. Either find common terms to replace the jargon, or find another joke.

7. *Bomb Gracefully* Every joketeller — even the top comics — has "died" at one time or another. It's not unusual to be greeted with absolute silence after telling a joke that had them rolling in the aisles just a few days ago. Psychologists have tried to analyze this phenomenon. Some say it's due to a hostile audience — filled with sadistic people gleefully watching a speaker sweat.

Sometimes a joke bombs because the audience is too small. A group of ten people or less will often be a silent audience, no matter how good the joke. That's because everyone is afraid to laugh for fear of being conspicuous. Also, one person's laughter tends to set others off. In a large audience you have greater potential for catalysts who will start the audience laughing.

If no laughter comes after your joke, don't express anger. Instead, try to capitalize on what happened. You might get a laugh from a no-response joke, for example, by saying, as you look down at your notes, "It says here, 'Pause for laughter.'"

Or you might say, "I knew I should have invited my mother."

Humor is as essential to a talk as seasoning to a good meal.

Using humor that is irrelevant to your message is as inappropriate as offering a drunk in the gutter a bottle of whiskey. Using humor doesn't mean that you should try to become a stand-up comic telling jokes. The only exception to this is to attempt a few jokes on yourself. This makes you look less superior and more human, permitting an audience's identification with you.

Tips for Beginning Professional Speakers
by Ed Hercer & Gene Perret
Condensed from *The Roundtable*

Let me give you three general rules for new speakers.
1. *Get Introduced*   No matter where you appear, it makes good sense to let someone else introduce you. Don't go up there cold. Carry an intro you've written yourself. Don't depend on the chairperson to be as clever as you are at introducing you effectively.
2. *Never Apologize*   If you're good enough to be asked to speak — and especially if you're being paid — then you don't have the right to make excuses to your audience. They expect the best . . . and any apologies on your part are a letdown to them.
3. *Be Prepared*   Maybe this should be No. 1 — because if you're prepared, you'll have taken steps to be introduced and you won't have to apologize — for anything.

People think it's expected of them that they start out with a quip. I'd hate to choke on the number of times I've heard, "A funny thing happened to me on the way . . ." or "I'm reminded, after that introduction, of a man who . . ." or "It's nice of you to invite me here and the situation reminds me. . . ." Why? Because it's expected.

I don't see that it is expected unless a funny story or one-liner can help juice up your point.

Humor is important only to the extent that it can move your talk along, provide meaningful commentary as a bonus for your listener.

Ask yourself these questions before you throw a joke into your talk:
1. Does it move the speech along?
2. Does it tie in to my main point, or subsidiary point?
3. Does it serve to provide comic relief, break up the audience's thought pattern or surprise them with its pertinence? or
4. Will it destroy the image I'm trying to create in my audience's mind?

Humor in a talk is a very serious matter. Don't use it lightly. Humor can set a fast pace for your talk. It can warm up your audience quicker than just about any other technique except for a startling different visual aid. It can build a bridge between you and your audience because it can establish you as "one of them."

But it can't work miracles. It can't save a poorly planned, sloppily executed presentation. It can't cover over a speaker's faults. Above all, it can't be substituted for a good central message.

Audiences WANT you to succeed, and they're willing to help someone achieve this.

1. *Show Enthusiasm* If you really believe in telling this story in the best way possible, the audience will feel it and help you.
2. *Push Animation* Deadpan comedians may appear immobile to you (Jackie Vernon, Bob Newhart), but if you watch them carefully, there's a great deal of animation in their voice, in their movement, in their body English.
3. *Make Yourself the Goat* People love it when a speaker makes himself the object of a joke. They feel safe. They feel superior. They feel comfortable.
4. *Wait Out Your Laughs* Sometimes new and untried speakers are so startled when they get a laugh, they step on their own lines. If you sense you've got a real rouser of a quip, be sure to plan on a pause to give the audience time to absorb, appreciate and laugh. But don't overdo this. There's nothing deader than a silence that a speaker arranged for to be filled by a laugh — and none is forthcoming. Move over quickly, in the event nobody understands the joke.
5. *Pick Local People* It's one thing to quote something Abe Lincoln said, but it localizes it if you're making a reference to Pete, the bartender down the street, who everyone knows can get off a good one now and then.

I don't think one person can tell another his or her best style for telling a joke. But I do think a person can be trained to use his voice, his motions, his body, to exert the most effective humorous approach to an audience.

Expert speakers use stories to catch and hold your interest, as well as to implant an unforgettable experience in your minds. Some less expert flub it, though, by not telling their listeners prior to the story what they intend to tell them.

I like the sandwich technique. Tell the audience the point you wish to make. Then give it back to them in the form of a story that makes the point again, only with a little easy-to-take humor. Then button up your talk with a final point.

Localizing always sells a story. Instead of talking about a man walking into a store, doesn't it bring it home more for you to envision Erik Estrada walking into Bo Derek's beauty parlor? Instead of telling about some nebulous somebody who doesn't bring visions of anything to a person's mind, isn't it smarter to say, "Jackie Gleason walks into Shelley Winters' weight-reducing parlor...."

The best anecdotes are self-deprecating stories you can tell on yourself.

If you're going to be serious about this business of comedy writing and/or humorous speaking, you'll do well to pick up some dramatics training.

If I had the say, every youngster in elementary school would receive dramatics training. I would make it mandatory, right up there with the other basics. Children have a head start on being "hams." It comes naturally to them; it's only the constant battering away by parents and maybe too much tv that causes them to lose interest in play-acting and dressing up. Halloween is one of your best indicators today that kids like to dress up and be somebody else, if only for a fun-filled trick-or-treat night. And the candy is their reward for taking time and trouble.

But there's a side benefit for writers/speakers in taking to the stage: It's a great way to drill yourself on audience reaction.

Try out your own material by performing it yourself, whether that's your bag or not. It certainly provides an insight akin to that of the veteran who has lived through the battle and survived, compared to the rookie soldier who wonders what the front lines are really like.

There's a piece of meat available to you that you can hone your fine comedy and speaking edge on.

It's called a "roast."

In business today, it isn't done that often . . . largely because it's hard to do right. It's also too much work, and roasts take the type of creativity and timing most people planning parties for others don't have.

Don't think it's easy to insult people on a level where not everybody in the audience knows their quirks and still manage not to hurt their feelings. There are two common mistakes among fledgling emcees; the first one is to denigrate with wit that's on the caustic side to pure insult. There's a definite difference. If a line is funny, it can support a little bit of sarcasm (provided it doesn't cut too close to a nerve), but the sarcasm without the wit is fatal . . . to the audience and the performer. Always be sure your lines are based first of all on humor, not just put-downs.

The second error is that people overstay their welcome. That's easy to do. Once it's done, it's almost impossible to eliminate. If you do it at this month's dinner, you'll get only half the reception you should get. This error has a long-lasting effect. You almost have to start from scratch to build a reputation again.

It's easier to overstay your welcome if your material isn't polished.

Audiences are essentially collectively egotistical.

Figure that when you walk into a room with a crowd of people, each of them is wearing a sign that says, "I want to feel important." Humor can fulfill that unspoken unconscious wish, and it's the wise speaker who understands this.

Comedian Bob Hope pays writers hundreds of thousands of dollars a year to "localize" his jokes.

Why did the troops like Bob Hope so much? First off, of course, because he was there. Secondly, though, and most important, he bothered to survey the local scene and toss it back to them. He cared enough to employ local humor.

Here are some ways you can localize humor in your talks?

1. *Study Your Group* Ask the program chairman, if there is one, about some of the recent discussions, projects, plans and affairs the group has conducted. There's always something going on within the organization that can be touched upon lightly and bring a smile to the lips of the members . . . even if it's a comment on the lunch or dinner just finished.

2. *Pick Something in Common* Local humor needs "inside" material. You wouldn't tell a Weight Watcher's joke at a mortician's convention because it wouldn't be pertinent. The relevance of humor lies in selecting something everyone knows about — and then taking off from there.

   Thus even results can be tailor-made.

3. *Build the Story to Fit the Situation* Don't just tell a joke that has no tie-in. Make it pertinent. Shaggy dog stories — the kind that go on endlessly with a trio of climaxes, the third being the punch line — have a good track record for pertinence. Some are downright impertinent, and that's what you want, something that will remain strongly in your listener's mind to get the point across.

4. *Don't Get Overly Cute* People like simple gags, not too elaborately staged and not ridiculously cute. By that I mean you shouldn't try to snow your audience with super-hyped-up gags that leave them limp — unless the situation calls for it. One of the most successful gags on *Laugh-In* in recent years, with a guest appearance by John Wayne, was a simple one. "I'd like to thank the *Laugh-In* staff," said the star, "for being so nice to me and treating me great. Besides, they all know I can beat the hell out of them."

   Profound? No. Simple? Yes. Direct and true? Right on. He didn't have to be cute — just typical John Wayne.

5. *Start with a Truism* Black comedian Slappy White has an opener that usually uncorks his audience's funnybone. "It's been said," he begins, "that one out of every four persons suffers from mental disorders (pause) . . . Now think about three of your friends . . . (audience begins to think and starts to giggle) . . . And if you don't think there's something a little funny about them . . . (more open laughter) . . . YOU'RE THE ONE!"

A recent version of the Bible took away a considerable amount of its lyrical quality. For instance, where Christ had said to the adulterous woman, "Go and sin no more," the 20th century editor had changed it to, "Don't sin." Somehow it loses something in the updating.

But how many times is your subject going to be as monumentally important as Biblical matters? It won't be. You'll be dealing with contemporary things, and the times are such that you'll have to deal with them crisply and succinctly.

Rudolph Flesch presents a table which shows how the length of the sentences affects the ease of reading:

AVERAGE SENTENCE LENGTH IN WORDS

VERY EASY	8 WORDS OR LESS
EASY	11
FAIRLY EASY	14
STANDARD	17
FAIRLY DIFFICULT	21
DIFFICULT	25
VERY DIFFICULT	29 OR MORE

The anti-Fleschians say that he oversimplifies, largely because this measurement doesn't take into account difficulty of words, sentence structure, etc. The pros say that he has the right idea, that too many people super-structure their writing to the extent that they get all tangled up in their own verbiage, that Flesch formulas are especially right for speakers because the mind in reading can absorb a long difficult sentence, while the ear cannot listen to and allow for one as readily.

His ideas are strong, they make sense, they flow. He projects power in his writing because it's so tight and crisp. He stresses two things: simplicity and effectiveness. He is a speaker's friend. More importantly, he's a friend of the audience.

So count the number of words you have in any sentence in your script which seems unusually long. (That last sentence, for instance, was 18.) Give yourself the acid test. Ask yourself if you can say the sentence aloud without stumbling. Try it. Then try saying it as two sentences.

It's a good idea to vary the length of sentences — and be counting words so that you're sincerely conscious of the length. Frequently you can chop excess words from the use of too many adjectives. Often you can find you'll gain a few by chopping adjectives.

Here's another tip: Check the long words in your speech. They, too, can be cut if they don't portray a simple meaning. I cite: utilization (why not "use"); enunciated ("said"); meticulous (why not "careful"); participate ("take part"); immemorial ("long ago"); rehabilitated ("restored").

Try your hand at substituting words on that list. The important thing to learn is that you have to shake the idea that long words make a good speech.

There are very few good judges of comedy, and they don't agree. The only sure ones are those that sit in the audience. The rest of us are merely making hopeful guesses.

As performers and speakers we sometimes tend to make ourselves the focal point. Why shouldn't we? The light is on us. We own the podium and the lectern. It can easily cause us to forget that comedy exists in the mind of the listeners.

The speaker sets the stage and paints the picture, but it is the image in the mind of the listeners that generates the comedy.

On one of Steve Martin's comedy albums he tells his audience that there is a large plumber's convention in attendance that night. He then goes on in his own zany style to tell a joke about a 3/4-inch Watson wrench that makes no sense at all. Then he has some fun wondering why those plumbers never showed up and why the joke got no laughs.

The opposite can also be true, though . . . an average gag can be a blockbuster.

Speakers have an obligation to learn a little bit about their audiences . . . not only what they want to hear, but what their opinions are on particular subjects.

For humorists, knowing their audiences throughly is not a luxury, it's a necessity.

Those of us who include humor in our presentations have "borrowed" stories from time to time.

You needn't feel guilty because the person we "borrowed" the anecdote from borrowed it from someone else anyway.

As a comedy writer, I don't condone stealing original material that a humorist paid good money for.

But some jokes fall into the realm of public domain. They're literally the property of all.

What is unforgivable, though, is to simply take the story and replant it into your speech.

If you're going to use an old joke in your presentation, make it peculiarly your own.

Bob Hope's material goes in rhythmic patters, peaks and valleys. I would read him monologue material over the phone, he'd say to me, "Where's the biggie?" He was looking for that joke that made the whole routine worth doing.

Comedy has to build to a crescendo and then taper off. Think of it as somewhat like a fireworks display. The audience reacts much the same way a crowd watching fireworks on the Fourth of July. You see the stream of light climbing skyward, then the explosion.

A great tried and true joke is like the explosion, but you can't put on a fireworks display with only that. You have to build it. That's where you can make a story YOUR STORY.

There is a children's verse that reads, "I'm a little teapot short and stout, this is my handle, this is my spout." It continues on and ends with, "Tip me over, pour me out." You recite this one with one hand on your hip and the other raised mimicking a teapot. The joke on this is a person who puts both hands on his hips and says, "I'm a little teapot short and stout. This is my handle, this is my . . . I'll be damned, I'm a sugar bowl."

Now because I'm a comedy writer I humanize this joke and make it mine. I tell the following story:

> My daughter once came home from kindergarten and told me she had this poem to recite and asked if I would help her with it. I said, "Honey, why don't I write some original material for you?" She thought for a moment and then said, "No, Dad, this is in front of the whole school and I want it to be good."
> But I didn't mind because I know kids don't understand. Besides she probably couldn't afford my material anyway.
> But that's the last time I ever offer her the special discount for members of the immediate family. Anyway I worked with her and rehearsed her and then came the night of the recital and my wife and I sat in the audience.

And then I do the story with the physical moves and in the voice of a child. It gets a nice reaction. Admittedly some of the people in the audience have heard the joke before, but never quite this way.

Then after the laugh, I'll say, "I hate children who get bigger laughs than their father," or "I hate kids who can ad-lib."

It has been changed from one joke to a routine with three little laughs, then the big explosion, then the little laugh or two on the way down.

In dealing with comedy it helps to deal in extremes. Reach for the bizarre and zany, even the grotesque.

Comedy is to mind what caricature is to the eye. A good caricature artist can spot those characteristics and define his subject and then exaggerate them, put a new perspective on them, again, almost make them grotesque. Yet the recognizability is never destroyed. In fact, it is often enhanced. It is sometimes easier to recognize a celebrity from a well-executed caricature than from a portrait.

The humorist does something similar. He or she spots something in the surrounding and then adds a new perspective to it.

Sometimes, the easiest way to accomplish this is to carry it to extremes. Take whichever topic you are exploring and imagine what would happen if you carried it to a ridiculous conclusion. Take facets of your topic and distort them out of all perspective to the rest of the topic. Think about your topic and envision in your mind a grotesque picture as a result of it.

Suppose we wanted to admit we had "stage fright." One symbol of stage fright was knees knocking. So we took that basic statement and tried to carry it to extremes. How much did your knees knock? We came up with the line, "My knees were really knocking when I gave my first speech in public. I asked someone afterwards how he liked the speech. He said, 'I don't know, I couldn't hear you. The drummer was playing too loud.'"

Once I had to do some material for a comic about Jackie Gleason's operation. Gleason had recovered sufficiently so he could be kidded about it. This was a classic exercise in exaggeration jokes.

> *I went to see Jackie Gleason in the hospital. He was in rooms 413, 414, and 415.*
>
> * * *
>
> *The operation took six hours. The first four hours were just to get him on the table.*
>
> * * *
>
> *He's fine now, but they're going to have to operate on him again. One of the doctors is missing.*

Phyllis Diller asked me many years ago to do some jokes about her cooking, and how bad it was. Again, you simply can't say the work in the kitchen is bad . . . it has to be BAD! So you have to ask what would happen if the cooking was so bad as to be dangerous or ridiculously foul. We exaggerated to get these lines:

> *My cooking is so bad, last Christmas the family chipped in and bought me an oven that flushes.*
>
> * * *
>
> *I once went out to my kitchen and caught a cockroach eating a Tum.*

Phyllis Diller had a joke in her routine about how big her mother-in-law, Moby Dick, was. I took that form and did many more jokes with different colors.

Once she wore a red, white, and blue dress, stood on the street corner, and a man threw a letter in her mouth. Once she wore a gray dress and an admiral boarded her.

This is not the only form of joke writing or humor, but when you're faced with a topic and are having trouble generating the funny lines, let your mind exaggerate, distort, and go to extremes.

12

Writing for Magazines and Publications

The Light Touch
by Roy Paul Nelson
Condensed from *Articles and Features*

The line between comedy and tragedy, as you know, runs thin and indistinct. Not that the light touch necessarily involves humor. It may mean, simply, a relaxed writing style. The trick is to use the light touch without hating yourself in the morning. The light touch can easily turn into the cute touch. One safeguard to take is to put a lightly-styled manuscript away for a few days and review it carefully once it has cooled.

A proven way of achieving a light touch — safe enough for anyone to try — is to pepper the manuscript with anecdotes.

A frequent complaint the beginning writer hears from an editor, if the writer is lucky enough to get a letter rather than a rejection slip, is that the article carries no anecdotes.

"It's one thing to describe a millionaire as frugal, but the description takes on much more meaning when you follow it with an incident in which he drove back from his office because he had forgotten his brown-bag lunch," says M.L. Stein, a journalism educator.

An anecdote can be described as a short — very short — story, usually no more than a paragraph or two in length, told to prove a point or breathe life into a generalization.

Anecdotes can precede or follow a generalization.

You need to look for anecdotes all the time. Finding a good anecdote should excite you as much as stumbling onto a little known fact.

Where do you find them? One way is to pick out key words, facts, or ideas in your manuscripts and look up what's been written on them in *The New York Times Index* or *Readers' Guide to Periodical Literature*. Failing to find anecdotes, writers sometimes make them up. But when you do create them, be sure they sound true and can be true. It's more important for anecdotes to be believable than to be true. Sometimes a made-up example sounds more plausible than one that actually happened.

The least the writer can do is let the reader know when an anecdote is made up. The writer can use an introductory line like: "This is the way it might have happened" or "The conversation might go like this."

Nels F.S. Ferre in *God's New Age* offers the anecdote — you could call it a parable — to explain some not-easy-to-understand terms:

> *Three baseball umpires were arguing.*
> *"I call balls and strikes exactly the way they come," said the first. He was an objectivist.*
> *"I can't do that," replied the second. "I call them balls and strikes just the way I see them." He was a subjectivist.*
> *But the third had an idea all his own.*
> *"They are neither balls nor strikes," he declared, "until I call them." He was an existentialist.*

Of course the anecdote is made up. But the reader understands that Ferre did not happen onto three real-life umpires engaged in so convenient a conversation.

Segregated Anecdotes For an occasional article, a writer may not want to integrate the anecdotes but may want to run them instead as little islands set off typographically from the article's regular flow.

Perhaps they will appear as boldface insets, or in italics, or even in colored ink.

The Joke A joke differs from an anecdote in that it makes no pretense that it actually happened. Here's an example from an article by William K. Zinsser.

> So closely is . . . [the fear of saltpeter] threaded into the American folklore that it even figures in our jokes. Only the other day I heard of a boy entering the army who was worried about his threatened maleness, so he asked his father if the food was saltpetered in his army days in World War I.
> "Of course," said the father.
> "Did it work?" asked the boy.
> "You know," the father replied, "it's just beginning to work."

Humor Abraham Lincoln said, "I have found in the course of a large experience that common people . . . are more easily informed through the medium of a broad and humorous illustration than in any other way." George Bernard Shaw said. "When a thing is funny, search it for a hidden truth."

There is a place, certainly, for humor in magazines and newspapers. Editors ask for humor in nonfiction as well as fiction. They also like to see some humor in pieces that treat serious subjects.

Philip Nobile asks in an article: "Which food is better for your health — American or Japanese? That depends on whether you prefer cancer in your colon or your stomach."

When in your writing you deal with someone known for humor, humor in your writing becomes almost mandatory. Not that you try to upstage your subject, but you do make good use of the humor he created, and you do it in a style appropriate to the subject. The beauty of Robert Lewis Taylor's biography of W.C. Fields is that, though adulatory, it is written with irreverence and understatement much in keeping with Fields' own manner. On Fields' reliance on whiskey as a tuberculosis cure: it was, according to Taylor, a "specific that probably would not withstand medical scrutiny." On Fields' lack of interest in gambling: "He felt that there was an ugly element of chance in gambling which made it possible for somebody other than himself to win."

Most writers find it easy to weave into their articles the anecdotes they uncover, but few writers appear to be comfortable with humor.

In *The Writer's Handbook* Sylvia Dee singles out the person who should try his hand at humor:

"Do you wake up in the morning with a feeling that Doomsday is rapidly approaching?

"Are you a morbid, morose, introverted, easily depressed, gloomy sad sack of an individual?

"If so, and you can write, I'd say you're well on your way to becoming a top-notch writer of humor."

The biographies of our humorists suggest that they are not the best adjusted of persons. Stephen Leacock said: "If a man has a genuine sense of humor he is apt to take a somewhat melancholy, or at least a disillusioned, view of life. Humor and disillusionment are twin sisters."

Elton Trueblood said: "It is not possible to have genuine humor or true wit without an extremely sound mind, which is always a mind capable of high seriousness and a sense of the tragic."

So far as the writer is concerned humor divides itself into (1) subject-matter humor (funny of itself) and (2) literary humor (funny in the phrasing).

It is easier to produce subject-matter humor than literary humor. But you need the ability to recognize the humorous event when it occurs.

The subject doesn't have to be an event. It can be an object. "An egg is funny," said Fred Allen, "an orange is not."

Richard Armour finds humor in the human body.

One form of subject-matter humor is gentle, reassuring, predictable. It celebrates ordinary events and everyday frustrations. It puts the writer in exactly the position of the reader. The reader responds: "Isn't it the truth!" It is the kind of humor that brings a smile — maybe a smile of recognition; it does not evoke a hearty laugh. The success of this kind of humor rests with genuineness of feeling and clarity of telling.

A variation of life-is-like-that humor is in-character humor, in which someone plays with a familiar role out of context. The opposite of in-character humor is out-of-character humor, in which someone plays a role completely different from what you would expect: an old lady uses hip language; a child talks like a grown-up.

Writers of subject-matter humor often write about themselves. They become the butt of the jokes. It is always safer making fun of yourself than making fun of others. Phyllis Diller had to give up exercising — "I can't stand the noise."

Hypocrisy is often an ingredient in this kind of humor. You make the case against some human weakness, perhaps with some disdain, but reveal yourself at the end as one who has the weakness, too. A character in a Peter DeVries novel says: "I can't stand name-dropping, as I once told Bea Lillie."

The humor in nonfiction may lie not in the subject itself but in the way it is described. The order of description — what comes first — can make the difference.

To many, humor is largely a matter of surprise, promising the reader one thing early in a sentence or paragraph and then delivering something quite different, as when Milton Berle says, "I had a wonderful compartment on the train on the way down. But the conductor kept locking me in at every station." Or when Woody Allen says, "My wife was an immature woman. I'd be in the bathroom taking a bath and she would walk right in and sink my boats." "Have a nice weekend, unless, of course, you have other plans," says a radio announcer. Earl Wilson quotes Rodney Dangerfield as saying this about his marriage: "We sleep in separate rooms, we have dinner apart, we take separate vacations — we're doing everything we can to keep our marriage together." Reggie Jackson, then of the Oakland Athletics, said of teammate Joe Rudi: "He's a misfit. He gets along with everyone on the club."

How to Write Humor Fillers for the *Reader's Digest*

by Betty Johnston
Condensed from *Writer's Digest*

What makes a good filler for *Reader's Digest?*

That's a tough question. Life would be simpler for filler contributors and editors alike if there were some precise formula for measuring out the ingredients of a good filler. But if there were a formula, the fillers would probably cease to be good. For variety is a prime consideration in the over-all selection of filler material — variety in length, in subject matter, in mood, in pace, in style. The element of unexpectedness which contributes to the success of a filler program can be present only because flexibility is fostered at the expense of formulas.

Still there are some generalizations that can be made. The word "filler" itself is perhaps unfortunate, suggesting as it does only the utilitarian aspect, the need to fill a gap. As one reader put it in sending a contribution to *Reader's Digest*. "I thought that maybe you could put it in the magazine just to cover up some unwanted space." The good filler goes far beyond simply covering the unwanted space, although that is of course an essential function. It may prompt the reader to laugh aloud, to gasp in surprise, or perhaps to say, "I didn't know that!" or "That really says it!" The basic criteria are pretty much the same, whether the filler is a pun or a ponderable, a factual eye opener or a sparkling quip, a poignant anecdote or a witty exchange.

A good filler is one that the reader will want to quote to a colleague or read aloud to a spouse — and perhaps even to savor again in solitude. To be quotable or tellable the filler needs a certain timeliness (and/or timelessness) and relevance. Although nostalgia is big these days, a quote or anecdote from the past or concerning past events should have some special application for today. For a general magazine like *The Digest,* a filler should be of broadest interest and appeal; it must concern something that readers know and care about, or would like to know about — or perhaps should know and care about. This does not mean that any subject is automatically ruled out. An item may concern astrophysics or astroturf, as long as it is clear to the general reader and in some way touches the funnybone.

What makes a poor filler? There are the obvious things to avoid: ethnic put-downs, out-and-out vulgarity, stories that ridicule the handicapped. Put-downs in general should be considered with some care. It's all right to deflate the know-it-all or the pompous bureaucrat, and to poke good-natured fun at the foibles and eccentricities of our fellow humans. But one quickly tires of the caustic comments that have nothing to recommend them beyond their sting. The story in which the teller is, in the end, laughing at himself may have a better chance of success than the one in which he's laughing at his mate, or his boss, or his neighbor.

Whatever his market, the contributor might ask himself: Is the story too complicated to hold reader interest? Is it specialized for the market? Is the incident one that's fun to participate in or hear about but doesn't quite come off on paper? Does it take too much space for what it says?

How do you go about finding good fillers? First, the oft-repeated advice: study your market. Read fillers intensively so that you will get an idea of the range of interest to be on the watch for.

Reader's Digest is dependent upon its filler contributors, who are a source of fresh and lively material, for both original and reprint items. If you do a great deal of reading, you may be in a position to turn up good reprint items. Newspapers, books, and regional small-circulation magazines may be good sources. Watch for clever headlines, short reports of unusual and funny incidents, anecdotes about well-known people, interesting or amusing ads or notices, provocative quotations. The filler contributors with a good ear for radio or TV (and a pen handy) may come up with a likely item. The observant person may spot an amusing sign in a store window or overhear an entertaining or revealing snatch of conversation. Keep an eye out for the funny or touching incident or encounter, and an ear out for the amusing or provocative remark.

If you study "Toward More Picturesque Speech," you will see it's an area for creativity — for the original one-liner pertinent or zany, the inventive play on words, the picturesque phrase or terse verse. It's also a good area for published items.

For our "Life in These United States" department, we invite only true unpublished anecdotes. Here the amateur probably has as good a chance as the professional, for success depends in large measure on being present at the right moment to participate in or observe the funny situation or the poignant scene. "Life in These United States" anecdotes may be tag-line stories with some added insight; they may have a philosophical twist or a regional slant.

True funny-situation and tag-line stories may also be suited to "Laughter, the Best Medicine." "Laughter" is primarily a joke department, including some oldies along with the latest stories going the rounds. There are pun stories, topical humor, quips from TV and night-club comedians, light satirical commentary.

Anecdotes about well-known people are wanted for "Personal Glimpses." These are most likely to come from published sources, but a good anecdote may also result from a personal encounter.

"All in a Day's Work" invites job-related humorous incidents and commentary — both unpublished accounts of true experiences and published items. We also want good college stories for "Campus Comedy," service-related humor for "Humor in Uniform," and celebrity remarks for "Quotable Quotes" and "Points to Ponder."

In addition to Digest filler departments ("Life in These United States," "Personal Glimpses," etc.), there are the bottom-of-the-page fillers, which cover as wide a range as the departments, all the way from one-liners to long, humorous anecdotes and short essays.

There are so many variables in the selection of filler material that there is nothing sure-fire in aiming at the filler market. It's a little like a treasure hunt — and the happy contributor is the one who enjoys the hunt even if the prize may elude his or her grasp.

13

Writing for Stand-Up Comics

Now Let's Write a Complete Monologue
by Ron Carver
Condensed from *How to Write Jokes*

Let us go through each step carefully to see how a writer starts from "scratch" and creates and constructs an entire monologue. We'll number each major step and give an example of the technique employed. In this way you will have a kind of mechanical blueprint of the entire process. Later you can follow these steps with your own original ideas, and draw from such practice your own personal writing techniques.

STEP I. THE NATURE OF THE PERFORMER

Take into consideration the type, personality and style of delivery of your comic (speech-maker or entertainer) in order to determine generally what kind of material your client can handle. Thus, if your comic "sells" best to an audience when he executes zany, fast-paced type material (like Jack Carter) it is obvious you must season your creation of his material with "bits of business" and chunks that fit this ability. If he does effectively a well-meaning or "dumb" characterization (like a George Gobel or Jackie Vernon), you must use this fact as a rack to hang your material on.

Even before you create the jokes, ask yourself what your comic's personality is like. Is he sarcastic and aggressive like Jack E. Leonard, Don Rickles or Joey Bishop? Is he political like Vaughn Meader? Topical like Bob Hope?

Now, let us say for the purposes of this test run that your comic's (proven-by-laughs) character, attitudes or style lends itself to complaining about domestic issues. In this case we must construct his material around his bitter attitude regarding his wife, children, living in the suburbs, his home, etc. (on the order of Alan King's style).

STEP II. THE NATURE OF THE AUDIENCE

Put down a note or two regarding the type of audience for whom your comic will be performing. It is important to keep the audience in mind as you write so that your material stays within boundaries acceptable to that audience. A nightclub audience is different from one at a PTA meeting — a "benefit" stage show is different from a private club banquet, etc. Thus, if you are writing for an audience of light bulb manufacturers at a convention, it's all right to use highly specific (or "inside") material. But for your general audience, stay with topics of general appeal (tv commercials, movies, mothers-in-law, children, dieting, doctors, cars, etc.).

Incidentally, do a little research. It can do your routine a world of good. It can give you ideas that can be springboards for quite a number of gags within your routine, and it will generally make you feel more secure when you write, knowing you have a few books or articles on the subject at your side. We also suggest that you get children's books whenever possible, as they provide more readily accessible material — being in digest or capsule form — and are not as technical or involved as the original adult books. Remember, if you get too high-brow, technical or obscure in the data within your monologue, you're back at the light bulb convention.

Let us assume for this test-run monologue that your comic's audience will be one attending a tv variety show to be broadcast nationally.

STEP III. THE MONOLOGUE AREA OR PREMISE

Here you can choose any logical area that fits the above-chosen comic — keeping in mind what is currently of interest to such a mass audience. To inspire us and define our topic, let's say there's been some recent national coverage of the "Little League" baseball teams. Most of the audience would then be familiar with this topic and it could be treated to fit your comic. Fine. Let us write a monologue on "Little Leagues" as our topic.

STEP IV. THE ASSOCIATION LIST

Now you put down on paper your typical associations relating to the "Little League" baseball teams, including any stray thoughts that occur to you while making the list, as follows:

Athletics/healthy exercise
Crowd in the stands (bleachers)
Coach drives team to ball park
Father-and-son activity
Pop is team coach (wife is real boss)
Kid tosses ball around house (breaks window, hits sis)
Last minute instructions (from wife)
Game-score (players fight with umpire) pop bottle thrown
Umpire
Betting
Lost game, wife sarcastic
Fresh kid
Kids gets a hit; father proud

Now several other items may occur to you which can help you create effective material. For instance, you remember that your entertainer can sing. Therefore, you might write a song for him to sing at the tag (or ending) of the monologue. Then you ask yourself how else your entertainer can further personalize this monologue, and it occurs to you he does a funny imitation of a talkative woman. You might be able to include this special ability somewhere. So you add the following to the association list:

SONG: Take Me Out To The Ballgame (Parody of new-lyrics)
        Comic does good "take-off" on woman

(Of course, your association list can be much longer than the above, but this partial list is sufficient to give you an idea of the type of items to choose.)

STEP V. CREATE THE JOKES

Now you bounce some thoughts off the above association list and try to come up with some jokes. You think aloud now — in typical "free-association" style, remembering how to place yourself in the role of the comic and his viewpoint on Little Leagues — something like the following.

(You say to yourself:) ATHLETICS/HEALTHY EXERCISE, huh? (Well, here's a thought:) "Clean body, clean mind — take your pick." This might be a funny line if I can find a reason for it in the monologue. Now I'll play around with the CROWD-IN-THE-STANDS item. (You think:) Don't they look funny when they're screaming for blood. (You write:) ". . . like a pack of gargoyles at a hanging . . . mine!"

What else do I suffer doing as a coach? (You read:) COACH DRIVES TEAM TO BALL PARK. (This starts you thinking:) Kids practice in the car. I might be able to rough out something using the element of misconstruction. Oh! Now I've got it! (Wait! I'll polish it. Now it reads:) "But the real excitement starts Saturday afternoons. The whole team piles into my car, and I drive them all over to the ball park. The kids practice pitching, hitting flies, swinging the bat around . . . then they all get out of the car . . . that is, what's left of it!"

(Next you think:) FATHER-AND-SON-ACTIVITY. Is it really? (But after trying, nothing funny occurs to you on this item, so you go on to the next item:)

POP IS COACH, WIFE IS BOSS. Ah ha! That reminds me of someone who said that mothers are taking over the game. Maybe I can use that idea. (You write out some roughs and then polish it to read:) "You think this is a father and son activity? I've got news! The mothers have taken over. You think when I was the coach of the team. I was coach! (shrugs: no) . . . My WIFE was coach! And if we lose a game, my wife can't face her friends. It's a new bit. You know how mothers scream at kids if they play ball in the house? My wife encourages it! My kid's knocked out every window in the house. If I shout at him, his mother says: Leave him alone . . . he's practicing . . . so he broke another window."

(Oops! That's the next item:) BREAKS WINDOW — I should be able to use that. (I'll apply the exaggeration element as follows:) "He broke every window in the house — our lawn has the sharpest blades of grass in town." (or another thought on this:) "We've got the only lawn in the neighborhood that glitters in the sunlight!"

(You think:) Now I have reason to do a "spank him" joke. (But you have the follow-up thought:) No, the wife wouldn't let me. (So you write:) "And if I grab him, my wife yells: Don't hit him, you'll injure his pitching arm! (Looks at audience suggestively) . . . Not where I'd hit him!"

(The next item is:) HITS HIS SISTER. Maybe the kid uses his sister as a target to perfect his pitching. If I catch him at it he'll have the usual excuse ready. (You play around with this idea and finally you come up with two possibilities:) "Once I caught him pitching balls at his little sister. I said: What are you doing??? He said: I'm using my head, pop. I screamed: You're using your sister's head! He said: Pretty clever, huh, pa? . . . I'm practicing how to hit a player and make it look like an accident."

It now occurs to me if he's to be a pitcher and my wife is intense about his winning, I could tease this thought a little, thus: "And I love when she says: Junior, you're pitching the game today, go out and warm up the old arm . . . OLD ARM! His arm is nine years old, already it's the *old arm!*"

(The next item is:) INSTRUCTIONS FROM WIFE — and that note I made regarding the comic's special ability comes to mind. Maybe I could have the father do a take-off on the talkative wife nagging him regarding the game, thus: "She gives me my last-minute instructions: She says: (in woman's nagging voice) Now listen. Casey Stengel . . . whatever you do, don't put that kid Charley Smith in to hit . . . his mother doesn't belong to our club . . . and don't criticize the umpire . . . my brother is sensitive . . . and tell our team to sharpen their spikes . . . it's okay, the other team has Blue Cross . . . and remind Junior to smile when he gets up to bat . . . there may be photographers. . .now listen, if you win the game, come right home . . . if you lose . . . there are plenty of motels."

Next, a joke regarding THE SCORE is needed. Maybe the kid could have a wild excuse for losing. (So you write:) "Then I noticed the score. . .sixty-eight to zero. I grabbed my kid and said: They're beating you sixty-eight runs to nothing! He said: What are you worrying for? Our team hasn't even been up to bat yet!"

Let's try THE PLAYERS FIGHT WITH THE UMPIRE idea. No joke occurs. Kids fight with each other maybe. Suppose my kid kicks the other kid but he's consistent — he has another excuse ready. (I'll play with this thought and then write:) "I said to my kid: What are you doing? Why did you kick that kid in the stomach?? He said: It's not my fault; he turned around!"

The next item is POP BOTTLE. The father of the other kid could throw it at me and knock me out. And when that happens my wife and kid couldn't care less. (I pursue these ideas on paper until I get:) 'Just then the other kid's father sent me a message secretly hidden in a pop bottle. WHAT! BOING!. . . When I woke up I was on a stretcher bleeding to death. My wife looked down at me and said: I suppose you're going to have one of your headaches again. Then my son ran up and said: Gee, Pa, good thing you stopped that bottle . . . someone might've got hurt!"

The UMPIRE item is next — no ideas occur. Okay, let's go on to the next item.

The BETTING ITEM: (I think:) There are no bookies for Little League Games — yet. Maybe the kids bet on the games themselves . . . trade toys and — wait a minute! I gotta better idea! (Quick! Let's write it before it vanishes:) "Suddenly a tough character grabs me, and pulls me aside, saying: (in character) Look, buddy, a word to the wise, if you want to stay healthy . . . I'm makin' book on it . . . so I want you should throw this game! Got it? . . . (to audience) Can you imagine the nerve of this eleven year old?. . . *girl*?"

FRESH KID is next. Now, suddenly a news item headlined in a recent sports page enters my thoughts regarding Pete Rose in a "spitting" incident. Maybe I could use it to teach good sportsmanship to my kid . . . maybe mention Reggie Jackson and Tom Seaver . . . or switch it to show how fresh my kid is. Here, I'll rough it out and polish it like this . . . (and while I'm at it a related stock gag occurs to me . . . Okay, I'll put both gags down:) "I said to my kid: What's the matter with you? Don't you want to grow up and pitch like Tom Seaver, and hit like Reggie Jackson? He said: Naw, I'd rather spit like Pete Rose! Well, maybe he'll change . . . next week he's gonna have his tenth birthday . . . if I let him."

The next item on the list is KID GETS A HIT. (It works out as follows:) "Finally, my Junior gets up to bat, and hits a home-run! I shouted: That's my boy! I taught him how to hit. The other coach yelled: Hey, stupid, they're supposed to use a bat, not their head. I said: Listen, a hit's a hit!"

STEP VI. ROUTINE THE JOKES

Now you look over your individual jokes with an eye to routining them. You suddenly realize that these jokes can be routined quite easily by placing the jokes about "family and house" in one group, what happens "before the game starts" in a second group, the jokes about the "game itself" in a third group and the "result of the game" at the end in a fourth group. So you:

1. Place the jokes in this new, improved order. Once they are spread out before you in some logical sequence, you may find ideas for more jokes (or how to polish them), fill-ins, throw-aways, follow-up gags, direction remarks for use in parentheses, etc. So you write in the jokes or corrections that occur to you; then you

2. Write the finish or ending of the monologue — in this case by doing a parody to the song-idea; then you

3. Write blend lines to form some reasonable and natural-sounding continuity (as demonstrated earlier in this lesson); and finally, when all this is complete,

4. You create an effective set-up for the opening of the monologue which will colorfully lead to the jokes as written.

The result of all this activity should then look something like a professional monologue.

Ethnic Humor
by Larry Wilde
Condensed from *The Complete Book of Ethnic Humor*

Wisecracks are usually insults. They are almost always exaggerated witticisms that overstate something about a particular person or thing.

The most popular of all exaggerations is the wisecrack that ridicules the special traits of an individual by means of absurd illustration. And this is the essence of ethnic humor.

The *American Heritage Dictionary* defines ethnic as a religious, racial, national, or cultural group. The following joke, told around Southern California, exemplifies the true substance of ethnicity in humor, for it encompasses no less than four races and three religious groups.

> Why is Sunday morning the best time to be on the Los Angeles Freeways?
> The Catholics are in church.
> The Protestants are still asleep.
> The Jews are in Palm Springs.
> The Indians are restricted to the reservation.
> The Chinese are stuffing fortune cookies.
> The Blacks are stealing hubcaps.
> And the Mexicans can't get their cars started.

The most popular kind of ethnic joke is the put-down joke, which ridicules specific "character traits" of a particular group. The person telling the joke wants you to believe that these traits are true.

We laugh at the images that the gag created. It conjures up certain recognizable ethnic characteristics. Though these traits are not true they are familiar and we laugh even though we know that the barbed jest has no basis in truth.

The jokes told about other minorities in America are, again, based on the behavior patterns that are known and generally accepted about that particular group.

If we were to take the eccentricities that are identifiable with specific nationalities and use their quirks and peculiarities to create a humorous situation we would have the following joke:

A cruise ship, with passengers from all over the world, was caught in a severe storm and wrecked on a remote and unexplored island.
Soon the island began to buzz with activity.
The GERMANS were drilling the natives into the Army. The JEWS opened up a department store. The ITALIANS began organizing some hookers and the FRENCH started a restaurant. The SCOTS were financing the whole thing and a couple of ENGLISHMEN were still standing around waiting to be introduced.

THE POLISH JOKE SYNDROME

What do they call a dance attended by a bunch of Polacks? A goof ball.

Polish Jokes are the best example of the barbed jest — best because there is no such thing as a Polish joke, per se. In Poland, almost all the jokes are political in nature. Poland has been a subjugated country and it is the Pole's way of coping with years of dictatorship and foreign intervention.

In America the very gags that poke fun at Poles are also told about the Irish, Blacks, Puerto Ricans, Mexicans, Gypsies, Swedes, Finns, Arabs, and the Indians. The following Polish jokes are also old as Italian jokes.

If you see a row of houses that all look alike, how can you tell which one is Italian? It's the one with the diving board over the cesspool.

★ ★ ★

Did you hear about the Italian who stayed up all night studying for his urine test?

In the early 1940's the popular joke craze on college campuses as well as in the war plants was *The Little Moron* jokes. The fad disappeared as soon as World War II ended. They surfaced again in the 1960's, only this time moron jokes were called Polish jokes.

It also depends on where you live. Around San Francisco, Polish jokes are called Portuguese jokes. In Canada, they are referred to as Newfie jokes (after the residents of Newfoundland), in South Dakota they are Norwegian jokes. Texans poke fun at the students of Texas Agricultural and Mechanical University who are, by and large, farmers. So as far as Texans are concerned, moron jokes or Polish jokes are really Aggie jokes.

If that isn't confusing enough, in France, Scottish jokes are attributed to the Swiss. In Sweden, moron jokes are told about the residents of Norway. Russians tell Czech jokes. The English tell moron jokes on the Irish.

THE SMILING IRISHMEN

Jokes about Irishmen began to flourish as the first immigrants from the Emerald Isle arrived on our shores in the 1840's.

They were naive — unsophisticated and totally unused to big city life. Before long their county bumpkin characteristics led them to be known as "greenhorns."

Around the turn of the century Irishmen began sending large numbers into three professions: politics, the priesthood, and the police. By escaping the ghettos and entering legitimate, respected work the Irish stepped up the rungs of society; and gags (moron jokes) about Irish ignorance and incompetence faded. Soon they were replaced with quips about councilmen, cops, and Catholics.

The Sons of Erin provided jokesmiths with additional subject material by their reputation for drinking and brawling. However, there is another element of humor that became part of the Irish comic spirit. It has been attributed to Obadiah Bull, an Irish attorney in London during the reign of Henry VII. Lawyer Bull was supposed to have been a notorious blunderer, often making statements that contradicted each other.

Soon other Irishmen got into the habit of making these utterances of paradox, which although appearing to have two opposite meanings turned out to have a logic all their own. They have since come to be known as *Irish Bulls:*

Policeman: Say, you, if you're gonna smoke here you'll have to either put out your pipe or go somewhere else.

★ ★ ★

Father Fallon: Abstinence is a wonderful thing.
MacNamara: Sure an' it is, Father, if practiced in moderation.

THERE WILL ALWAYS BE AN ENGLAND

Often Irish humor is mistakenly lumped together with the English, which quickly raises the ire of any true Irishman. There is a lot that is funny about the British. Again, national idiosyncracies provide the jokemakers with much material.

The English have a reputation for being terribly reserved, even standoffish. Their attitude toward sex seems Victorian, yet homosexuality appears to be accepted and practiced rather openly. The

British become comically absurd when trying to explain their point of view in their typical superior manner:

> Sir Reginal Farthington was on trial before the high court of Australia for the crime of molesting an ostrich. "Before passing sentence," announced the judge, "do you having anything to say?" "Your honor," said the Englishman, "if I'd have known you were going to make such a fuss about it, I'd have married the bloody bird!"

THE RED MAN

> Did you hear about the Algonquin Chief who named his daughter "ninety-nine cents" because she was always under a buck?

That is the kind of joke Americans find funny about Indians. But what do American Indians laugh at? An example of a favorite joke would be an animal outwitting a human being.

The essence of true Indian humor is almost childlike. It is innocent and simple, unencumbered with subtlety. Pranks are a key source of laughter. If there was such a thing as an Indian stand-up comedian, he would be a prankster not a joketeller. His technique would be visual not verbal.

THE FUNNY FAR EAST

The Western world does not understand many things about the mysterious Far Easterners. Their sense of humor is one of them.

The word joke in Chinese is literally translated to mean "smile talk." Orientals rarely laugh out loud. They are amused. They smile. However, there are certain idiosyncrasies to poke fun at, in particular the Oriental's transposition of the l and r sounds when they speak English,

> Did you hear about the new Japanese camera, on the market? When you trip the shutter, it goes "crick!"

THE BLACK COMIC SPIRIT

Blacks discovered what Jews had learned thousands of years ago: that humor is the way to reduce tension by attacking whatever threatens us.

"Music played a large role in the survival of the black people in America," wrote Redd Foxx and Norma Miller in their *Encyclopedia of Black Humor.* "That . . . and a sense of humor that just couldn't be enslaved."

The "nigras" became expert at imitating their master's mannerisms. They poked fun at the white man by mimicking him through impersonations and comic impressions guaranteed to evoke belly laughs. They strutted and pranced and mocked the cockiness of the oppressive plantation owners to the delight of their fellow slaves.

Blacks have been snickering at "whitey" ever since. Like the Jews, blacks developed a grin-and-bear-it attitude toward their unfortunate predicament. The following joke illustrates the bridge blacks have crossed in humor from slavery to the Seventies:

> *An NAACP official telephoned the Library of Congress and told the chief librarian that the library had 18,000 books with the word "nigger" in them and that all the books had to be removed in a week.*
> *"But," protested the librarian, "we have 50,000 volumes with the word 'bastard' in them."*
> *"I know," said the official, "but you bastards aren't organized."*

THE JEWISH SENSE OF HUMOR

Jewish jokes are a thing apart. Some are interchangeable with those directed at other minorities, but most are stories indigenous to the Jews.

Actually, Jewish jokes form the foundation for all ethnic humor. One reason is that Jews have been a minority longer than any other group and historically have been used as the butt of biting barbs. Another, and more important, reason is that humor is part and parcel of the Jewish culture.

Lenny Bruce, ahead of his time with his poignant comedic insights, was a student of his craft. Bruce is credited with the humor formula: *Tragedy + Time = Satire.*

This equation is the cornerstone for most Jewish humor. Business failure, family heartbreak, Hitler's holocaust, sorrows of every nature provide subjects that have been joked about by Jews.

This ability to laugh at adversity seems to be the key to Jewish survival. Paradoxically, it has also been the spring that nurtured the development of the "American sense of humor." Much of the comedy as it exists today on the stage, in motion pictures, and television has been created, molded, and delivered by Jewish comedians and comedy writer.

Only because Jews are joke-oriented could the following story have come about. It is the absolute refinement of the Jewish sense of humor:

Morton and Fogel were discussing humor over lunch. "Do Jews react differently when they hear a joke?" asked Morton.

"What a question!" replied Fogel. "If you tell an Englishman a joke he'll laugh at it three times. Once, when you tell it, again when you explain it and third time when he understands the point."

"Tell a German the same joke, he'll laugh twice. Both times to be polite. There won't be a third time, because he'll never get the point."

"Tell the same joke to an American, he will laugh once, immediately, because he'll get it right away."

"But," said Fogel, "when you tell the joke to a Jew . . ."

"Yes?" asked Morton.

"When you tell the same joke to a Jew, he won't laugh at all. Instead he'll say, 'It's an old joke — and besides, you told it all wrong!'"

SEX AND ETHNIC HUMOR

It is common knowledge among comedians that jokes with erotic content evoke the biggest response from any audience. Since sexual mores in America have always been couched in the Puritanical ethic, the mere mention on stage of mating allows the crowd to release whatever frustrations or hang-ups they have about the subject.

The second most powerful comedic weapon for the nightclub comic is the ethnic joke. A story about a dress manufacturer can be funny — tell it about a Jewish manufacturer of ladies apparel and you add a dimension that can turn the same story into a scream.

An audience can identify emotionally with specifics. The story becomes funnier when the audience can visualize the person concerned. It is emotion that causes the big laugh. Tell a mother-in-law joke to an unwed college student and he might smile. Relate it to a married man who isn't particularly fond of his wife's mother and you get a laugh of recognition, of identification.

THE AMERICAN SENSE OF HUMOR

Americans can trace their ancestors to countries all over the world and are proud of the land of their fathers. But now they live in America. In the land of the free. So it is that Poles can laugh at Polish jokes, Jews will scream at Jewish jokes, Irishmen are convulsed by Irish jokes and so on down the line.

As Will Rogers once said, "Everything is funny as long as it is happening to somebody else." Ethnic humor is an integral part of our heritage. It will be with us as long as we are a nation of many peoples from many lands and as long as we are able to laugh at ourselves. Laughter is the tonic that keeps Americans healthy.

14

Writing for TV Sitcoms

The Do's and Don'ts of Sitcom Writing

Most viewers watch tv primarily for entertainment, and sitcoms fulfill this universal need. "The medium is not designed to command the depths of people's attention," claims Sheldon Leonard.

Season after season, 15 to 18 of the top-20-rated programs are sitcoms. Eager producers, anxious advertisers and program hungry networks are hunting for writers who can maintain high ratings. The demand is so great that producers can not satisfy the public's hearty appetite, and it is a seller's market for those few writers who can consistently produce acceptable material. They not only make good bread, but then eat steak.

Until they learn the importance of being earners, however, comedy writers start being very lean and hungry.

THE SCARCE COMEDY-TV

Sitcom writers kid each other with this greeting: "What a silly job, being a comedy writer . . . you're making *how much?*"

In 1981, $100,000 a year was the average income for those few top sitcom writers; a half-hour sitcom script (23-25 minutes playing time) was worth at least $6,000; Garry Marshall, executive producer of *Laverne and Shirley, Mork and Mindy,* and *Happy Days,* claimed that sitcom writing was the most overpaid business in America.

Not only are there more sitcoms than ever before, but also each show needs several writers. Six or more writers usually create each of twenty-six episodes for those shows that run a full year's season. Some shows, such as *I Love Lucy, All in the Family,* and *M*A*S*H,* ran for over ten years. In the fall of 1981, there were 32 sitcoms in production. And five times that many — that had received network or advertiser encouragement — were in various phases of development. No wonder sitcom writers and ski professionals are the only people who don't dread winter.

Good new writers are also in demand because established writers go on to earn $20,000 a week rewriting shows as producers or as hyphenated executives such as writer-director or writer-producer, leaving a gap for new people.

Established writers earn money, even if they burn out. *I Love Lucy, Ozzie and Harriet, Father Knows Best,* and so many other shows we know *too well* have been in national syndication since the 1950's. Sometimes reruns begin while the show is still in original production, so you can receive a double income for the show you are writing. Even in your old age, the nurse will help you endorse your checks. The distributors of *All in the Family* claim that there is never a time when the show is not playing somewhere around the globe. And with all that money, its writers are probably playing somewhere around the globe, too.

Upon reflection, to be a sitcom writer, you must reflect your world, not through an ordinary mirror but through, what Bert Andrews calls, "a Coney Island mirror that distorts and makes amusing every little incident, foible and idiosyncrasy. . . ."

You must be aware of many serious limitations to the creative boundaries. A successful sitcom must satisfy the production companies, the stars, the networks, the sponsors, the critics and finally, and most importantly, a large enough segment of the viewing public to outdistance all competitive programming. It must also conform to certain legal and federal guidelines and, lately, it must be aware of the public organizations which have become self-appointed watchdogs over such issues as sex and violence.

Since you must please-please the audience, a writer's script takes into consideration public demographics: for example, the major consumer market is young women between 18 and 49, purchasers of billions of dollars of consumer goods. Men of brawn (and some brains) are attractive to this audience, so "machos" get more than their fair share of exposure, compared to well-built young ladies in "jiggle" shows, who get too much exposure. In addition, stereotyping characters, who purposely do not conform to preconceived notions, is one of the most common comedy techniques.

One of the first things you must learn before writing commercially saleable sitcom material is that imitation is not only the better part of flattery, it is also the better part of tv. Before you learn to compose classical music, you play the classics.

It's the same with sitcom writing. *All in the Family, M*A*S*H*, and *The Jeffersons* may not be classical literature, but for the tv sitcom neophyte, they are the textbook of today.

One of the first and best ways to attain skill in sitcom writing is to write for an existing show. Many writers are discovered when they submit their spec scripts to series story editors. There are plenty of shows to choose from. The *TV Market List* averages over 72 shows in production requiring new scripts.

But not every show is suitable for new writers. In order to decide which shows seem worth risking your reputation over, you first have to decide which show is especially relevant for your writing style and preferences.

Find a group of shows that reflect the type of humor you like and feel easy with; watch all the shows that are similar to each other, and select one of them to write for. While you concentrate on the chosen show, do not ignore the others. They are a bank of information, plot ideas, character analysis, and who knows, they may even entertain you.

HOW SITCOMS REFLECT EACH OTHER

Tolstoy's success with *War and Peace* rests on people's fascination with the recurring themes of love and war. All literary works draw on a few well-loved themes for their popularity: romance, adventure, poignancy, sex and violence, to name a few. Following all the great literary masters, you must humbly imitate existing successes, though try not to stay humble for long. *I Married Joan* succeeded because *I Love Lucy* was popular. In the fifties, aspiring comedy writers realized that families were a successful theme, so by the early sixties there were about sixty similar family-oriented sitcoms, *Mama, Make Room for Daddy,* and *The Goldbergs*. Following the success of *The Phil Silvers Show,* about a dozen comedy service shows have marched in step, including *Hogan's Heroes, Sergeant Bilko, F. Troop,* and *Gomer Pyle.*

The early sixties saw many apparitions, including *The Munsters, Mr. Ed,* and *My Favorite Martian*. There were about ten fantastic shows concerning witches and similar spell-binding themes. Women have starred in over twenty girlie sitcoms like *My Girl, Margie, Private Secretary,* and *Susanna*. Hillbillies, cops, showbiz, and other themes have been successfully imitated by writers.

TV sitcom writers also learn to recognize interesting characters in existing shows and create lucrative spinoffs around them. Some early sitcoms were spinoffs from stage shows, such as the vaudeville of Lucille Ball and Desi Arnez, which developed into *I Love Lucy*.

All in the Family was transformed from a British series called *Till Death Do Us Part!*

Americanizing a British sitcom earned money, so it was tried again: *Sanford and Son* was produced from *Steptoe and Son*, *Three's Company* retained its British name, and *The Two of Us* was derived from *Two's Company*.

All In The Family created its own spinoffs. Archie's neighbors *The Jeffersons* found their own appeal as an upwardly mobile black family in a white-dominated luxury apartment block. Edith's cousin Maude got in on the act with her own show and her own spinoff, *Good Times*. The irascible Archie could not be lost to tv, even without Edith, so he created his own spinoff series, *Archie Bunker's Place*.

Not all spinoffs are created from regular characters, however. The versatile talents of comedian Robin Williams shone when he delivered a deluge of one-liners as Mork in *Happy Days*, so he was developed for *Mork and Mindy*. *Laverne and Shirley* also first appeared in *Happy Days*.

IT'S THE SAME OLD STORY

When you can discern how sitcoms resemble each other, you can begin to see recurring story lines within the various shows. If you can't watch all the sitcoms, read the story outline in *TV Guide* to identify the crux of each story. It is a solid theory that unless you can summarize your plot in one simple sentence, it is probably too complex.

Humor is a type of magic, and just as a magician uses tried and tested tricks to intrigue his audience, so you should use well-tracked funny situations: just display them in novel ways.

The heart of every sitcom is the "What if . . ." conflict/situation. Once you have carefully developed the physical and psychological attitudes of each character within a selected environment, the plot fabrication becomes easier if you think of situations where your identifiable character is placed in unique, frequently uncomfortable conflicts.

The following are twelve of the most common recurring themes which have been popular with audiences since the beginning of motion picture production — the grandfather of all contemporary sitcoms.

1. Every sitcom places people in close contact with each other, and then lets their *natural aggressions* feed upon the basic situation. Husbands compete with wives in every family-oriented show, and their children compete not only with each other, but also with their

parents. From the days of *Father Knows Best* to *Too Close for Comfort,* when fathers knew least, family affiliations have flared into feuding. You must create laughter by the interplay of characters. Use illness, prejudice, death and cream pies to make your characters interact with each other.

Satirize social types; Bob Newhart was a psychiatrist, Jeannie was a genie. But do not produce normal expectations of stereotypes. Exaggerate them to tease the audience with unexpected characteristics, like a black rock musician with a Ph.D. in psychology, or an accountant who plays practical jokes.

Someone is always the fall guy. The fall guy evokes our sympathy because we resent the superior attitudes of the straight man and his dominating attitudes. We are all fall guys in some situations, and we retain the desire to see fall guys get even for us. Sheldon Leonard reminds us, "This is human, too — to watch the stupidities of others, to feel a bit superior."

2. *The work-place* also provides sitcoms with the antagonisms upon which they thrive. Workers resent bosses and each other. Sergeant Bilko was one of the many subordinate characters who made us laugh. The Governor's staff in *Benson* backbite and insult each other for humorous effects. In every sitcom, as in life, close proximity produces emnity; but your sitcom writing must reveal the farce around the friction.

Names are an essential part of aggressive dialogue, for they express the character's personality before the person even speaks or acts. "Hot Lips" is appropriate for her passions. An early radio show called "Duffy's Tavern" presented characters called "Abigail Puddletum," "Dr. Slaughter" and a racehorse called "Stumblebum." "Archie" and "Edith" sound like blue collar, down-home beer drinkers while "Hawkeye Pierce" and "Trapper John" sound as though they should drink martinis, even at war. Archie Bunker was named for the bunk he talks. Choose names to match preconceived notions about characters. Names create *soft stereotypes*.

3. One essential ingredient of drama is that the audience is kept in mystery about known facts. In comedy, it is frequently the reverse: the audience knows what is hidden from the characters. This helps to create one of comedy's greatest themes — *mistaken assumption* by the fall guy.

Lucy tried to hide her identity by impersonating a clown to get into her husband's nightclub act. In *The Two of Us,* a corpse was concealed from a character; Jack, in *Three's Company,* was introduced to Janet's parents as her husband; The Jeffersons' new maid mistook the Jeffersons for hired help.

There would be very few sitcom plots if all the characters were forced in the opening scene to abide by George Washington's "I shall not tell a lie" credo.

4. Intrusions in the form of people, objects, and events which *disturb the equilibrium* crop up in every series. One way that intrusions occur is through long-lost or unexpected visitors. Edith's old flame was featured in *All in the Family*; an old friend of Jack's in *Three's Company* turned out to be a prostitute; a bus-load of Chinese tourists visited Nan in the first episode of *The Two of Us*; Jo, in *Facts of Life*, learned that her father had been released from prison and was coming to visit her.

5. The oldest of all emotions, which never ceases to produce absurdities, is heartbreak. Hawkeye fell for a Korean aristocrat; in another *M*A*S*H* episode his old flame was already married by the time she joined his unit.

6. *Moral goodness and ethical principles* often lead to satirical trouble, such as when Edith was the lone dissenter in a murder trial jury, or when Mary Tyler Moore wanted to go to her high school reunion without a date. They are often connected with group identity, especially to show the position in society of women or ethnic minorities. Lucy was the first of several women to try to liberate herself. She did it by trying to enter showbiz, despite Ricky's desire to keep her in the kitchen. Mary Tyler Moore, Rhoda and Maude were others who rubbed against male dominance. Ethnic characters were accused of becoming culturally whitened in *Different Strokes* and *Chico and the Man*.

7. *Sympathy for the disadvantaged* is becoming much more common. Sitcoms do not convey the nihilism of *Saturday Night Live*. Blair, in *Facts of Life*, learned to respect her handicapped cousin. Arnold befriended a cripple. Even muggers learned to respect their elderly victims in *Mork and Mindy*.

8. A close variation is *serious physical mishaps*. Hawkeye and the Fonze both went temporarily blind from accidents. Amnesia is a popular outcome of any bang on the head. Every accident known has been used — at one time or another — on tv, permitting the leads to be strapped to the rack in hospital beds with broken limbs stuck out at every angle.

Accidents need not be life or death: the plumbing broke in *The Two of Us*, and the *M*A*S*H* unit was kept in the dark with a lightbulb shortage, and kept in fear when their bus broke down.

9. Everybody wants *something of value* — money, promotion, award, material product — and creates havoc to get it. The more oddball the request, the better. Hawkeye needed boots; the Jeffersons needed a maid; Lucy wanted John Wayne's footprints. The most frequent need is for money; it is the one that audiences most easily identify with. Amos'n Andy were always short of cash; Sgt. Bilko was always short of someone else's cash (his show was originally called *You'll Never Get Rich*). Ralph, in *The Honeymooners*, constantly searched for the one great scheme that would make him rich.

10. Many episodes revolve around the *failure of a lead character to cope with a new situation* — at home, on the job, in social events. A new pupil in *Facts of Life* upsets Blair's dominance . . . for thirty minutes. For several years, the Jeffersons were a new situation in an all-white apartment block. Becoming unemployed was a new situation which upset Archie. Lou Grant had to cope with his wife leaving him.

11. "We just took *ordinary situations and exaggerated them,*" Lucille Ball once admitted.

12. When you are searching for "What if . . . ?" situations, learn to spot what is usable from your everyday existence. Trouble? Who doesn't have any? Garry Marshall advises, "If an experience is painful to you, don't block it out. Save it. Maybe in three days it will be funny."

Not all sitcom dialogue is humorous. Researchers have reported that only 35% of a sitcom's time utilizes humorous material. Much comedy involves serious situations which are highlighted by comic relief. Sitcoms generally contain about one third humor. The remaining two thirds reflect Sheldon Leonard's warning, "If you must have a straight scene it should lead directly into something that is going to be very funny."

Whatever problems you tackle, always support moral goodness. Characters continually fight for right against wrong . . . though their beliefs as to what is right and what is wrong vary. The conclusion of your plot should indicate that overprotective parents are all right, because they really are for their children's well-being, and recalcitrant kids come out all right, because they are learning about life. Unless you deliberately introduce a true villain everyone in your sitcoms must always act in good faith, though never in agreement with each other. In *Laverne and Shirley,* the girls broke into their boss's office, lied, cheated, and did all the wrong things, but in innocence! Sitcom characters are above the normal rules of morality, because they are goofy and lovable, but never wicked.

Remember that situations for script episodes are decided six months before their air date and final scripts are taped, or filmed, three to six weeks in advance of their air dates. There will be a wait between sending out your material to an agent and his getting a producer to read it. Therefore work a year in advance. That's normal. What happens if the show you are working on is cancelled? That's normal too!

Send for a script to the show for which you wish to write. Stick as closely as possible to an existing script when you write. Use the same length scenes, number of words in dialogue and other similar patterns to conform as closely as possible to the existing format.

To analyze a show, watch it regularly; tape it on video or audio cassette; read scripts (which can be obtained from the producer). You must know the sets used by your show, and most shows use only three sets.

Learn the "point of view" of the star. You obviously could not have written liberal views for Archie, nor prejudiced ones for Hawkeye, submission for Mary Tyler Moore, nor brilliance for Laverne.

You must know the supporting cast in the show, intimately, and remember to include them in the story.

Time your show for length of scenes, sets and commercial breaks. Learn the total length of running time available to you.

There can be as many as eleven short scenes in a twenty-five-minute episode. Usually there are about six or seven. The first act often consists of about five scenes and the second about two or three. The two acts are separated by a 1½- 2-minute commercial break. The last scene before the mid-commercial break must end on a cliffhanger, to sustain audience interest.

TIMING ELEMENTS OF A *HAPPY DAYS* EPISODE (THREE SETS)

ACTION	APPROXIMATE TIME (minutes)		
Introduction	1		
1st Commercial Break	1	Introduction	Total 2
ACT ONE			
Scene 1	3		
Scene 2	½		
Scene 3	½		
Scene 4	2¾		
Scene 5	1		
Scene 6	4		
2nd Commercial Break	1½	Act One	Total 13¼
ACT TWO			
Scene 1	1½		
Scene 2	3½		
Scene 3	2¾		
Scene 4	1¾		
Scene 5	3		
3rd Commercial Break	1	Act Two	Total 13½
TAG			
Scene 1	¾		
End Titles	½	Program	Total 30:00

Total Breakdown (minutes)	
Titles	¾
Commercials	3½
Playing Time	25¾
Playing Time	25¾
Total	30:00

When you get used to timing your show, you can begin to add essential information, such as how many characters appear in each episode, how many scenes are used, and their locations. Then you can build up a chart of information for several episodes and write to conform to the series range of attributes.

You can't throw a lot of eggs up in the air and hatch a plot. Your plot is no more than a good excuse for your characters to interact in a comedy sketch. Even if a general lies dying in *M*A*S*H*, Hawkeye's wit is what really matters. It is the interaction of your characters rather than a story that creates comedy. And most important, interaction of characters with the star of the show. Garry Marshall claims that the biggest single error in new talent is to write for outside characters. He does not want *Laverne and Shirley* episodes with a garbage man or mailman in the limelight. Laverne and Shirley are the stars, and demand 80% of your dialogue. Let your star shine brightly as the center of all attention. The audience has been conditioned to see the whole show as a vehicle for the star. Don't fight it!

CREATING A SCENE

Scenes usually start out sensibly, but then get silly, and end abruptly with a cut to the next scene. *M*A*S*H* often opened with shots of serious operations, then the banter removed the seriousness.

When you have decided on one or more "what if?" ideas, expand their possibilities into a page-long outline. Brainstorm your ideas with friends, let them help suggest how well-known characters would respond to your situations. When you have an idea outline, divide it into parts for each act. Then break it down into scenes which match the show's format.

Some writers prefer to go straight into a rough treatment of the dialogue and work with revisions of that. Whatever you do next will be filled with weaknesses, false starts and brilliance, though not in that order! It will be a beginning to a re-writing process that never seems to end.

Most sitcoms open with a minute of introductory welcome which serves to capture audience attention and present a happy opening. No matter how tense your situations become within the episode, your story should usually end happily, too. This construction is reassuring for the audience which looks forward to familiar situations each week.

Although your endings should resolve the immediate situation, they do not resolve the inherent tensions of the series.

When you have written your episode for an existing series you should create at least six other episode outlines to accompany your script. You may also consider developing a portfolio which contains original material for your own comedy shows.

TV is a visual medium, so what we see must be as entertaining as what we hear. Klinger wore ladies' clothing, the Fonze was famous for his thumbs-up salute. When your plot is finished, think of how you can add visual comedy to your character.

It is not a mark of a poor writer to write in one particular style, but it is a mark of a poor writer not to develop a unique style and utilize it appropriately. You can only develop your style by writing . . . you must learn from every comedian and every show you watch, but only by your own writing charts will you reach your own style. Selma Diamond advises, "I think you learn by doing it. I only learned by doing. I just kept writing and writing and I'm still writing."

Even at the final stages, the same motto is true as the one you need to start humor writing. "If at first you don't succeed, you are in the best company."

Television Comedy Techniques
by Daniel E. Garvey & William L. Rivers
Condensed from *Broadcast Writing*

Television comedy usually means situation comedy. The "sitcom" has a continuing cast of characters, some basic theme, and usually a half-hour running time. Its customary format consists of a first act, a commercial, a second act, a commercial, and a tag. A few open with a teaser before the first commercial. The script must almost always give plenty of exposure to the stars of the show and should use the continuing characters. It is fairly common to introduce one new character in an episode — someone who appears only in that episode.

It is important to know which characters carry most of the action. While Barney Miller is nominally the star of the series that carries his name, action is divided fairly even among the main continuing characters, and episodes frequently feature interaction between one of the continuing characters and a noncontinuing character. Retaining the theme and key characters is an important element of situation comedy. The writer should not tinker too much with the customary form and style of the show.

THE PLOT

Plotting a situation comedy can be difficult. You need to think of a problem that you can introduce to the audience quickly, develop rapidly, and solve by the end of the show. Moreover, that problem has to carry the weight of the vehicle for 50 or more jokes or funny lines.

Plots can, and often do, deal with serious problems, even though the problem always provides opportunities for some funny lines or action.

You can begin to look for a plot idea by imagining a typical day in the life of one of the main characters.

A less subtle approach is simply to look about for a social problem that the show has not yet tackled, since that is the basis of so many comedies today. How can the main characters of the program become plausibly involved with the problem? Often you may have to use a noncontinuing character. Suppose, for instance, you decide to stick your neck out and do a program on venereal disease. You're not likely to have one of the main characters contract one of these diseases, but a main character could provide advice and help to a noncontinuing character with some such problem.

Be careful of the one-gag plot. Inexperienced writers often sit down and think, "Gee, wouldn't it be funny if . . ." and come up with some hilarious idea — but one that will not sustain a half hour of jokes.

In a series that centers on one character, you will usually have to set out the basic problem before the first five minutes of the program are gone. You can elaborate on this, bringing it to the final crisis and solution in the second act.

However, if you are working with a program that gives fairly equal weight to several different characters, you may need only a relatively weak plot line to string together segments involving the various characters. In such a case, you can introduce at the start of the show what the unifying theme will be, but you do not have to concern yourself so much about when specific events occur in the script. We'll call these two techniques "tight plotting" and "loose plotting," and take a look at each one.

Tight Plotting For a tightly plotted story, first answer these two questions carefully. What sort of jam does the main character get into? How does he or she get out of it at the end? Here you have the "bookends" of your plot. Pay particular attention to the way the problem is to be solved at the end, because this must be both quick and funny. If it isn't, you probably should put the story aside and work on another one.

Now working backward, sketch in the major crisis of the plot, which should come immediately before the solution. Then sketch in a lesser but funny crisis for just before the second commercial. Now, before adding any further complications to the plot, begin writing down all the gags you can think of that fit each of the crises you have outlined. If the situations do not help you to generate plenty of gags, then you may need to consider another plot.

Comedy writer Abe Burrows has written, "In radio and television you have to bowl the audience over in the first thirty seconds of your show. If there's the smallest hint of dullness, the audience switches to another station. The slogan in tv is 'Grab'em Quick!'" The writers of *Three's Company* know that rule. The script opens with a sight gag of Stanley Roper carefully seasoning his scrambled eggs, bite by bite. There are six verbal gags in the first two minutes of the script. Then the pace slackens to one or two jokes per minute as the plot is developed. In the next scene, the writers give us four gags in the first minute, and then they slow the pace to allow more plot development. At no point in the script do we find more than a minute passing without at least one joke. When things are really rolling, the gags come every five or six seconds.

Obviously, you don't depend upon plot alone for this much humor. It must be developed from the traits and personalities of the characters on the screen. Sometimes this consists simply of the old comedy standard of one character providing the "straight" line and the other the gag. However, a clever writer can make several successive lines funny by having each speaker relate to what was said by the other in the previous line. Here's an example from the script we are analyzing. The comedy is relatively low-key, but each line is designed to draw a laugh. Roper and Jack are discussing Roper's lunch, which Roper says was "great."

>JACK: Really? What did you have?
>ROPER: Peanut butter sandwich.
>JACK: We must exchange recipes sometime.
>ROPER: Nothing to it. All you need is two slices of bread, some peanut butter. And a knife.
>JACK: Gee, I wish I had time to write that down.
>ROPER: What do they teach you in that cooking school?

The lines are not big laughs, but they keep the audience chuckling.

The basic idea is that tightly plotted comedy is simple but well thought out. It moves from crisis to crisis, finally reaching the major crisis and then quickly moving to a simple resolution of the characters. It is from these interchanges that most of your funny lines and action will come. The jokes must come at frequent intervals. The number of jokes may slack off a bit during the development of the plot — but there still must be some jokes.

Loose Plotting In a loosely plotted script, there is less attention paid to the development of plot line and more to the interplay between characters. There is always some plot, but the buildup of crises may be absent and the solution to the problem may pack little punch.

It may not always be the case, but in general the loosely plotted script has to provide more interplay among different characters. Because there is little plot to keep the audience occupied, the dialogue has to keep the audience laughing. *Barney Miller* is a good example of a series in which most episodes have relatively loose plots. The interplay of the main characters carries the show.

Since little time is required for plot development, more can be devoted to humor. More is not necessarily better. A comedy show needs to produce at least one gag per minute of playing time. Most will do considerably better. But quantity is not the determining factor. It is the mood you create in which to tell the jokes that gives a program a feeling of being funny. That probably is why tightly plotted series seem to hold up better than loosely plotted ones.

SITUATIONS

The Misperceptions One or more characters of a comedy often labor under misperceptions. Usually these are resolved by the end of the program, but in some cases they can be a continuing element of the program. For example, Stanley Roper's belief that Jack Tripper in *Three's Company* is a homosexual is an integral part of the plot. It is also a fairly common comedy situation to have the misperception entirely accidental.

In the British series *Faulty Towers,* Basil Fawlty mistakes a deadbeat guest for the hotel inspector in one episode and showers him with service while maltreating the actual hotel inspector. At times, the misperception may be double, with two characters, each having the wrong idea about the other. A fairly ancient plot line is the boy courting the girl because he thinks she is rich only to find out she is courting him for the same reason.

The Imagined Predicament In its extremes, the misperception becomes the imagined predicament. Many comedies have been built around the somewhat morbid idea of a character mistakenly believing he or she is dying. Numerous supposed catastrophes — loss of job, eviction, and such — can be the basis for comedy.

Fooling the Audience With misperceptions and imagined predicaments, the audience is usually let in on the gag. However, it is possible to keep the audience in the dark, letting them learn at the end that they've been taken in, too. This is a fairly risky procedure because it cannot contribute much to the story until the end. It usually serves to provide some zany ending to the story.

Reversed Roles This gimmick is an old favorite for comedy. Opera abounds in "trouser roles," roles to be sung by women who are supposed to be men posing as women.

Most modern comedies take a more plausible approach of simply having two people trade roles, such as a husband staying home to care for the children while his wife works.

Reversal of sex roles is an obvious and easy approach, but role reversal can take place between any two characters, regardless of sex. The theme is almost always the same: People do not appreciate their own jobs or the difficulties of another's job until they've tried it.

A change of character traits is often the theme of comedy scripts. A greedy character becomes generous. A mean character becomes kindly. However, if you are dealing with a continuing character in television, you must have the character revert to "normal" at the end of the script.

Unorthodox Viewpoints Again, what makes these a basis for comedy is stereotyping. We expect old people to act a certain way. We expect ministers to act a certain way. We expect women to act one way and men another. Any character running counter to these stereotypes can be funny.

Funny Actions These can consist of doing something ordinary in an unordinary way, or they can be odd actions that no one does ordinarily. It is surprising that there is not more visual humor in television. The reason seems to be primarily that it is harder to think up. Not, of course, that you cannot think of some actions that are funny, but it is difficult to find funny actions that fit the characters and plot of a given story. Moreover, the visual humor has to be good. A pie in the face continues to be somewhat funny because the audience has a general idea what is going to happen from the moment the pie is picked up. But pratfalls and pies in the face are far too familiar to the audience to get much of a laugh without some special angle.

Three's Company uses visual humor in the tag.

> JACK: Now drink. But — be sure and drink from this side of the glass . . .
> (POINTS TO SIDE NEAREST HIM)
> And never from this side of the glass.
> (POINTS TO THE SIDE FARTHEST FROM HIM)
> CHRISSY: Why can't you drink from that side?
> JACK: Because if you drink from that side
> (DRINKS FROM FAR SIDE AND AS HE TILTS GLASS, MILK SPILLS DOWN HIS SHIRT FRONT)
> . . . It'll spill all over you.

DIALOGUE

Most comedy, of course, is verbal comedy. Here are a few types:

Put-downs In the *Three's Company* script, Mrs. Roper inquires of Stanley if he thinks her new nightgown is sexy. Roper replies, "Please, Helen, not while I'm eating!" The audience can become annoyed if sympathetic characters are the targets of too many cruel remarks. At the least, some sort of retribution is expected.

Retorts. One of the most common types of funny line, the retort is usually a line that responds to a put-down. In the put-down cited earlier, when Stanley Roper tells his wife, "Not while I'm eating," she snaps back, "Or when you're sleeping, or when you're working or while you're sitting or standing or . . . ."

Analogies and Descriptions Describing her first day working in the cafeteria, Mrs. Roper says:

> MRS. ROPER: Did you ever see the movie "Earthquake"?
> CHRISSY: The cafeteria looked like that?
> MRS. ROPER: Only when things quieted down after the rush hour.

Malapropisms A standard element of humor, these are usually linked with dialect of some sort. Comedian Norm Crosby has made a career out of monologues full of malapropisms such as his description of Samson and the "uncircumscribed Philistines."

Perhaps the greatest contemporary source of malapropisms is

Archie Bunker, who, like Crosby, confuses "circumcised" with "circumscribed," and who loves to eat "smashed potatoes." The writers often set the audience up for a Bunkerism by having Bunker preface it with the phrase "she's one of them what ya call your 'lemians.'"

Backhanded Compliments These are comments intended to be complimentary by the persons making them, but sounding awful to everyone else. Often they tie in with some character trait of the person making the compliment. When hillbilly programs were popular, they abounded in comments like, "Miss Emmy Lou, you're purtier 'n a plate of hog jowls and collard greens."

Double Meanings Many, of course, are not suitable for use on the air. In the old *Here's Lucy* series, Mary Jane's boyfriend cracks a very poor joke. Mary Jane says loyally, "Don't you just love him? He's so full of fun!" and Lucy responds, "Yeah, he's full of it."

Keep in mind that the audience must fully understand both meanings of the words used. The first use of them must seem logical in the context, and the second use must be unexpected.

Dialect This rich old resource of humor must be used with caution these days. It must never appear that you are demeaning a group by making fun of the way its members talk.

Note how the writer in *The New Temperatures Rising Show* used tricks of word placement to provide a Yiddish dialect for Dr. Mercy's temporary roommate, Bernie Margolies:

> PAUL: Mr. Margolies, getting agitated is not good for me.
> MARGOLIES: And for me, it's good? Three times last night they woke me up to give me sleeping pills.
> PAUL: I'll make a note of your complaints.
> MARGOLIES: Where are you going to get all the paper?
> (PAUL PRESSES THE BUZZER FRANTICALLY.)
> MARGOLIES: Go ahead ring. You know what you'll get from ringing? Muscle cramps, you'll get. They won't answer. But I must congratulate you for hiring the handicapped. Who else would give a job to deaf nurses?

Word Distortion to Illustrate Character If you do use this technique for a gag, you must spell phonetically what the actor is supposed to say. *Saturday Night Live* made fun — some would say cruel fun — of Barbara Walters' difficulties with the letter *r*. A good many people would question whether it is in good taste to ridicule someone who has a speech defect, even though stammering, lisping, and other speech defects have been fodder for comedians for centuries. Probably the writer is on safer ground if the pronunciations are affectations. Whenever the female character pops on camera calling everyone "dahling," the audience will immediately assume the role is meant to be that of a supercilious snob, and probably a comic one.

Spoonerisms This form has definite limits. Either it is good for one or two gags treated as accidental slips of the tongue or it is necessary to create a character who has as a trait the frequent making of spoonerisms.

One obvious problem in using spoonerisms is that the audience must figure out what was actually meant. This can be tricky. The spoonerism is customarily made by transposing the first letters of two words in a sentence. Generally speaking, when you use spoonerisms, you are going to have to give the audience a little time to think about the meaning of the statement — and that can be risky in comedy. Spoonerisms sometimes play in scenes about drinks: "Bartender, you fulled my glass to fill!" It is difficult to make them carry much of the burden of comedy.

Puns Reputed to be the lowest form of humor, the pun remains popular. But for most broadcast humor, it is often too difficult to set up the background for a pun. Very often the pun is a sort of intentional spoonerism, transposing the first letters of words to give them new meanings or transposing whole words in expressions. However, while the spoonerism may result in nonsense words, the words created by transposition in puns should have meanings of their own. Such puns always bring a groan, and that is what they are intended to do. Part of the humor of the pun is the labored wording required to achieve the goal. The audience mutters, "Oh, no!" but it does chuckle.

Silly Rhymes Again there is relatively little time for this sort of humor because it is too difficult to find a plausible reason for interjecting it into a plot. When used, it normally is found in variety-type humor rather than situation comedy. The obvious advantage to rhyme is that it has built-in foreshadowing. The word required to complete the rhyme is usually obvious — and often dirty — and the humor frequently stems from the clever way in which the person reciting avoids using the improper rhyme. This can be either by substituting an unexpected rhyme, which is usually funniest, or by turning the unacceptable word into the stem of a longer word.

Parody and Satire These are among the favorite devices of student writers. Unfortunately, they are among the most difficult forms of comedy to write and perform, and as a result, often fall flat. Parody makes fun of some verbal style.

Parody for broadcast writing is often a parody of specific programs or popular films. It can also be a parody of a type of film or program. *Saturday Night Live* frequently parodied television news programs. The *Carol Burnett Show* used to parody both specific films and styles of film. Parody is a form that lends itself best to revue-type programs rather than series.

Satire, on the other hand, makes fun of social and political customs. Often the technique is exaggeration or carrying something to a ridiculous extreme.

Non Sequiturs In everyday life, we assume that specific causes lead to known effects and that two and two should equal four. In non-sequitur humor, the tables are turned. The answers do not logically follow from the questions, and the resulting twisted logic amuses us. Goodman Ace used to write wacky non-sequitur dialogue for his wife, Jane, in their old radio series, *Mr. Ace and Jane*. Here's a sample:

> JANE: Hello, dear (DOOR CLOSES)
> ACE: Well, Jane, what brings you downtown this early?
> JANE: Just fine. Hello, Mr. Norris. How are you?
> NORRIS: I've been a little under the weather lately, Mrs. Ace.
> JANE: Yes, isn't it?

The Unexpected Answer If you analyze most comedy dialogue you will find that the fact that the response to a statement is a surprise, whether logical or illogical, is what brings on the laughter.

> LAMONT: WHAT"S THAT HORSE DOING IN THE KITCHEN???
> FRED: I don't know . . . you saw him last.
> LAMONT: POP . . . I WANT AN ANSWER!!!
> FRED: Well, it's very simple . . .
> LAMONT: I DON'T WANT A LIE!!!
> FRED: It's getting harder.

Sometimes, the explanation of an unexpected answer is what gets the laughs. Asked why her husband hasn't returned a phone call, Jane Ace says she's just taken four showers. Asked what that has to do with it, she explains, "The phone always rings when I'm in the shower."

Comedy writers usually work closely with the performers who will be reading their lines. Changes are frequent. One danger in writing comedy is that by the time the material has been rehearsed and rewritten many times, good material begins to seem stale. Comedy writers can easily lose perspective. It is a good idea to have someone read or view your material fresh. That will help you decide whether a joke you have lost faith in really is a failure or whether you have simply seen and heard it too many times in the rehearsal.

In television comedy you must grab your audience at once. Scripts often open with visual humor. The reason is fairly simple. Any verbal humor requires some preparatory dialogue. Visual humor, if well planned, can be instantly funny to the audience. Concentrate heavy doses of humor at the start of the program, just before the end of the first act, and at the end of the show. Never let more than 60 seconds pass without giving the audience something to laugh at.

In the 30-minute weekly series, you normally have just a bit over 23 minutes to tell your story. That includes a "tag" at the end, so the actual story has to be wound up in under 23 minutes. The existence of continuing characters in this series is a godsend to the writer because they are already known to the audience. You do not have to explain that this character is cheap, that one smart, and that one a skirt-chase.

When a new character is introduced to the series or is brought in for one or two shows, the writer and actor must both work miracles to help the audience understand the character. This is one reason that television characters tend to lack subtlety.

Dialogue, too, must replace action that would take time or cost too much. In a feature film, you might show a couple walking home through the park. In a series, they come through the door into the living room, and the girl says: "Thank you for walking me home, David. I love walking in the park this time of year."

Details also help build your characters. Think about a female character you are developing. She is to be rich and beautiful. Her dialogue may be written as standard English, and she may sound slightly "cultured." She may smoke, possibly using the cigarette holder. She may drink, but certainly not beer. She probably prefers champagne. She does not chew gum. Television may be faulted for preserving "class" stereotypes, but given the 23-minute format of most shows, the writer would be hard put to work without them.

Since most comedy programs are series programs, the producers prefer it if the comedy is not too topical, because topical humor dates programs in reruns or when sold in syndication.

A few elements that appear frequently as the basis for television humor:

1. SITUATIONS

a. *Misperceptions*, either by one character about another or by both about each other. Example: He mistakes her for the new secretary; she thinks he's an escaped convict.

b. *The imagined predicament*. Example: She misunderstands a telegram and thinks she's being evicted.

c. *The misled audience*. This follows the same line as (a) and (b), but the audience is not let in on the gag until the end.

d. *Reversed roles*. Example: He decides to stay home with the kids; she goes to work at the boiler factory.

e. *Unorthodox viewpoints*. Example: The 75-year-old maiden aunt turns out to be a swinger.

f. *Funny action*. Examples: He strains the spaghetti with a tennis racket; she roller skates in the supermarket.

2. DIALOGUE

a. *Put-downs*. Example: Basil Fawlty's wonderfully nasty line, "The people in room 14 have never seen chairs before."

b. *Retorts*. Example: "If you were my kid, I'd poison you." "If you were my father, I'd drink the poison."

c. *Analogies and descriptions*. Example: "He's got a head like a glass of stale beer."

d. *Malapropisms*. Example: Norm Crosby's monologue reference to the "uncircumscribed Philistines."

e. *Backhanded compliments*. Example: "You're as pretty as a plate of hog jowls."

f. *Double meanings*. Example: Henny Youngman's classic "Take my wife . . . please!"

g. *Dialect,* which must be used with caution. For example, Fred Allen used to play the character of a Chinese detective Won Long Pan. He would invariably discover a revolver, and in what Allen seemed to think was a Chinese accent, would cry: "A luwalawa.!"

h. *Word distortion* to illustrate character. For example, in the days when there was a Nash automobile, Jim Backus used to play a rich snob who would always "Cadillac" rather than gnash (Nash) his teeth.

i. *Spoonerisms*. Example: "I fulled my glass too fill."

j. *Puns*. Example: "Haven't you heard of 'mountaineers'?" "No. Have mountain ears heard of me?"

k. *Silly rhymes*. Example: Gary Moore's old shaggy dog recitation about "Hugh the blue gnu."

Your job is to see to it that funny things continue to happen throughout the show. Humor doesn't just build to one gag; there must be a continual flow of gags or the audience quickly tires. You need about 20 good gags for one half-hour comedy. Coming up with that much humor is a tremendous task, which is one reason why comedy is often written by teams.

NBC Fact Sheet: The Marketing of Television Properties
by Submission Department
NBC, West Coast

The market for all television properties for network broadcasting is extremely limited, since the network schedule covers only a certain number of hours daily.

It has been estimated that the chances for an individual to sell a television series are approximately the same as getting a play produced in a Broadway theater. In Hollywood alone there are roughly two thousand professional tv writers. As you might expect, the competition among those professional writers for the very few television opportunities is intense.

There are many complex creative and technical factors involved in writing for television — factors not generally apparent to even the most astute of inexperienced writers.

The vast majority of series carried on the networks are obtained from outside producers, agencies, studios and packagers. Perhaps you could interest one of these outside companies in investing the necessary time and money to develop your material or idea for marketing. By consulting the trade papers of the industry (*Weekly Variety, Broadcasting Magazine,* for instance), you will find many references to the active producers in the field. The Thursday edition of both *Daily Variety* and *Hollywood Reporter* publish a *Tv Film Production Chart,* which lists studios and their personnel involved in current production.

It would usually be to your advantage to secure the services of a literary agent to market your work. Agents are aware of script needs on various programs. Many studios and production centers refuse to examine outside material unless it is submitted through an agent.

A list of established agents can be obtained from THE WRITERS GUILD OF AMERICA WEST, 8955 Beverly Boulevard, Los Angeles, California, 90048; or the ACADEMY PLAYERS DIRECTORY SUPPLEMENT, 8949 Wilshire Boulevard, Beverly Hills, California, 90211.

Looking for Mr. Right: Writer's Guide to Agents
by Oscar Millard
Condensed from *Los Angeles Times*

It could be argued that, for a young writer, the selection of an agent is more important than the selection of a spouse. If a bad wife makes life hell, you can always move out; a bad agent can destroy you through inertia. An agent virtually holds a writer's life in his hands, a responsibility of which many seem unaware and to which most are indifferent.

So the selection of a good agent, especially early in one's career, is crucial. The catch is, you don't select your agent, he selects you. That is the first God-like attribute of the agent. You approach him humbly and pray he will look upon you and your works and find them good. Of the 106 Hollywood literary agents signatory to the Writers Guild Artists Manager Agreement, only 18 are willing to consider material from a novice. Few of the willing 18 are called good agents.

What is a good agent? At social gatherings I've heard horror stories about agents — among them my own, with whom I was well pleased — and tales extolling the virtues of agents whom I regarded as ineffectual, glib phonies. One man's leech is another man's paragon. An agent who returns your calls within 48 hours, reads your material within six weeks and submits it may be considered a good agent. But their names are legion who will not extend themselves that far.

When I arrived in Hollywood, I had had two books published. One of them, *Uncensored,* had been bought by 20th Century-Fox. It was filmed in London, directed by Anthony Asquith and starred Eric Portman, a prominent English actor of the time, but no Hollywood agent would represent me because I was considered a novice: "Based on the novel by . . ." was not regarded as a movie credit.

In the fullness of time, I wrote a picture starring Loretta Young, based on a story by Clare Booth Luce. It was nominated for the Screenwriters Guild Award and 20th signed me to a term contract. The day the contract item appeared in the trades, the agents also appeared. Men who wouldn't let me into their office now invited me to lunch at good tables in the best restaurants.

It is known as romancing a client. Leeches, I thought, while cheerfully accepting the invitations and eating high off the hog, lending a distraught ear to the earnest assurances that my host, better than any other agent in town, would be able rapidly to improve my contract and that my career depended on his personal efforts to promote it. Agents love the word "personal." They will always personally take care of everything, and they close their letters with "Best personal regards." What is an impersonal regard? Fred Allen said you can place all the sincerity in Hollywood in a flea's navel and still have room for three caraway seeds and the heart of an agent.

Time was, before tv, when the Hollywood literary agent's prime mission was selling clients. This carried the seldom mentioned ancillary duty of periodically reassuring the producers that their writers were "performing," i.e., actually writing, not nursing chronic hangovers. Selling material, which consisted simply of dumping it on a story editors's desk, was secondary because few established screenwriters ever wrote except on salary. A term contract was more profitable than the sale of a novel or a screenplay. Fifty thousand dollars was a big price for the movie rights to a novel. The rights to *The Graduate* went for $25,000. Today a million dollars is not unusual.

Agents' egos have swollen commensuratley — in some, disproportionately — to the point of their assuming the mantle of Divinity. From being mere peddlers practicing the admirable philosophy of "sell it, don't smell it," they have become critics, seers of trends and arbiters of taste. They speak of their credibility and the absolute need to believe in a story before sending it out in their agency's covers. This means a writer must now strive first to please his agent.

Some years ago, I wrote an offbeat rape story before rape became, so to speak, the "in" thing. "No one will ever go for that," said my agent when I sought his reaction after a month's silence. I eventually wrote the story as a novel. It was published in hardcover and paperback, praised by the late Robert Kirsch of *The L.A. Times*, commended by *The New York Times* and optioned three times for movie production. Had I not in the meantime changed to an agent with more contemporary tastes, the story manuscript still would be gathering dust.

A New York literary agent, after reading a short story of mine, advanced several cogent reasons why it wouldn't sell, but he tried it anyway on *The Atlantic Monthly,* which promptly accepted it and gave it *The Atlantic Award.*

When an agent contracts to represent a writer, there is an implied if not explicit agreement to give his material its chance in the marketplace irrespective of his assessment of its salability. Failure to go on is one of the most common complaints made by writers against agents.

It makes no more sense for an agent to refuse to submit a client's work, assuming it is of professional caliber, than for a Fuller Brush Man to refuse to peddle a floor polish because he thinks it stinks. It implies an assumption of divine omniscience for an agent to affirm that because he doesn't like a property, it is ipso facto unsalable. When one considers that the bread and butter of the majority of agents derives from sales to television, any mention of taste delivered with a straight face suggests a total absence of any sense of the ridiculous.

The agent who could predict success or forecast failure would be worth not 10 but 90%. But they don't make their fortunes as a result of their prescient selection of material or their virtuoso performance in selling it. Except in the case of pre-sold best-sellers, most stories reach the screen not as a result of high-power agenting but of a chance happening. Deal making is, in fact, the agent's main function of value to the client.

According to current Hollywood cliché, the agent has become the czar. Like all Hollywood clichés, this one contains an element of fantasy. To the extent that it has any validity, it is true only of a small group of superagents that represents a roster of established writers, directors and bankable players with whom they can put together packages that give them clout far greater than that of the individual elements. Their percipience may be judged by the annual film turkeyfest and the 90% flop rate that is a feature of every tv season.

So, put not thy trust in princes nor thy faith in agents. If you are hot, you don't need an agent, you need a Hollywood-wise lawyer. If you're not hot, the agent doesn't need you. His working hours will be devoted to the clients who bring in the most money. If you have written something that he regards as promising, he may accept you on his list on the chance that you may write something sensational or get yourself a job, on which he will, of course, take 10%.

But meanwhile you will be among the last to have your call returned, and it may take him two months to read your latest masterpiece. As for getting you an assignment, a development deal or a staff job on a tv series, do not hold your breath. In January of this year, when producers began stockpiling scripts, there were 359 writers working on features and 1,030 in tv. The Writers Guild West has 5,790 members. Good luck!

Writer's Representatives
The Screenwriter's Handbook

Unless otherwise stated, all addresses are in Los Angeles, California, area code (213).

ABRAMS-RUBALOFF & ASSOCIATES — 273-5711
9012 Beverly Blvd. (90048)

ADAMS, BRET, LIMITED — 656-6420
8282 Sunset Blvd. (90046)
36 E. 61st St., — (212) 752-7864
New York, New York (10021)

ADAMS, RAY & ROSENBERG — 278-3000
9200 Sunset Blvd., PH 25 (90060)

AIMEE ENTERTAINMENT ASSOCIATION — 872-0374
14241 Ventura Blvd. — 990-6996
Sherman Oaks, Calif (91423)

ALVARADO, CARLOS, AGENCY — 652-0272
8820 Sunset Blvd. (90060)

AMBER, VELVET AGENCY — 464-8184
6515 Sunset Blvd., Suite 200A (90028)

AMSEL, FRED & ASSOCIATTES — 277-2035
312 S. Beverly Dr., Suite R,
Beverly Hills, Calif. (90212)

ARCARA, BAUMAN & HILLER ARTISTS' MANAGERS — 271-5601
9220 Sunset Blvd. (90069)
850 7th Aven., Suite 1201
New York, New York (10019) — (212) 757 0098

ARTISTS CAREER MANAGEMENT — 278-9157
9157 Sunset Blvd., #206 (90069)

ASSOCIATED BOOKING CORPORATION — 273-5600
9595 Wilshire Blvd., Beverly Hills, Calif. (90212)

BARR, RICKEY/GILLEY, GEORGIA — 659-0141
8721 Sunset Blvd., Suite 210 (90069)

BARSKIN AGENCY, THE — 657-5740
8730 Sunset Blvd., Suite #501 (90069)

BART/LEVY ASSOICATES, INC. — 550-1060
9169 Sunset Blvd. (90069)

BEAKEL & JENNINGS AGENCY ARTISTS' MANAGERS — 274-5418
9615 Brighton Way, Suite 314,
Beverly Hills, Calif. (90210)

BELCOURT ARTISTS 222 N. Canon Dr., Suite 204 Beverly Hills, Calif. (90210)	276-6205
BELLEVUE LITERARY AGENCY Kirkeby Center, Suite 1034 10889 Wilshire Blvd. (90024)	478-9470
BLAKE, WILLIAM, AGENCY/WEST TALENT INTERNATIONAL 1888 Century Park East (90067)	274-0321
BLOOM, BECKETT, LEVY & SHORR 449 S. Beverly Dr., Beverly Hills, Calif. (90212)	553-4850
BLUMENTHAL ARTISTS AGENCY 435 S. La Cienega Blvd. (90048)	656-1451
BRADY, CHRISTINA, AGENCY 11818 Wilshire Blvd. (90025)	473-2708
BRAND AGENCY 8721 Sunset Blvd. (90069)	657-2870
BRANDON & BARAD ASSOCIATES 9046 Sunset Blvd. (90069)	273-6273
BRESLER, WOLFF, COTA & LIVINGSTON 190 N. Canon Dr., Beverly Hills, Calif., (90210)	278-3200
BREWIS, ALEX, AGENCY 8721 Sunset Blvd. (90069)	274-9874
BRIDGETOWN MUSIC CORPORATION 723½ N. Glendora Ave., La Puente, Calif. (91744)	333-5288 283-1830
BROWN, NED, INCORPORATED 407 N. Maple Dr., Suite 228 Beverly Hills, Calif. (90210)	276-1131
CALDER AGENCY, THE 8749 Sunset Blvd. (90069)	652-3380
CAMBRIDGE COMPANY, THE 9000 Sunset Blvd., Suite 814 (90069)	657-2125 666-1920
CARTER AGENCY, INC., THE 1801 Avenue of the Stars, Suite 640 (90067)	277-2683
CENTURY ARTISTS, LITC. 9744 Wilshire Blvd., Suite 206 Beverly Hills, Calif. (90212)	273-4366
CHANDLER, RITA, AGENCY 8282 Sunset Blvd. (90069)	656-4042
CHARTER MANAGEMENT 9000 Sunset Blvd. (90069)	278-1690
CHARTWELL ARTISTS, LTD. 1901 Avenue of the Stars (90067)	553-3600
CHASIN-PARK-CITRON AGENCY 9255 Sunset Blvd. (90069)	273-7190

COLLIER, SHIRLEY, AGENCY 270-4500
1127 Stradella Rd. (90024)
(Representatives in all foreign countries)

COLTON, KINGSLEY & ASSOCIATES, INC. 277-5491
321 S. Beverly Dr., Beverly Hills, Calif. (90212)

COMPASS MANAGEMENT, INC. 271-5122
211 S. Beverly Dr., Beverly Hills, Calif. (90212)

CONNOR-CORFINO, ASSOCIATES, INC. 981-1133
14241 Ventura Blvd. Sherman Oaks, Calif. (91423)

CONTEMPORARY-KORMAN ARTIST, LTD. 278-8250
Contemporary Artist Building
132 Lasky Dr., Beverly Hills, Calif. (90212)

CONWAY, BEN & ASSOC. 271-8133
999 N. Doheny Dr., #403 (90069)

CORALIE JR., AGENCY 766-9501
4789 Vineland, N. Hollywood, Calif. (91602)

COSAY, WERNER & ASSOCIATES 550-1535
9744 Wilshire Blvd., Beverly Hills, Calif. (90212)

CREATIVE ARTISTS AGENCY, INC. 277-4545
1888 Century Park East, Suite 1400 (90067)

CUMBER, LIL, ATTRACTIONS AGENCY 469-1919
6515 Sunset Blvd., Suite 408 (90028)

DADE/ROSEN ASSOCIATES 278-7077
999 N. Doheny Dr., Suite 102 (90069)

DANSON ARTISTS' AGENCY 769-3100
19732 Riverside Dr., N. Holywood, Calif. (91602)

DIAMOND ARTISTS, LTD. 654-5960
8400 Sunset Blvd. (90069)
119 W. 57th St. (212) C17-3025
New York, New York (10019)

EISENBACK-GREENE-DUCHOW, INC. 659-3420
760 N. La Cienega Blvd. (90069)

FERRELL, CAROL, AGENCY 466-8311
6331 Hollywood Blvd., #828 (90028)

FIELDS, JACK & ASSOCIATES 278-1333
9255 Sunset Blvd., Suite 1105 (90069)

FILM ARTIST MANAGEMENT ENTERPRISES, INC. 656-7590
8278 Sunset Blvd., (90046)

FISCHER, SY, COMPANY, THE 273-3575
9255 Sunset Blvd., (90069)

FLEMING, PETER, AGENCY 271-5693
9046 Sunset Blvd., Suite 206 (90069)

GERSH, PHIL, AGENCY, INC. 274-6611
222 N. Canon Dr., Beverly Hills, Calif. (90210)

GIVSON, CARTER J., AGENCY 274-8813
9000 Sunset Blvd. (90069)

GOLDFARB/LEWIS AGENCY 659-5955
Falcon Gold, Inc., 8733 Sunset Blvd. (90069)

GOLDSTEIN, ALLEN & ASSOC., LTD. 278-5005
9301 Wilshire Blvd., Beverly Hills, Calif. (90210)

GORDEAN-FRIEDMAN AGENCY, INC., THE 273-4195
9229 Sunset Blvd. (90069)

GRANITE AGENCY, THE 943-8283
1920 S. La Cienega Blvd., Suite 205 (90034)

GRASHIN, MAURI, AGENCY 652-5168
8730 Sunset Blvd. (90069)

GREEN, IVAN, AGENCY, THE 277-1541
1900 Avenue of the STars, Suite 1070 (90067)

GREENE, GLORIA, CREATIVE EXPRESSIONS 274-7611
439 La Cienega Blvd. (90048)

GROSSMAN, LARRY & ASSOCIATES, INC. 550-8127
9229 Sunset Blvd., Suite 502 (90069)

HALLIBURTON, JEANNE, AGENCY 466-6138
5205 Hollywood Blvd., Suite 203 (900270D2

HALSEY, REECE, AGENCY 652-2409
8733 Sunset Blvd. (90069) 652-7595

HAMILBURG, MITCHEL J., AGENCY 657-1501
292 S. La Cienega Blvd., Suite 212,
Beverly Hills, Calif. (90211)

HENDERSON/HOGAN AGENCY, INC. 274-7815
247 S. Beverly Dr., Beverly Hills, Calif. (90212)
200 W. 57th St. New York, New York (10019) (212) 765-5190

HOLLYWOOD, DANIEL, THEATRICAL MANAGEMENT, LTD. 550-0570
9200 Sunset Blvd., Suite 808 (90069)

HUSSONG, ROBERT G., AGENCY, INC. 655-2534
8271 Melrose Ave., Suite 108 (90046)

HYLAND-DE LAUER, LITERARY AGENCY 278-0300
8961 Sunset Blvd. (90069)

I.M. AGENCY LTD. 277-1376
1888 Century Park East (90067)

INTERNATIONAL CREATIVE MANAGEMENT 550-4000
8899 Beverly Blvd. (90048)
40 West 57th Street,
New York, New York (10019) (212) 556-5600

INTERNATIONAL LITERARY AGENTS, LTD. 275l-8779
Peri Winkler, 9601 Wilshire Blvd., Suite 300
Beverly Hills, Calif. (90210)

IRWIN, LOU, AGENCY 553-4775
9901 Durant Dr., Suite A, Beverly Hills, Calif. (90212)

ISER, BEVERLY KAHN AGENCY 657-8693
9701 Wilshire Blvd., Suite 710
Beverly Hills, Calif. (90212)

JACKSON, IONE J. 293-8833
4306 S. Crenshaw Blvd. (90008)

JOSEPH, L.H., JR. & ASSOCIATES 651-2322
8344 Melrose Ave. (90069)

KAHN-PENNEY AGENCY 656-4042
8282 Sunset Blvd. (90046)

KANE, MERRILY, AGENCY 550-8874
9171 Wilshire Blvd., Suite 310
Beverly Hills, Calif. (90210)

KARLIN, LARRY, AGENCY 550-0570
9200 Sunset Blvd. (90069)

KOHNER, PAUL-LEVY, MICHAEL AGENCY 550-1060
9169 Sunset Blvd. (90069)

KURLAND, NORMAN, AGENCY, THE 274-8921
9701 Wilshire Blvd., Suite 800
Beverly Hills, Calif. (90212)

LARSEN, MICHAEL-POMADA, ELIZABETH,
LITERARY AGENTS (415) 673-0939
1029 Jones St., San Francisco, Calif. (94109)

LAZAR, IRVING PAUL, AGENCY 275-6153
211 S. Beverly Drive
Beverly Hills, Calif. (90212)

LENNY, JACK, ASSOCIATES 271-2174
9701 Wilshire Blvd.
Beverly Hills, Calif. (90212)
140 W. 58th Street
New York, New York (10019) (212) 582-0270

LEVEE, GORDON B., AGENCY 652-0012
8721 SUnset Blvd., Suite 103 (90069)

LEVERING, LILLIA ARTIST' MANAGER 874-9591
P.O. Box 1447 (90028)

LEWIS, HENRY, AGENCY 275-5129
9172 Sunset Blvd. (90069)

LITTMANN, ROBERT, COMPANY, THE 278-1572
409 N. Camden Drive,
Beverly Hills, Calif (90210)

LOO, BESSIE, AGENCY 657-5888
8746 Sunset Blvd. (90069)

LOVELL & ASSOCIATES 659-8476
8730 Sunset Blvd. (90069)

LYONS, GRACE, AGENCY 652-5290
8732 Sunset Blvd. (90069)

MAJOR TALENT AGENCY, INC. 820-5841
12301 Wilshire Blvd., Suite 515 (90025)

MAKRSON, RAYA L. LITERARY AGENCY 552-2083
Artists' Manager 997-6699
1888 Century Park East, Suite 1015 (90067) 778-6788

MCCLENDON, ERNESTINE, ENTERPRISES, INC. 654-4425
8440 Sunset Blvd., Suite M05 (90069)

MCHUGH, JAMES, AGENCY 651-2770
8150 Beverly Blvd., Suite 206 (90048)

MCKIERNAN & GURROLA 746-3550
1150 S. Olive St., Suite 1400 (90015)

MEDFORD, BEC, AGENCY 271-7021
9440 Santa Monica Blvd., Suite 403 (92120)

MEIKLEJOHN, WILLIAM, ASSOCIATES 273-2566
9250 Wilshire Blvd.,
Beverly Hills, Calif (90212)

MESSENGER, FRED, AGENCY 654-2800
8265 Sunset Blvd. (90046)

M.E.W. COMPANY 653-4731
151 N. San Vicente Blvd.
Beverly Hills, Calif (90211)

MILLER, STUART M., CO., THE 659-8131
8693 Wilshire Blvd., Suite 206
Beverly Hills, Calif (90211)

MISHKIN AGENCY, INC., THE 274-5261
9255 Sunset Blvd. (90069)

MOLSON-STANTON ASSOCIATES AGENCY, INC. 477-1262
10889 Wilshire Blvd., Suite 929 (90024)

MONTAIGNE, EVE, AGENCY 980-3770
10546 Burbank Blvd., Suite 3
N. Hollywood, Calif (91601)

MONTGOMERY, JO, AGENCY, ARTISTS' MANAGER 980-5899
4429 Carpenter Ave. (91604)

MOORE, LOLA, ARTIST MANAGER 276-6097
9172 Sunset Blvd. (90069)

MORRIS, WILLIAM, AGENCY, INC 274-7451
151 El Camino, 272-4111
Beverly Hills, Calif (90212)
1350 Avenue of the Americas
New York, New York (10019) (212) 586-5100

MOSS AGENCY, LTD 653-2900
113 N. San Vicente Blvd., Suite 302
Beverly Hills, Calif (90211)

MOSS, MARVIN, ARTISTS' MANAGER 274-8483
9200 Sunset Blvd., Suite 601 (90069)

MULTIMEDIA PRODUCT DEVELOPMENT, INC. 276-6246
170 S. Beverly Dr.
Beverly Hills, Calif (90212)

MURPHY, MARY, CONTESSA, JOSEPH, AGENCY 985-4241
10701 Riverside Drive
Toluca Lake, Calif (91602)

NOVEMBER NINTH MANAGEMENT 553-4123
9021 Melrose Ave., Suite 301 (90069)

OLIVER, MAURINE & ASSOCIATES 657-1250
8746 Sunset Blvd. (90069)

OTIS, DOROTHY DAY, AGENCY 461-4911
6430 Sunset Blvd., Suite 1203 (90028)

PEARSON, BEN, AGENCY 451-8414
606 Wilshire Blvd., Suite 614 (90401)

PICKMAN COMPANY, THE 273-8273
9025 Wilshire Blvd., Suite 303
Beverly Hills, Calif (90211)

PLESHETTE, LYNN, AGENCY 465-0428
2643 Creston Dr. (90068)

PORTNOY, MILDRED O., AGENCY 851-5426
11969 Ventura Blvd. (91604)

PREMIERE ARTISTS & PRODUCTIONS AGENCY 651-3545
Artists' Manager
6399 Wilshire Blvd., Suite 506 (90048)

PROGRESSIVE ARTISTS AGENCY 553-8561
400 S. Beverly Dr.
Beverly Hills, Calif (90212)

RAISON, ROBERT, ASSOCIATES 274-7217
9575 Lime Orchard Rd.
Beverly Hills, Calif. (90210)

RAPER ENTERPRISES AGENCY 461-5033
6311 Yucca (90026)

ROBARDS, BILL, GENCY 845-8547
4421 Riverside Dr.
Toluca Lake, Calif. (91505)

ROBINSON & ASSOCIATES 275-6114
132 S. Rodeo Dr.
Beverly Hills, Calif. (90212)

ROBINSON-WEINTRAUB & ASSOCIATES, INC. 653-5802
554 S. San Vicente, Suite 3 (90048)

ROGERS, PHILIP & ASSOC. 275-5278
9046 Sunset Blvd. (90069)

ROSE, HAROLD, ARTISTS, LTD 652-3961
8530 Wilshire Blvd.
Beverly Hills, Calif. (90211)

ROSEMARY MANAGEMENT 826-3453
11520 San Vicente Blvd., Suite 210 (90049)

RUBEN, SANDY ROTH 271-7209
9418 Wilshire Blvd.
Beverly Hills, Calif (90212)

RUBY, BETTY, TALENT AGENCY 466-6652
1741 Ivar Ave., Suite 119 (90028)

SALKOW, IRVIN, AGENCY 276-3141
450 N. Roxbury Dr.
Beverly Hills, Calif (90210)

SCHALLERT, JOHN W. AGENCY 276-2044
450 N. Roxbury Dr.
Beverly Hills, Calif. (90210)

SCHECHTER, IRV, COMPANY 278-8070
404 N. Roxbury Dr., #800
Beverly Hills, Calif (90210)

SCHULLER, WILLIAM, AGENCY 273-4000
9110 Sunset Blvd. (90069)

SEALOCK, LOIS, AGENCY 473-7130
1609 Westwood Blvd., Suite 204 (90024)

SHAPIRA, DAVID & ASSOCIATES, LTD. 278-2742
9171 Wilshire Blvd. Suite 525
Beverly Hills, Calif (90210)

SHAPIRO-LICHTMAN, ARTISTS' MANAGER 274-5135
9200 Sunset Blvd.
Penthouse Suite #7-8 (90069)

SHAW, GLENN, AGENCY 851-6262
3330 Barham Blvd., Suite 103 (90068)

SHEPHERD, DON, AGENCY 467-3535
1680 Vine Street, Suite 1105 (90028)

SHERMAN, CHARLIE, AGENCY 660-0000
6311 Yucca St. (90028)

SHERRELL, LEW, AGENCY, LTD. 461-9955
7060 Hollywood Blvd. (90028)

SIEGEL, JEROME, ASSOCIATES, INC. 652-6033
8733 Sunset Blvd., Suite 202 (90069)

SINDELL AGENCY, THE 820-2069
11706 Montana Ave. (90049)

SOLOWAY, ARNOLD, ASSOCIATES 550-1300
118 S. Beverly Dr., Suite 226
Beverly Hills, Calif. (90212)

STANLEY, MARGIE, AGENCY 466-3289
1418 N. Highland Ave. (90028)

STIEFEL OFFICE, THE 274-7333
9255 Sunset Blvd, Suite 609 (90069)

STONER, PATRICIA, ARTISTS' REPRESENTATIVES 980-4449
12069 Ventura Place (91604)

SUGHO, LARRY, AGENCY 657-1450
1047 N. La Cienega Blvd., Suite 303 (90069)

SWANSON, H.N., INC. 652-5385
8523 Sunset Blvd. (90069)

TALENT, INC. 462-0913
1421 N. McCadden Place (90028)

TANNEN, HERB & ASSOCIATES 466-6191
6640 Sunset Blvd., Suite 203 (90028)

TAYLOR, WILLIAM, AGENCY 550-7271
9000 Sunset Blvd., #805 (90069)

TOBIAS, HERB & ASSOCIATES, INC. 277-6211
1901 Avenue of the Stars, Suite 840 (90067)

TODD, DAVID & CAMARILLO, JAMES 550-1790
9348 Santa Monica Blvd., Suite 101
Beverly Hills, Calif (90210)

TREJOS & TREJOS LITERARY AGENCY, ARTISTS'S MANAGER 538-2945
18235 Avalon Blvd.
Carson, Calif. (90746)

TRUE AGENCY 874-8474
7513 Fountain (90046)

TWENTIETH CENTURY ARTISTS 990-8580
13273 Ventura Blvd., Suite 211 (91604)

UFLAND AGENCY, INC., THE 273-9441
190 N. Canon Dr.
Beverly Hills, Calif (90210)

VITT, ANGIE, AGENCY 276-1646
9172 Sunset Blvd. (90069)

WEBB, RUTH 274-4311
9229 Sunset Blvd., Suite 509 (90069)

WEINER, JACK, AGENCY 652-1140
8721 Sunset Blvd. (90069)

WEINTRAUB, MURRY, AGENCY 274-6352
8230 Beverly Blvd., Suite 23 (90048)

WEITZMAN, LEW & ASSOCIATES, INC. 278-5562
9171 Wilshire Blvd, Suite 406
Beverly Hills, Calif. (90210)

WITZER, TED, AGENCY 278-1926
9441 Wilshire Blvd., Suite 214
Beverly Hills, Calif. (90212)

WORMSER, JACK, AGENCY, INC. 874-3050
1717 N. Highland Ave., Suite 414 (90028)

WOSK, SYLVIA, AGENCY 274-8063
429 S. La Cienega Blvd. (90048)

DAN WRIGHT
c/o WRIGHT, ANN ASSOCIATES, LTD. 655-5040
8422 Melrose Place (90069)
c/o WRIGHT, ANN REPRESENTATIVES, INC.
136 East 57th Street
New York, New York (10022) (212) 832-0100
c/o WRIGHT, ANN REPRESENTATIVES, INC.
333 Alcazar Ave.
Coral Gables, Fla. (305) 445-2505

WRITERS & ARTISTS AGENCY 550-8030
9720 Wilshire Blvd.,
Beverly Hills, Clalif. (90212)
162 W. 56th St.,
New York, New York (10019) (212) 246-9029

ZIEGLER, DISKANT & ROTH, INC. 278-0070
9255 Sunset Blvd. (90069)

Contracts and Rights
Condensed from *Scriptwriter's News*

Contracts and subsidiary rights are among the most neglected areas of a script writer's expertise and knowledge. These agreements, or contracts, are the legal documents which grant producers, television networks, movie companies or other parties the rights to use your material for performance.

Most script writers in tv, theatre, radio, cable and film rely on their agents to answer their questions about the contracts, rights, copyrights and other legal matters in general. It is also wise, however, for you to be knowledgeable. After all, these contracts determine your personal income and usually involve a great deal of money.

First of all, be aware of the fact that agents who work in the entertainment industry wield tremendous power. Although most agents are honest and above-board, it is better to have a working knowledge of what you are signing. Script writers need agents, but agents can't survive without writers.

One clause in your typical contract which often causes some unnecessary concern is the so-called "pay-or-play" paragraph. This clause (briefly stated) means that the producer, after reaching mutually agreeable financial terms with the writer, signing a standard contract, and abiding by its stipulations, still has no obligation to use the script in any manner whatsoever.

Another common clause requires the script writer to promise that any and all material submitted to the producer is original. One method of protecting yourself is to place a fixed monetary ceiling on the amount of indemnity that you would ever be required to pay to the producer — regardless of the damages.

The "credit clause" is another important element. Contractual promises for such credits as "created by," "based on an original idea by" or simply "written by" — especially if they appear before the story, or in the case of television, if the credit appears on all episodes of a series, regardless of the length of its run, and regardless of the original writer's involvement in that particular episode — can mean more than any dollar amount for the beginning scripter, and are valuable to all writers.

The clauses about subsidiary rights are the most crucial ones for the script writer. These are agreements you make between yourself and the producer which determine what he can and can not do with what you have written beyond what was initially agreed upon. Subsidiary rights are usually the largest income-producing area for a producer.

These subsidiary benefits may include paperback, movie and television, serialization and book club rights.

You may not be able to successfully sell your material without sacrificing some of these subsidiary rights as part of the deal; but you must be knowledgeable. After you've signed it's too late.

Both the *Writer's Guild of America* (555 West 57th Street, New York, NY 10019) and the *Dramatists Guild* (234 West 44th Street, New York, NY 10036) are helpful in providing contract information. The Writers Guild has a sample "Minimum Basic Agreement" and an accompanying rate sheet which can be purchased (whether or not you are a member of the guild) for about $12.

The Dramatists Guild has sample contacts available for both Broadway and Off Broadway plays and musicals, for about $2 each.

A new copyright law was passed in 1976, and went into effect January 1978. It is an author's law. Copyright is automatically granted to the author from the date of "creation." This is not the same thing as having the copyright registered with the Office of Copyright in Washington. The U.S. Copyright Office has just installed a 24-hour "hotline" which script writers can call, request form "PA" and leave an address to which it can be mailed. The number is (202) 287-9100.

Copyright is now good for the life of the author plus 50 years after his death. R. R. Bowker has published the very useful and comprehensive *Copyright Handbook* ($14.95) and such organizations as the *Association of American Publishers* have issued pamphlets such as the AAP's "Overview of the New Copyright Law" which give a helpful summary of the most important aspects of the new law. In addition, the copyright office itself (Library of Congress, Washington, DC 20559) will provide circulars, forms and information regarding the new law free of charge. One of their most helpful circulars is "Highlights of the New Copyright Law," and another is called "Duration of Copyright Under the New Law." Both are free.

There is tremendous variance in both the manner and amount of payment for scripts. A rule-of-thumb which many script writers aim for as final compensation is roughly 10% of the total cost of the production. Regardless of the final arrangement, it is always wise to receive payment as you complete certain specified obligations. One suggested system of paying script writers is: 25% upon signing the initial contract; 25% upon submission of a treatment or rough draft of the script; 25% upon submission of the final shooting script; and the final 25% upon completion of the filming or taping, or on opening night.

Producers and agents who contract for scripts will want to retain as much of the potential income as possible. Writers must remember, however, that they too can negotiate, deal, and actively work towards viable contracts which favor career advancement and financial success.

15

Writing for Print Cartoons

Gag Writing for Cartoons
by Jack Markow
Condensed from *Cartoonist's and Gag Writer's Handbook*

Ideas dealing with diverse subjects may have a common denominator.

1. *Hidden Element* The idea may picture a scuba diver in the sea or an astronaut in space, but the basic gag ingredient is something hidden from one or more characters in the picture. The remainder of the cast in the funny episode usually knows what is taking place. The reader knows all that is going on. This gives him a feeling of superiority over the comic character ignorant of his present or future harassment.

2. *Understatement* The formula for this type of gag is the creation of a picture that carries great turmoil and excitement. Something violent and/or something unusual is happening in the picture. In contrast, the caption is quiet, understated. The person speaking ignores the obvious, and is almost oblivious of the chaos, crisis, confusion, or oddity of the scene.

Two classics from *The New Yorker:*

> *Fencing school. One swordsman lops off the head of his opponent, and says: "Touche!"* (James Thurber)

★ ★ ★

> *Trapeze artist, high above the circus crowd, fails to catch his partner. He says: "Oops, sorry!"* (George Shanks)

The cartoon character in his remarks skirts the importance of the eye-catching event taking place or which has taken place, and usually makes "small talk." This shifting of weight, this accent on the unimportant, throws the cartoon situation off balance and provides a surprise diversion for the reader.

Other examples:

> *Theater on fire. Man on stage reads from notes to seated audience: "The management has asked me to make the following announcement."*

Many understatement cartoons come in the form of a question.

> *Dentist's office. Patient has rocketed through ceiling — shown by large hole and plaster everywhere. Dentist, holding drill, stands on chair, looks through the hole, and asks: "Did I hit a nerve?"* (Al Johns, Saturday Evening Post)

3. *The Reverse* Writers of humor have long played with the topsy-turvey, the opposite, for quips that take the reader unawares.

There are two approaches to building a reverse cartoon.

(a) The caption may be twisted. The main impact remains in the conversational line. The picture, usually an ordinary scene, is just an adjunct to illustrate the quip — as in this cartoon.

> *Doctor holding x-ray of beautiful girl: "What's a joint like this doing in a nice girl like you?"*

(b) The Reverse may be a visual reverse rather than a verbal one. Visual reverse, or "sight gags," usually do not require a caption. Examples:

> *Two horses playing "horse shoes" with human shoes.*

★ ★ ★

> *Two nude girls, in a nudist camp, discussing a nude man hiding in the bushes. "Disgusting! He always looks at you like he's mentally dressing you."*

4. *Huge and Tiny*   Here, a tremendous, important happening in the picture is deflated by an insignificant item (usually brought out in the caption). The air in an enormous balloon of authority is released by a little pin prick. Complete visual thinking is required as a base for these ideas. Large shapes, pageantry, huge crowds — definite items like mammoth sculpture and paintings, tall buildings, high mountains, tremendous monuments, parades — all lend themselves to this kind of gag.

Some examples where a mole hill is made out of a mountain:

> *After driving through endless winding roads, trailer truck has delivered huge generator to power plant at the top of a mountain. Power plant manager: "Good heavens, man! We're D.C. not A.C.!"* (Richard Decker, The New Yorker)

★ ★ ★

> *Man about to be shot by firing squad is offered cigarette by officer, and says: "It's awfully kind of you — but I'm trying to give up smoking."* (R. Taylor, The New Yorker)

★ ★ ★

> *Movie director is sitting on camera boom looking down at mob of thousands of extras who are groping around on the ground. He yells: "Well, it's a hell of a time to lose a contact lens."* (Donald Reilly, Saturday Evening Post)

5. *Antique and Modern*   These ideas are accomplished by introducing today's customs, habits, manners, and word usage into a setting of another era. Conversely, ancient items and customs are used in a contemporary setting. This device may revolve on the gag line alone — a modern caption being used with a picture showing some aspect of Victorian living, for example. Or language and customs of olden times may provide the caption to accompany a present-day picture.

The transition may also be made in the picture itself — old items in present-day picture.

The transition may also be made in the picture itself — an old item in a present-day scene and our latest gadget projected into a scene of the past. This is a fertile field for the idea-maker, but care must be taken that the situation is worked out so it will be believable.

Two examples from *The New Yorker:*

> *Charios. Addams uses the extremes of antique and modern in his cartoon showing animals two by two, entering a space rocket to the moon (not a Noah's ark).*

★ ★ ★

> *Steinberg depicts a crook togged in colonial costume holding up owner of present-day antique shoppe with an old pistol.*

6. *Shop Talking* When other devices fail momentarily, a further approach to capturing that elusive idea is that shop talk angle. The language of a trade, business, or profession is the focal point of this kind of idea. This device is valuable in slanting humor for trade papers. This type of cartoon is also used widely by general magazines. Conception usually starts with the caption — and an appropriate picture (usually lurking in back of the mind) is used for this illustration.

> *Waitress to executives in dining room of motion picture studio: "Our super-super colossal lunch today consists of a gargantuan salad, a stupendous soup, and a four star super-gigantic double-feature entree surrounded by a galaxy of scintillating vegetables. 'Excellent,' says Dribinger of the* Times. *'Solid, with a touch of pure whimsey,' says Blobington of the* Tribune.*"*

Footnote on Shop Talking: Many cartoonists make a career of working for trade journals alone. These publications are numerous and many use cartoons. Various trade papers, unaccustomed to printing comics, would do so if they received material properly slanted to their specialized field. The trade journal cartoonist does research on products, manufacturing, working habits, and other items indigenous to each field brought out in these magazines. The resulting cartoons, if slanted right, sometimes bring surprisingly high prices. The lingo of the trade or profession provides an additional jumping-off place for the creation of ideas to fit these trade papers.

7. *Habits and Customs* Certain customs or habits of people, nations, strata of society, professions and trades may be converted into idea material. While the Shop Talking device deals primarily with words, Habits and Customs use a more visual approach in sparking a gag. In the antique/modern idea the old is brought into the new and

the new into the old; in satirizing manners and mores, regional and special fashions and practices, still contemporary, are shifted and brought into contact with the living ways of other regions, other peoples and other trades and professions. Examples:

> *Space man just emerging from his rocket which has landed on another planet is startled by a man from Mars who shows him typical French post cards and says: "Pssst!"* (Joe Farris, Climax)

★ ★ ★

> *Anthropologists riding in a jeep have draped a fossilized animal over the fender of their car, as is customary with hunters of modern game.* (Charles Addams, The New Yorker)

    8. *Surprise Ending Caption* This type of cartoon is based entirely on the gag line. The caption begins as a commonplace statement and zooms into an unexpected ending. As an example, an old bromide: "It's easy to stop smoking — I've done it many times." The picture, usually of two people conversing, plays a relatively minor role in the overall humor content. Illustrating a surprise ending caption results in a static picture, in most cases. Typecasting of the characters is required, but the background is unimportant in projecting the gag. This quiet type of idea actually poses a more difficult problem for its illustrator than the gag which requires more action and broader expressions. The cartoonist, drawing a conversational piece, cannot sink his teeth into the usual kind of cartoonist's goodies such as extreme exaggeration, vigorous motion, and the lively play of facial features. Therefore, confronted with many gags of this category, he must seek different backgrounds for each, and make his picture as interesting as he can — in design, composition, and tonal effects.

    Surprise ending gags are a bonanza for cartoon quip quoters and are heavily rerun in *Reader's Digest* since these carry their own weight without the help of a picture. From the Cartoon Quips department of *Reader's Digest:*

> *One girl to another: "He popped the big question all right — who do I think will win the National League Pennant?"* (Jerry Marcus, Saturday Evening Post)

★ ★ ★

> *Girl introducing one beau to another: "Albert, this is Edward. Edward, this is goodby."* (Leo Garel, Saturday Evening Post)

Here are those examples, all with the same scene showing two chorus girls talking:

"I think a girl should marry for love — I'm going to fall in love with the first millionaire I meet."

★ ★ ★

"We quarreled over the wedding plans — he wanted somebody else as a bride."

★ ★ ★

"After four martinis, my husband turns into a disgusting beast and after the fifth, I pass out altogether."

Experienced cartoonists and other idea-producing people know that it is comparatively simple to originate gags on one set subject. The comic strip man, fortunate in his firm foundation of a cast of characters, has little difficulty in meeting his quota of 365 ideas a year. His readers, fully indoctrinated to the foibles and idiosyncrasies of his little men, women, children, and animals, are ready to accept gags which individually do not have to be strong — but collectively have their appeal in a continuing pattern satirizing the traits and habits of his comic family. In most strips the formula is set, and only the ingredients vary somewhat from day to day to add freshness and spice. (How many variations have been made on the theme of the Dagwood super-sandwich, on Popeye's partnership with spinach, on Dennis being Mr. Wilson's menace?)

One device valuable as a start in idea producing is the "breaking down" method. Here, one general subject is broken down into smaller and smaller categories. This scheme worked well when cartoonists had to hold to one subject for the old comic weeklies. It helps today in slanting for specialized magazines — and it is even a good aid for general ideas. While the mind should not be too restricted in its wanderings far afield for that idea, an anchor sometimes helps in achieving a quota of gags quickly and efficiently.

Inspiration For general inspiration, each idea deviser should have his own collection of great published cartoons, those he considers classics. Just as the painter looks at museum masterpieces for stimulation, so should the cartoonist enjoy his collection — not at this time for the definite purpose of switching — but as a tonic to set the general temper of the ideas he is going to produce. A look at some good solid gags will help him set his sights high, will aid him in the quest for quality in his own idea output.

Taking a topic like "Office," he breaks it down into many subdivisions. These may be boss, secretary, late to work, clock watcher, water cooler, filing cabinet, desks, typewriter, parties, collections, salary, salesman, receptionist, switchboard, lunch. Sometimes, further dissection is necessary. For example: "typewriter" translated into smaller subjects — ribbon, broken key, carriage. Gag devices are the transference. An object is transferred to a setting unusual for it. Office water cooler in the middle of a desert, filing cabinet on a raft at sea, switchboard outside an igloo are some situations that may be tried as a gag beginning.

For specialized gags such as those used in book review supplements and magazines, the same breaking down method is employed. Example: *Books* — writers, publishers, critics, writer's wife, manuscript, publisher's office, bookseller, customer, etc. The subject "book," for instance, examined for weight, size and shape became a *New York Times Book Review* cartoon:

> *Book seller, staggering under the load of a large flat stone covered with hieroglyphics, says to customer: "Here's the first edition you wanted."*

Clichés Bromides, ancient enough to have become classics, have inspired idea-creators for many years. Cartoons based on these trite lines are used extensively in sophisticated magazines like *The New Yorker,* in down-to-earth trade papers in advertisements, and in greeting cards. The older and more familiar the expression — providing it still is in common usage — the better! To the writer of humor it is stimulating as a rare vintage wine.

The Non-Literal Clichés Because this expression is such a well-known and comfortable friend, a surprise picture — way out from the usual illustration expected to go with the old caption — is a necessity. While the picture with a new and exciting twist is the main ingredient which gets the laugh, an addition of reasonableness helps. A timely, topical picture (based on such innovations as electronics or space flight, for example) hooked up with one of these old-hat expressions makes a fine marriage.

Try the caption "straight." If that doesn't work, change a word or two still retaining the basic meaning of the line. Other approaches to the cliché line are the adding of words to devise a surprise ending caption, and twisting of words to provide a reverse gag.

Using one line from our list, *"Darling, they're playing our song!",* we try it in reverse — "Darling, they're not playing our song!" This has possibilities, but failing to get a picture immediately, we attack the original line in another way. This is an expression that ordinarily evokes a sentimental picture — something quite serious. Here is something to work on — puncturing of the serious-romantic, with a silly picture that will offset the sober caption.

Additional words tacked onto the original cliché are considered. The word "song" sparks the title of a classical piece. The title is lengthened and other liberties are taken with it, and when delivered with preciseness following the romantic first half of the caption, the whole line becomes ridiculous.

> *A symphony hall with the two principles depicted as intellectuals, with a large orchestra.*
>
> *"Darling, they're playing our song next — the andante cantabile movement from Mozart's Concerto for the bassoon and muted flutes, opus 147, number 12."*

In concentrating on a cliché caption, the imaginative idea man visualizes various types to act out the line. He also visualizes a variety of scenes. By doing this, he can get the utmost mileage from just one cliché, and use it as a base for different, salable ideas. Examples:

> *A couple of corpulent characters with "Darling, they're playing our song!" The materialistic thought of food brings love sparks to the fat couple's eye.*

★ ★ ★

> *The gadget of a dinner bell and the setting on a luxury liner at sea — entirely believable as a gourmet's paradise.*

Lenny Herman, illustrating this line for *Argosy Magazine,* shunned the use of musical instruments. Instead, he showed two women drivers in a minor collision outside a garage, with their fenders all banged up. One garage mechanic says joyfully to another: "Listen, they're playing our song!"

In completing ideas, you may have to make minor changes in the caption, to synchronize caption and picture. These consist mostly of pronouns and exclamations — embellishments which have no bearing on the main conception of the idea. However, when one important word is changed, we have a caption with an entirely new meaning — and one which will bring to mind more of a variety of pictures.

> Original: *"He called me a dirty name!"*

★ ★ ★

> Revision: *(Prisoner in fistfight) "He called me a dirty number!"*

Back to the use of animals in connection with cliché lines. The following remark is trite when uttered by a human, but a real gag when two chickens converse: "Some day I'd like to settle down on a farm and raise chickens."

Another example of the reverse version: (Marriage Bureau) Man to marriage broker about prospective wife, "May I have a look at her in the moonlight?"

Take an old phrase, select one of its words that has different meanings, directly illustrate one of its off-beat meanings — and you have a literal cliché cartoon. Involved here is a play on words, a certain pun quality. Puns ordinarily do not have wide usage in magazine cartoons but they do have their innings in certain publishing areas, notably the studio greeting card and in advertising. Cartoon trends constantly shift and the pun may be used more in magazines some day. Virgil Partch (VIP) has been doing this form of gaggery for many years.

Some examples of Partch's handling of the literal cliché:

> *Navy signalman is waving tiny semaphore flags at another ship. Officers says to him: "OK, Kosgriff, enough of that small talk!" (Look)*

★ ★ ★

> *Downhearted Turk is wearing very long hat. Friends asks: "Why such a long fez, Abdul?" (Look)*

LIST OF READY-MADE CAPTIONS

Whether searching for the non-literal or literal cliché idea, the following list will help spark original gags, and should inspire new and different drawings to go with each caption.

> "Why don't you watch where you're going?"
> "Mind if I look at it in the daylight?"
> "I never could understand what he sees in her."
> "He got up on the wrong side of the bed today."
> "This is the happiest day of my life."
> "It costs more to live nowadays."
> "His face is an inscrutable mask."
> "Nothing like a cup of coffee to wake you up in the morning."
> "Take a card — any card!"
> "I'll make him eat humble pie!"
> "May I see your driver's license?"
> "Keep this under your hat — "
> "Her hair was so long she could sit on it."
> "You're not fit to touch the hem of her skirt."
> "Visiting hours are over!"
> "He's put her on a pedestal."

"We can't make up our minds whether to buy or build."
"I'm just giving you one hour to get out of town.!"
"Father has cut me off without a cent."
"She reminds me of someone, but I can't think who."
"I don't think he's found himself yet."
"I get tired of it, but it's the only thing I know."
"Please don't feel it's necessary to make conversation."
"Anything for a friend."
"He'd give you the shirt off his back."
"My hair is a mess."
"Who dealt this mess?"
"All I know is what I read in the papers."
"It takes a thief to catch a thief."
"My feet are killing me."
"I'll try anything once."
"To coin a phrase. . ."
"Don't change horses in midstream."
"Once over light."
"It's coming out of my ears."
"I don't know what's come over John lately."
"New at this job, aren't you?"
"Lifelike, isn't it?"
"Relax dear, I can explain everything."
"It's within a stone's throw of the railroad station."
"Hi, babe, what are you doing tonight?"
"What shall I say if anyone calls?"
"Who shall I say is calling?"
"May I borrow a cup of sugar?"
"Darling, there's no one in the world but you."
"Say, are you following me?"
"Stop me if you've heard this one."
"Follow that car!"
"A simple yes or no will be sufficient."
"Standing room only."
"I'll make a man of him yet."
"It's as clean as a whistle."
"Grindall is under the weather today."
"'Taint a fit night out for man nor beast."
"Pull over to the curb."
"Oh, I can't complain — ."
"I smell something burning."
"How about one for the road?"
"Fish biting, today?"
"He carries his office in his hat."
"May I quote you?"
"All leaves are cancelled."
"Have you read any good books lately?"
"What's the good word?"
"I'm just browsing."
"You men are all alike."
"Is my slip showing?"
"Selling out — must vacate."
"It's a speciality of the house."
"I don't know anything about art, but I know what I like."
"She's quite a home body."
"Either he goes, or I go."

"Don't fight it, just let yourself go."
"Two containers of coffee — to go."
"Take a letter!"
"He's in a rut."
"He's pouring his heart out."
"This takes the cake."
"I haven't got a thing to wear."
"Travel is broadening."
"He's in the driver's seat."
"We now bring you the blow by blow account — "
"This little pig went to market, this little pig stayed home."
"You must give me a buzz some day."
"Try this one for size."
"Go away and never darken my door again."
"Mind if I look over your shoulder while you work?"
"It isn't polite to point."
"You should have seen the one that got away."
"We're going to have it done over this spring."
"He'll burn himself out before his time."
"I want to get this off my chest."
"Say when!"
"What are you going to be when you grow up?"
"Everyone has money these days."
"The more I think about it, the madder I get."
"Watch out for a trick play, men."
"He just stepped out — but we expect him back any minute."
"The next question was sent in by Mrs. B — "
"They went that way."
"I simply can't go on living without him."
"She's trying to combine marriage and a career."
"It's nice for a man to have a hobby."
"I'm writing a letter to my Congressman."
"It's such a nice day, we decided to walk."
"A penny saved is a penny earned."
"Under Construction — Proceed at Your Own Risk."
"I can get it for you wholesale."
"It's just puppy love."
"I think Dobson is overstepping his authority."
"Please don't get up."
"But first — a word from our sponsor."
"It's the first dollar I ever earned."
"Don't pigeonhole the matter."
"Let's lay our cards on the table."
"Don't give me the third degree."
"That's the bone of contention."
"It was a slip of the tongue."
"What are you, man or mouse?"
"He made the best of a bad bargain."
"You took the words right out of my mouth."
"I don't know what I'd do without you."
"He's an Indian giver."
"Where have you been keeping yourself lately?"
"She had the last word, as usual!"
"Once upon a time — "
"Let's steal a march on him."
"I'm at a complete standstill."

"It's no bed of roses."
"Let's throw out a feeler, men!"
"You have the advantage of me."
"To put it in a nutshell — "
"He plays second fiddle."
"He always keeps his two feet on the ground."
"It's not the heat, it's the humidity."
"I hope I'm not intruding."
"He has a skeleton in his closet."
"Time and tide await no man."
"Stop dogging my foot steps."
"He's not my type."
"I sold him a bill of goods."
"Two's company, three's a crowd."
"You don't know the half of it."
"He has money to burn."
"He's rolling in wealth."
"Let's see how the other half lives."
"She's my better half."
"He's the chip off the old block."
"He's following in my footsteps."
"Here comes the bearer of good tidings."
"He swept her off her feet."
"Do you think money grows on trees?"
"If you don't see what you want, ask for it."
"You're an Indian giver."
"Did you have a hard day at the office?"
"He's in the chips."
"Give him an inch and he'll take a mile."
"Money is the root of all evil."
"Where there's a will, there's a way."
"A fool and his money are soon parted."
"Don't handle the merchandise."
"He's seen better days."
"He's a gentleman of the old school."
"Let's paint the town red."
"She's growing old gracefully."
"This is so sudden."
"He's in the prime of life."
"He believes in striking while the iron is hot."
"I'm turning over a new leaf."
"You can't change a leopard's spots."
"Only one to a customer."
"These are dog days."
"Sauce for goose, is sauce for the gander."
"You can't eat your cake, and have it."
"Having a wonderful time, wish you were here."
"Woman's work is never done."
"Everything's in ship-shape order."
"He's in conference."
"I'm a stranger in town myself."
"Don't keep me in the dark."
"We're just made for each other."
"I was just an innocent bystander."
"I'm trying to catch his eye."
"It's right under your nose."

"Well, out of sight, out of mind."
"He lives by his wits."
"I'll give him a piece of my mind."
"Handle with care."
"This side up."
"It was just a slip of the tongue."
"I'm sitting up with a sick friend."
"Will you have one lump or two?"
"This is one of those days when everything seems to go wrong."
"My fate is in your hands."
"No down payment necessary."
"I've got you covered."
"Shake well before using."
"He thinks he's pulling the wool over my eyes."
"I can buy it just for a song."
"Build a better mouse trap, and the world will beat a path to your door."
"George Washington slept here."
"It's the pot calling the kettle black."
"See here, my fine feathered friend!"
"They're playing our song."
"We all have to go sometime."

Cartooning: Style and Marketing
by Robb W. Winwood

Over the years I have established my own list of common criteria that I consistently find in the more effective cartoons. They are subjective of course but in reality they fall in line nicely with the ideas of Jack Markow, and they do appear repeatedly in most syndicated cartoons.

1. The focus is always on the character, or character action, not the situation he is in.
2. A simple line of logic or illogic runs throughout the entire cartoon strip, and every action or comment builds on this.
3. A character always looks pretty much the same in every panel. He may change expression of course but his general characteristics are constant.
4. Every panel is self-sufficient.
5. Dialogue may foreshadow something to come, but rarely refers to something already stated. To do this is to add needless repetition.
6. There are never more than four well-defined characters in a panel. There may be more figures, but they are usually drawn into the shadows and are nondescript.
7. Dialogue is always pithy and never excessive.

The Publishing Process The *1981 Writer's Market* has the following tips on the process of becoming published.

Study the market place. Research the types of periodicals that will print your cartoons.

Look for a market that doesn't buy all rights; if possible retain as many reprint rights as is comfortable, but don't be too demanding either. The idea is to get published.

Try to find a buyer who pays on acceptance. This way you are assured of the benefit.

Don't send in extremely timely cartoons as it may take months before the cartoon is printed, and the humor will undoubtedly be lost with time.

Know the subject you are cartooning and bring new light to it. Clever cartooning is always unique and unusual.

On Submission Always put the final drawing on stiff Bristol board paper and use black India ink. Most magazine cartooning is reproduced in black and white so there is little need for color in the initial draft. Type captions three to four inches below the cartoon images. Some publications will shoot directly from the original drawing. Others will assign another artist to redo the work. Captions will be added in the proper place by the printer. If unusual dialogue is used send a separate sheet with an explanation of its use. Always print your name and address on the back of the cartoon in the upper lefthand corner. Attach the cartoon to a separate piece of cardboard with paper clips or rubberbands so there will be no damage in the mailing process. Mark the envelope — "Illustration, Do Not Bend or Fold."

Many times a gag writer will come up with a funny idea and caption for a cartoon and is unable to draw it. Usually a rough sketch is drawn and the caption is sent on a 3x5 card. Only send one gag on a card with a very scant outline of the situation so the artist will know exactly what is required. In most cases a gag writer will send in 10 to 20 gags at a time.

The gag writer and the artist are partners. In most instances the profits are split on a 50/50 basis although sometimes an established artist with an already existing cartoon strip will demand a fuller share. There is a tremendous need for good captioned gags so even though the gag writer does no art his services are in great demand.

On Creator Rights The object is of course to get exposure through publication. As one becomes more widely known and gains a professional reputation, i.e., becomes more valuable to the publisher, his negotiating leverage is increased. So will the ability to retain rights to reprint.

As of January 1, 1978, a new copyright law went into effect. This law protects writing and artwork by recognizing that the creator of the work is its owner and as the owner is entitled to all rights, benefits and privileges that ownership entails.

A copyright now extends from the completion of the work to 50 years after the death of the artist. Even if you create under an anonymous name or a pseudonym your rights are protected from 100 years after the completion date or 75 years after publication — whichever comes first and is shorter.

A copyright covers your work whether it is registered or not. However, registration does allow certain advantages in the event of an infringement law suit, so in some cases it is a very good idea to register a copyright.

When publishing cartoons you should never send the same cartoon to two different publications without notifying them first. And it is suggested that you send only one cartoon to one publisher. If that publisher rejects the idea then you can send to someone else. There are six types of publishing rights.

1. *First serial rights:* The artist offers the newspaper or magazine the right to publish the cartoon for the first time. All other rights to the art belong to the artist.
2. *Second serial rights (reprint):* This gives the periodical the opportunity to print the cartoon after it has already appeared in some other source. The income from the reprint right is normally split evenly between the artist and the first publisher.
3. *All rights:* A cartoonist will usually sell all rights with a cartoon. This means that he forfeits the right to reprint elsewhere. Most cartoonists will work in a work-for-hire situation, meaning all rights are retained by the publisher and the artist cannot reprint the cartoon in its present form.
4. *Simultaneous rights:* Two publications with no overlapping circulation areas may be willing to buy simultaneous rights to a cartoon. Many religious publications will do this. Always advise the editors involved when a simultaneous submission is in action.
5. *Foreign serial rights:* If you sold only first U.S. serial rights to an American publication, a foreign publication may be willing to buy printed cartoons which have already been released.
6. *Syndication rights:* When involved with syndication a cartoonist sells all rights to the syndicate in a work-for-hire relationship. The syndicate in turn distributes the cartoons in many different publications around the country or world. The artist/gag writer will receive from 40 to 60% of the gross proceeds, although many times the syndicate will retain an artist on a salary basis. To become involved with a syndicate usually 7 to 10 samples of the cartoon work are needed.

Here is a complete listing of syndicates and other buying sources.

The Cartoon Writer's Agents
Condensed from *The Writer's Market*

Raeavena, 36 Winslow Road, Trumbull, CT 06611. "Gagwriters should send around 12 gags. Keep descriptions short," Pays 25% commission. Returns rejected material "as soon as possible."

Dorothy Bond Enterprises, 2450 N. Washtenaw Ave., Chicago, IL 60647. When we receive your gag, it is carefully reviewed and, if we think it's salable, it is drawn up at once and sent on its quick way to a wide list of top cartoon buyers. Pays 30% of the sale check "the same day we receive it." Tips: "Be professional and type your gags on 3x5 cards with your name and address on the back, and always enclose SASE (and if you want us to tell you why we rejected your gags, let us know). Please, no clips or rubber bands, or letters with your submissions. We want to sell them as badly as you do. Trust us, and good luck to us both.

Bill Boynansky, Apt. 13/20, Ansonia Hotel, 2109 Broadway, New York, NY 10023. (212) 787-7690. Submit 15-20 gags at one time. Pays 25% for regular, 35% for captionless; all others — regular payment.

Ashleigh Brilliant, 117 W. Valerio St., Santa Barbara, CA 93101. Pays $10. Any interested writer not completely familiar with my work should first send $1 for my catalog of 1,000 examples. Otherwise, their time and mine will be wasted."

Joe Busciglio, 420 W. North Bay, Tampa, FL 33603. Pays 25% commission on sale.

Comedy Unlimited, Suite 625, Jack Tar Office Bldg., 1255 Post St., San Francisco, CA 94109. Contact: Jim Curtis. "We are exclusively concerned with material intended for oral presentation."

Thomas W. Davie, 1407 S. Tyler, Tacoma, WA 98405 Prefers batches of 5-25. Pays 25% commission.

Lee DeGrott, Box 115, Ambler, PA 19002. Pays 25% on sales.

George Dole, Box 3168, Sarasota, FL 33578. Submit 12 gags at one time. Pays 25% commission.

James Estes, 1103 Callahan, Amarilla, TX 79106. Submit 10-20 gags "clear, concise ideas set down without excessive wordiness." Tips: "I think even time-worn subjects can be made funny by talented people. I place no restrictions on what sort of writers."

Charles Hendrick, Jr., Old Fort Ave., Kennebunkport, ME 04046. Submit 10 gags at a time. Pays 50% of commission.

David R. Howell, Box 170, Porterville, CA 93258 (209) 781-5885. Pays 25-30% commission. Tips: "Try to write gags for special markets that can, if need be, also sell to general markets."

Larry (KAZ) Katzman, 101 Central Park W., Apt. 4B, New York, NY 10023 (212) 724-7862. Submit 12-15 gags at one time. Pays 25% commission. "I use only medical (doctor, nurse, hospital) gags; no others."

Jeff Keate, 1322 Ensenada DR., Orlando, FL 32807. Pays 25% commission. Needs: General situation and timely gags, sports gags (all sports in season) for "Time Out" sport panel. "Be funny. No puns. No oldies. No old-hat situations." Tips: "Study publications using cartoons to get the 'slant.'"

Steve Kell, 733 Waimea Dr., El Cajon, CA 92021. (714) 440-5749. Submit gags in batches of 10-15. Pays 25%.

Reamer Keller, Box 3557, Lantana, FL 33462 (305) 58202436. Submit gags in batches of 20-30. Pays 25%.

Milo Kinn, 1413 SW Cambridge ST., Seattle WA 98106. Pays 25% commission. Tips: "The cartoon should be a funny picture or situation — not just 2 people talking. Gags demeaning or putting down females (dumb wife; dumb blond type) do not seem to sell as well as others."

Lo Linkert, 1333 Vivian Place, Port Coquitlam, British Columbia, Canada V3C 2T9. Batches of 10-25 gags. Pays 25% commission: $50 for greeting card ideas. Needs: Clean, general topical, medical, family, office, outdoors gags: captionless ideas; greeting card ideas. No puns, please, nor hippy, beatnik, or pro-male subjects."

Art McCourt, Box 210346, Dallas TX 75211 (214) 339-6865. Submit 10-15 gags at one time. Pays 25% commission. "No crowds, TV, mothers-in-laws or desert islands."

Masters Agency, Box 427, Capitola CA 95010. Editorial Director: George Crenshaw. Pays $10/gag. Single panel cartoons, needed quarterly: pays $15/cartoon.

Bill Maul, 644 Willowood Ave., Altamonte Springs, FL 32701. 10-15 in a batch. Pays 25%; "raises to 30% after a successful collaboration period." The writer should concentrate on general, family-type gags. Topics such as TV current events and trends warrant special consideration. Sight gags are always desirable."

Harold B. Money ("HALM"), 1206 Dover Ave., Wilmington DE 19805 (302) 994-0272. Submit 10-15/batch. Pays 25% on sales to $15; 30% thereafter. Strictly girlie slant gags with a fresh viewpoint and "punchy" gaglines. No general or trade journal gags. No orgy scenes, VD gags, flashers, brides and groom, or multi-panel ideas."

Ray Morin, 140 Hamilton Ave., Meriden CT 06450 (203) 237-4500. Submit 7-10 gags at one time. Pays 25% commission. I do 95% of my own gags, but am willing to look."

Michael J. ("SKI") Pellowski, Box 726, Bound Brook, NJ 08805. Sometimes buys juvenile gags and riddles for 25¢ each for use in joke books. Pays $1-5 outright purchase. Buys performable comedy material for outright fee and polishes same for sale. Will look at anything that can be performed in night clubs or on TV. "I use few if any cartoon ideas. My need is for material for comedians and joke books, not for speakers or DJs."

Irv Phillips, 2807 E. Sylvia St., Phoenix AZ 85032. Pays 25% commission; $10 minimum.

Dom Rinaldo, 29 Bay, 20 St., Brooklyn, NY 11214. Keep gag brief. Pays 25%. Needs: "Girlie, family and trade. No golf gags, or making fun of religion." Tips: "I like to see gags that are no good without the picture (cartoon)." Pays 25%.

Lee Rubin, 9 Murray Ave., Port Washington, NY 11050. Interested in gags concerning eyesight, eyeglasses and optometrists. Pays 40% commission.

Frank ("DEAC") Sematones, 5226 Mt. Alifan Dr., San Diego, CA 92111. (714) 279-7178. Pays 25% commission. Needs: Male, sexy, girlie. "Must be new, fresh and funny."

Jospeh Serrano, Box 42, Gloucester, MA 01930. Pays 25% commission.

Ed Shipley, 4725 Homesdale Ave., Baltimore, MD 21206. Pays 25%. Needs: General, computer, office and machine shop gags. "I am doing mostly trade journal cartoons." No medical gags.

John W. Side, 335 Wells St., Darlington, WI 53530. Interested in "small-town, local happening gags with a general slant." Pays 25% commission.

Scott Smith, 170 Madison Ave., Danville, KY 40422. (606) 236-9390. 10-15/batch. Pays 25%. "No 'small island in the middle of the ocean' type subjects, nor women drivers, husband/wife dumb jokes."

John Stinger, Box 241, Pineville, PA 18946. Interested in general, family and general business gags. Would like to see more captionless sight gags. Pays 25% commission; "more to top writers."

Tom Stratton, S. 4211 Lake Shore Rd., Hamburg, NY 14075. In batches of 10. "I don't want to be inundated — I can't swim." Needs: General, sex, and off-the-wall humor. "An oblique way of looking at things. Nothing normal."

Bob Thaves, Box 67, Manhattan Beach, CA 90266. 25% commission. Needs: Gags "dealing with anything except raw sex."

Marvin Townsend, 631 W. 88th St., Kansas City, MO 64114. Prefers batches of 12 gags. Pays 25% commission. Interested in gags with a trade journal of business slant, such as office executives, professional engineers, plant managers, doctors, etc.

Bardulf Ueland, Halstad, MN 56548. Pays 25% commission. Needs: General, family, medical and farm gags. No sex.

Art Winburg, 21 McKinley Ave., Jamestown, NY 14701. Pays 25% commission. Needs: All types of gags; general, family, trade and professional journals, adventure, sports, medical, children's magazines. Would prefer not to see gags about "smoke signals, flying carpets, moon men, harems or cannibals with some person in cooking pot."

16

Writing for Greeting Cards

Write Studio Cards and Still Have Time for Sex
by Bob Hammerquist
Condensed from *A Guide to Greeting Card Writing*

Compared to the more traditional types of greeting cards, the studio format is still quite new, a mere teenager. They just seemed to appear in the early fifties, coming from any number of small, independent, and somewhat adventurous types who wanted a new way to sell greeting cards. The huge and near-huge manufacturers at first looked upon the studios as something akin to a New Leftist at the 35th Class Reunion. However, with a prognosis of longevity, and with their present image as a profit maker, 2,850,000 card manufacturers have, as of this date, laid claim to their birth.

If you plan to write studio cards, it doesn't hurt to appreciate as many styles and types of humor as possible. There are outlets for all of them. Risque ideas or slightly blue material can be either outrageously funny or plain smut masquerading as humor. Satire and parody can be subtle and penetratingly funny. They can also be smug, bitter, self-righteous, and just plain dull.

I am personally from the bedroom/belly button/bedpan school. I am betting that bathrooms and bedrooms will be around approximately as long as navels, and that onrushing generations are going to discover, much to their delight, that some very funny things, indeed, do happen in these areas:

[outside] [man and woman]
It's your ANNIVERSARY . . . Don't just stand there!

CONNUBULATE!!
CONGRATULATIONS!

★ ★ ★

[outside] For You in the Hospital
This card contains no uncouth remarks, risque humor, or crude jokes.

It offers instead a thoughtfully chosen wish to comfort and cheer you during your hours of restful healing . . .

[inside] . . . May your bedpan always be warm!
HOPE YOU'RE DOING WELL!

Please don't flood the market with belly button gags, bedpan gags, or sex gags!!! There is no outstanding shortage in these particular categories. But if your bedroom, belly button, or bathroom gag is really a good one. . . .

What are we looking for? First of all: Are they widely sendable? It has to relate to a situation! Somebody's having a birthday, remember? Or someone is sick, or is having an anniversary, or is going on a trip, or is a very special type of friend, or is having a toenail transplant. Something pretty specific.

Obviously card buyers want to communicate with people they care for, and they have chosen studio cards because they want to do so in an informal manner. As a writer, you're simply offering them a choice of messages for the communication. Think about this constantly when you're writing card material. You're not writing for a TV or nightclub comedian, or a comic strip, or for any other medium where anything goes. You're writing studio greeting cards.

Here are a few examples of what I would consider very sendable greeting cards:

> [outside] Sorry you're so sick!
>
> [inside]   Hate to see someone so yummy feeling so crummy!

* * *

> [outside] Like a vintage wine, we get nicer with age . . .
>
> [inside]   . . . though our kegs may be starting to swell . . .
> HAPPY BIRTHDAY

Notice that the word "I" doesn't appear. That's because using the word "I" or "my" limits the number of potential senders of each card to one. It makes the card unsendable by married couples or a whole gang of people. It's not a forbidden word, exactly; plenty of studio cards are sent by individual persons, but it's a word that should be left out unless it's needed.

Next consideration — are the cards clever or funny?

> [outside] Congratulations on your success . . . but then, why shouldn't you be successful!?
>
> [inside]   You've got more brains in your head than most people have in their little finger!!!

And yet another consideration — are your ideas short and to the point? Most of the good ones are funny (or cute) and as short as possible. Very few words — but, hopefully, the right words. . .the ones that move the idea across quickly and smoothly without clouding it up. For the most part, these words don't just happen. They have been selected, judged, trimmed, positioned, invented, etc. For instance:

> [outside] Just a friendly little "Hi!" for your birthday . . .
>
> [inside]   . . . 'cause it's cheaper than a friendly little present!
> HAPPY DAY!

GREETING CARDS

Part of the idea-gathering process is simply keeping your eyes and ears open, and thinking greeting cards twenty-four hours a day.

Look and listen for ideas! Tv, radio, movies, theater, chatter over cocktails and coffee breaks, popular phrases, customs, issues, attitudes and anxieties that reach crests of concern (morality, living costs, etc.), articles and cartoons in magazines and newspapers, and office jokes.

[outside] [animated rock, singing]
Happy birthday to you . . .
Happy birthday to you . . .
Happy birthday to you-oo . . .
Happy birthday to you . . .

[inside] Just a little rock music for your birthday . . .

If you're going to write studio ideas, you have to assume, nitty-gritty-wise, that life is absurd.

Living in these United States makes it that much easier to come up with stuff like this:

[outside] For your Birthday I was going to bake you one of your favorite treats . . .

[inside] . . . but how do you bake beer???
HAPPY BIRTHDAY!

★ ★ ★

[outside] HEY, MOM
For a special Mother's Day treat you get to have breakfast in bed. Just check off what you want from the menu . . .

[inside] [on homemade menu]
MENU
Cookies   Chocolate Bars
Potato chips   Pepperoni Pizza

Pop   Ice Cream
Milkshake   French Fries
HAPPY MOTHER'S DAY!

★ ★ ★

[outside] Granny had a word for birthdays

[inside] The word was "CRAP!"
HAPPY DAY

On a writing day, I shoot for thirty or forty ideas. Set yourself a realistic goal and strive to reach it.

Fortunately, you will not have to sustain your creative energies fulltime. When you have a few hundred ideas going, you will spend more than a little time keeping records of where they are, who has bought what, who needs what, and when. If you're inefficient, which you'll remember was a prerequisite of being a studio card writer, you will never have enough stamps or envelopes and the typewriter ribbon will always be sideways. When you get a few thousand ideas going, confusion escalates. Naturally, you will also spend three or four days a month just hauling sacks of money to the bank.

All of these little time-consumers are part of running a small business, and, although boring, they at least make you eager to get back to writing — and that's the way you should come to it.

Another little involvement that can eat up hours is artwork. If you honestly feel you have no talent in this area, just type out your ideas plain. If they're good, they'll sell. If, however, you like to sketch little comic figures, and can do it quickly, fine. It can't hurt. This type of artwork will not turn a bad idea into a good one, but it can put any idea into a more impressive package.

Almost all editors have certain types of ideas they do no want to see, but what is not wanted varies from editor to editor. No sex stuff, please! No bedpan or belly button gags! No topical ideas! No trick folds! No brand names! No too-cutesy-pie. Different companies have an image to maintain or protect, or, for one reason or another, they have found that certain types of ideas just do not sell in their particular line.

If an editor states he doesn't want to see a particular type of idea, don't keep throwing it in his face, or give him advice about his unimaginative approach to publishing.

For instance, here is a studio idea that had to go to the right type of company. It would have been a waste of everyone's time to send it out indiscriminately:

>[outside] Happy Mother's Day, Mom dear . . . and although I don't usually talk this way, I want you to know I think you're . . .
>
>[inside] . . . one helluva nice MOTHER!

The problem word is "helluva," and it's the basis for the whole idea; but there are a few companies that wouldn't touch this type of thing, even though it would be classified as a "cute" idea.

A word about integrity. The honesty of the companies, as well as of yourself, should be dictated, if not by sheer morality, at least by common sense. They are not going to make copies of your ideas or artwork and return the originals to you with a rejection slip. If you feed the junk, they wouldn't want to steal it even if they were bandits. If you're valuable to them as a contributor, they want to keep you happy. Trust them!

In return, you don't play hanky-panky with ideas. The editors have a built-in sensitivity to most ideas that have been used before. As mentioned before, borrowing an idea from a source other than greeting cards and converting it to a card situation is not exactly plagiarism, you understand, but borrowing from another greeting card without giving it an original twist of your own is something else again.

The future of studio cards, along with the future of greeting cards in general, looks good.

Studios are like the people who enjoy sending and receiving them: the young and those who think young. A little more direct, uncluttered, and candid, but not way, way out or completely demented:

> [outside]   Happy Birthday to a typical red-blooded American guy!
>
> [inside]   32% warm blood . . . 68% cold beer . . .

Humor Writing for Greeting Cards

by Larry Sandman
Condensed from *A Guide to Greeting Card Writing*

There are perhaps twenty studio writers for every humorous writer submitting greeting card ideas today. This means the competition in the studio market is twenty times as stiff as the competition in the humorous market (give or take a few times).

A lot of people have overlooked the humorous market simply because they don't really know the line is there. Many writers, I believe, think that "humorous" is just another name for "studio." Not true. Humorous cards are a distinct line of greetings that express a sentiment in a funny, clever, or cute way. The name "humorous" is in itself deceiving. It suggests that all the cards are funny, which isn't true. Many humorous cards are more "sweet" than funny. Other humorous cards tend more toward the clever. They aim to make you smile, not laugh. Then there are the humorous cards that are actually intended to be funny:

> [outside]   It's Father's Day and you deserve a 21-gun salute . . .
>
> [inside]   . . . or at least a couple of "shots"!
> HAPPY FATHER' DAY!

The difference between this and a studio card is in the way it's illustrated. In fact, what distinguishes humorous cards from all the other lines is the way they're illustrated. Humorous cards are actually written with a particular illustration or situation in mind. It's for this reason that many people in the business refer to them as "illustrated" cards.

When you write a humorous card, it is best to start out thinking visually. Think of how the idea could be illustrated. While it takes some extra thought to visualize a card, humorous cards do allow the writer a high degree of flexibility. Unlike studios and unlike most informals, humorous cards do not have a standard size or shape.

The sentiments, too, can be done in many ways. They can be short prose, not unlike studio sentiments:

GREETING CARDS 253

    [outside]   [photo of two pigs]
                     Let's get together on your birthday . . .

    [inside]   . . . and have a snort or two!

Or they can be something totally unique, not quite like anything you'll find in any other line:

    [outside]   (designed to look like an insurance policy)

                     GOOD HEALTH POLICY
                             of the
                     CONVALESCENT BENEFIT
                        ASSOCIATION
                        Issued by the
                     Good Health Underwriters

    [inside]   The Convalescent Benefit Association
                    Underwriters for GOOD HEALTH Inc.
                    under the law of the state of health
                         and happiness
                          THIS POLICY
                        entitles the holder

            M _____
                        to a speedy recovery
                   an end to all aches and pains,
                         and years of
                   HEALTH, HAPPINESS, AND
                       CONTENTMENT

    Humorous cards can be divided into several established formats. One of the oldest, and still one of the most popular, formats is the long illustrated verse, in which each individual phrase is separately illustrated.

    All illustrated verses have several things in common. They lend themselves well to illustration, they all progress to a logical conclusion, and they all carry legitimate me-to-you messages. They're dressed up to be light and fun, but their underlying messages are uniformly warm and pleasant.

    Another type of humorous format is the "parody." Many things can be the basis for a humorous parody card: newspapers, magazines, wanted posters, book covers — even other cards make likely targets for humorous parodies.

    Parodies take a good deal of time and work, and so they rarely come from freelancers. If well done, however, such works would command a premium price in some companies. There are countless things that could lend themselves to parodies, things from diplomas to stock certificates to confession magazines.

Related to parodies, though not quite the same, are signs, badges, and certificates.

Another humorous format is the "photo tie-in" card. This is a humorous card which features a photograph — often an animated object, or a cartoon character dropped into a photographic setting:

    [outside]   [photo: close-up of a pumpkin — pumpkin has dropped-in cartoon eyes and smile]
You're not getting older . . .

    [inside]   You're just getting ripe!
HAPPY BIRTHDAY!

Another popular format is the humorous "mechanical" card. These were quite popular several years ago, but they declined somewhat when their production costs started becoming prohibitive. Mechanical cards are particularly appealing to customers because there is some sort of action when the card is opened.

One common type of mechanical card is the pop-up, a card in which part of the inside design pops up as the card is opened. The sentiment in a pop-up card should tie in with the mechanical action:

    [outside]   [tired-looking mare]
THE OLD GRAY MARE
Ain't what she used to be . . .

    [inside]   [mare kicking, hind legs pop up]
But there's plenty of KICK
in the OLD TALE yet!
HAPPY BIRTHDAY!

Another type of mechanical is what is called a slider. This is a card that is folded and die-cut in such a way that part of the inside slides when the card is opened. One particularly effective slider is the following card which features a slot machine. When the card is opened, three birthday cakes slide into view in the three windows of the machine:

    [outside]   Slotted for a birthday?

    [inside]   Pullin' for a happy one for you!

Special die-cuts provide yet another humorous format:

        [die-cut hole in fence; see through to what appears to be the legs of a slender young woman]

[outside]   A Birthday "Peephole"
For men only!
Just peek inside and you'll see sumpin' cute!
[inside design: cow; legs that appeared to belong to a woman belong to the cow]

[inside]   Here she is, Mister!
Ain't she a Beaut!
HAPPY BIRTHDAY,
YOU OL' REPROBATE!

There are opportunities in humorous cards for the writer who doesn't mind putting in a lot of time on a single idea. You have to familiarize yourself with all the different types of folds, and you have to be constantly on the lookout for new ideas that can be adapted into successful humorous cards.

You'll want to spend a lot of time at greeting card counters becoming acquainted with the kinds of cards that different companies are making.

The National Association of Greeting Card Publishers (170 Mason St., Greenwich, Connecticut 06830) puts out a list of publishers that will consider freelance ideas, and details needs and payment rates.

Amberly Greeting Card Co., Box 37902, Cincinnati 45222

American Greetings Corp., 10500 American Rd., Cleveland 44144

Barker Greeting Card Co., Rust Craft Park, Dedham, Massachusetts 02026

Charm Craft Publishers, Inc., 34 34th St., Brooklyn, New York 11232

Custom Card of Canada, Ltd., 1239 Adanac St., Vancouver, British Columbia, Canada V6A2C8

The Drawing Board, Inc., 256 Regal Row, Dallas 75221

Fran Mar Greeting Cards, Ltd., Box 1057, Mt. Vernon, New York 10550

Freedom Greeting Card Co., Inc., 409-1/2 Canal's End Rd., Bristol, Pennsylvania 19007

Gibson Greeting Cards, Inc., 2100 section Rd., Cincinnati 45237

Vivian Greene, Inc., 15240 NW 60th Ave., Miami Lakes, Florida 33014

Hallmark Cards, Inc., Contemporary Design Dept., 25th and McGee, Kansas City, Missouri 64141

Mark 1, 1733 W. Irving Park Rd., Chicago 60613

Norcross, Inc., 950 Airport Rd., West Chester, Pennsylvania 19380

The Paramount Line, Inc., 400 Pine St., Pawtucket, Rhode Island 02863

Rust Craft Greeting Cards, Inc., Rust Craft Park, Dedham, Massachusetts 02026

Sunshine Art Studios, Inc., 45 Warwick St., Springfield, Massachusetts 01101

Warner Press Publishers, 1200 E. 5th St., Box 2499, Anderson, Indiana 46011

17

Writing for Advertising

Johnny Carson thinks that the funniest things on tv are the commercials. He proves it annually by devoting a good part of one program to the best humor commercials of the year.

Shirley Polykoff wrote the tongue-in-cheek ad for Clairol hair coloring — "Does she or doesn't she? Only her hairdresser knows for sure." The whimsy not only propelled Clairol to millions of dollars of sales, but jetted Shirley into the Advertising Hall of Fame and shortly thereafter into her own multi-million dollar business.

Stan Freberg gets $25,000 just to write one 30-second tv commercial for Jeno's frozen pizza. The former comedy team of Dick and Bert charged $10,000 and up to write one 60-second radio spot. Even modestly successful writers of humor advertising in print, radio and tv pick up $1,500 per script.

Humor ads are growing in popularity. Said John Martins, "Humorous advertising is doing the job. The American consumer has so many distractions, so much to do, so much information clamoring for his attention, that off-beat advertising is about the only decent way of getting and holding his attention." Adds Freberg, whose company uses the motto *Ars Gratia Pecuniae* (art for the sake of money), "I'm not convinced that advertising is necessary, but if we must live with it, the idea is to make it bearable. The advertising business does not have the right to bore the blazes out of 200 million Americans. Even a bad humor ad is less boring that watching arrows running around people's stomachs."

The humor club membership includes many of the biggest names in advertising: Coca Cola, Polaroid, Xerox, General Mills, Bic Pen, Alka Seltzer, E.F. Hutton, Blue Nun wine, Chiffon margarine, Exxon, *Time,* Kellogg's, Heinz, Huffy bags, Stroh's and Miller beers, and scores of other blue-chip corporations. Typical of the humor value is the rationale of Timex executive Paul Kuavis: "We have to take the consumer by the shirt to say, 'We've got something different.' "

It is also used successfully by some of the smallest advertisers in the country: Larry Robinson, a San Francisco Chevy dealer in Superman leotards flew from car to car extolling each virtue and price. "Of course I feel silly sometimes," he said, "but I'd rather be silly and sell cars than look nice and go broke." In St. Louis, appliance dealer Steve Mizerany cavorted in a churning washing machine, rollerskated through his stores and chatted with pet monkeys. In Kansas City, a Ford dealer co-starred with a cow, and at the end of his "low, low price" pitch, the camera focused on the cow's udder over the words, "and that's no bull."

The most successful cracker-barrel humorist since Will Rogers is Frank Perdue, an East Coast chicken wholesaler who hinted that he critically examined every one of his millions of farm poultry with the theme, "It takes a tough man to make a tender chicken." The public loved this scrawny, tough talking chicken plucker with an egg-shaped head and a nose like a beak. He not only has his name on every chicken, he looks like one, too.

But humor is the most difficult of all advertising copywriting. Advertising is a very subjective business. While it is heavily researched, there are few hard facts — as in science or math — that are unqualified.

Put down rules on how to create winning advertising and, undoubtably, someone will soon break the rules and score a product smash that will be, like Wendy's, "hot and juicy."

Advertising is first a business, secondly an art form. Product success is measured at the cash register and your personal success is measured at the bank, not necessarily by the award certificates.

Give 100 creative directors the same assignment with the same set of facts and you will, of course, get 100 different campaigns. Unless someone tried them all, it would be impossible to predict which one would succeed best.

Controversy is epidemic in the profession, and your ability to win debates is as much a skill as the ability to create ideas.

For example, there are those who are strongly for (or against) such creative concepts as testimonial advertising using paid celebrity endorsers. You can get into fist fights in creative meetings when the subject of comparative advertising comes up — where a client's ad evaluates his competitor's by name. Some think it effectively and dramatically permits the public to have the facts. Others think it's an unethical cheap shot because only the client selects the battleground on which the public must compare competition.

There are those who believe in limiting the advertising message content to one unique selling proposition (U.S.P.) and repeating it ad nauseam. There are just as many who believe facts don't count, but a brand image (or brand personality) subliminally affects the consumer to believe that the Marlboro man "is me and my kind of product."

There are those who believe in sex symbols and there are others who are convinced you should keep your fantasies in the bedroom. There are specialists who are convinced that mail order or retail price advertising is the only "true" advertising and that the rest is as wishy as cheap perfume.

And finally, there are those, like John Kenneth Galbraith and Ralph Nader, who believe that advertising misleads the public, is wasteful and is a misallocation of the nation's resources.

It is in this climate that your humor advertising material must struggle.

Those for humor, like Stan Freberg, believe that "the listener has been beaten about the ear with the baseball bat of hard sell for so long that it is a little hard to get the message through the scar tissue."

Ed Graham, Jr., believes that "commercials should be created to appeal to a sense of enjoyment rather than a sense of logic. Humor advertising causes sales to go up." But academic researchers have not been able to verify Graham's contention. Today all that research indicates is that there is no difference in attitude change or retention between humorous and serious versions of the same message. The best that Brian Sternthal and C. Samuel Craig, professors who assessed the role of humor in persuasion experiments, can speculate is that since "most commercials are perceived to be dull, then the addition of humor may enhance the audience's perception of the message source."

Critics agree on one major point. All the world may love a clown, but nobody buys from one. Andy Rooney claims, "Humor doesn't have much stature in this country, and I think that's because there isn't any in the Bible."

John Caples went one step further. "Copy should sell, not just entertain. Remember, there's not one funny line in the two most influential books ever written — the Bible and the Sears catalog."

There are a long list of theoretical hypotheses that are used by both sides to support their pro or con contentions.

1. Since people enjoy humor, it may help infiltrate advertising defenses, but people's involvement, even laughter, can distract from the sales message.

2. Humor advertising encourages the retelling of the funny parts, but anywhere from 50 to 89% of the audience, who can remember the amusing content, cannot recall the name of the product or the sponsor.

3. Before learning can become effective, you must secure your audience's attention, and people find that humor quickly attracts attention, but if they're in the mood to be entertained, they resent being tricked into a sneaky sales message.

4. Humor enhances persuasion by interfering with the process of counter-arguing and thereby reduces sales resistance, but it can negatively affect the favorable perception of the product by those who feel that the humor is in questionable taste.

5. Humor is an antidote to the monotonous sameness of advertising formats, but humor ads, frequently self-satisfying and self-conscious, often go over the head of the audience.

6. Good humor advertising must have clever copy, but the humor point of view may not focus on the important sales points that a consumer may need in order to justify a purchase.

7. Humor is successful only when it entertains the public, but advertising is successful only when it sells the public. Unfortunately, says Herman Davis, humor has two chances to fail. It can be unfunny and fail, or it can be funny but fail because the heavy desire to be witty or clever obfuscates the product value.

In addition to the theoretical controversy, the creative strategy is complicated by other important marketing facts:

Most products in each category are almost impossible to differentiate on the basis of performance or taste. More often than not, the public conception of the product difference is a result of product positioning through advertising.

There is an overwhelming amount of information attempting to get through to the public, and every day each one of us is exposed to approximately 750, perhaps as many as 1,000, advertising messages. If you could remember one from yesterday, you would be a very perceptive individual.

The public has become increasingly sophisticated and increasingly skeptical — not only about advertising and products, but about all institutions, public and private. In 1975 approximately 61% of the public felt advertising "insults my intelligence." By 1980, the figure had risen 10% and the total negative audience reached an impressive two out of three people interviewed. "The consumer is not a moron," said David Olgilvy. "She is also your wife."

Each year thousands of new products come onto the market, and while only 10% are successful, that still means that nearly half of the products we purchase today were not on the market 10 years ago. Therefore, advertising must be more effective than just maintaining brand share. It must also focus on need, it must introduce a product which fulfills that need, and finally it must convince the public that the sponsor's product is better than any competition.

The cost of advertising production, media, research and promotion has made it too expensive to experiment except under very controlled conditions. More importantly, it has made the prospect of failure so terrifying that a pernicious disease, which Richard Karp called "youth fogyism," breeds timidity and play-it-safe attitudes among middle management on both the agency and the client sides. Bill Dana once wrote a joke in which his character, Jose Jiminez, is a rancher. "The name of my ranch is the Bar Nine, Circle Z, Rocking O, Flying W, Lazy R, Crazy Eight, Bar Seven, Happy Tow, Flying Nun, Lazy Six, Bar Five ranch. But we don't have many cattle. Very few survive the branding." The same can be said about selling humor ads. Considering the multi-level hierarchy for decision-making in agencies, and these obstacles doubled again on the client side, it is a wonder any humor "survives the branding."

But wonder of wonders, statistics indicate that there were 42,000 different tv commercials last year and approximately 18% used humor, depending upon your definition of humor.

The above figure includes all spots which used one or more verbal gimmicks (puns, understatements, one-liners and epigrams), humor celebrities, or audio-visual situations involving satire, irony or something graphically ludicrous. (And, the joke goes, some of this humor was intentional.)

Of the seven to eight thousand tv commercials which used humor, a higher percentage were noted in some respect by the public when compared to recall responses of all other types of advertising.

The problem with all this marketing mastication is that scholars attempt to equate humor advertising effectiveness with persuasion. No research has delved into the results conditioned by repeated exposures of humor vs. straight-sell ads. I suspect that the results would show that quality humor attracts attention more, softens up the recipient more and is more memorable.

It would also show that the name of the brand (and sometimes the name of the advertiser) becomes a friendlier symbol, and everything else being equal (quality, taste, price, availabilty, etc.), scores its biggest achievement at the retail store when the consumer has to make that split-second buying decision. Quality humor has as many varieties as Heinz, but it is not a panacea for inferiority.

Humor advertising also wins a higher proportion of industry awards, and this generates columns of favorable publicity for those agencies and creative people involved. Louis Auchincloss once wrote: "Prizes are for the birds. They fill the head of one writer with vanity and 30 others with misery." My advice is quite the opposite. Don't be put off from competing. When you are successful in the advertising humor writing, or even perceived to be successful, awards help financial rewards become bigger and easier.

THIRTEEN RULES FOR ADVERTISING HUMOR WRITING

A smart man learns from his own mistakes; a wise man learns from the mistakes of others.

Whether you are writing humor for advertising print, broadcast, mail order, highway posters, t-shirts, store signs or table cards, there are at least thirteen general rules that apply to all ad humor and are essential knowledge for any professional writer.

1. *Do not let the plot of your story bury the attention of the product* — i.e., don't take the spotlight off the star. How do you know when this is happening? Ken Roman said that if you could remove the product from the commercial and still have an understandable story, then you have made the product insignificant.

2. *Don't panic when the client says he wants a hard sell commercial.* There is no such thing as hard sell or soft sell. When the commercial effect is irritating, repetitious, mundane, prosaic and obvious, the public labels it "hard sell." When the commercial turns out to be humorous imagery or analogic, the public labels it "soft sell." Nobody likes to be "sold," so any label is just a way of perceiving the public's attitude toward the product. And to a client, "hard sell" means that he will sell merchandise and not waste his money — that's all folks!

3. *Humor comes second — the facts come first!* The object of humor advertising is not entertainment, it is intended solely to encourage the recipient of the message to "buy" something — a product, an idea, a vote, even inaction ("Perform a death-defying act — stop smoking"). Entertainment is the modus operandi, not the objective. If the result of the humor ad — in fact, any advertisement — is not request for action, then the message opportunity has not been properly utilized. An ad must first contain the information you wish the purchaser to act upon, then you can mix in the sweetener.

4. *Do not kid the product!* In order to sell, you must build up respect for what you're selling. In order to buy, a consumer must need or want the product, not the humor. A great deal of entertaining advertising copy works on the theory that everything else is interesting except the product. Do not let your witty and clever copy get in the

way of the product. The product must be the star and everything else in the commercial must be part of the supporting cast.

5. *Do not associate your product with a negative for the sake of humor.* Perrier bottled water once ran a radio commercial in which Socrates, tasting his fatal beverage of hemlock, said, "It's good, but it's not Perrier." Funny? Yes. Good advertising? No!

6. *The name of your product must be indelibly imprinted.* Research at Ohio University by undergraduates in advertising and humor writing classes indicated that where the second- or third-ranked brand used humor, half the time the brand name recall went to the brand with the biggest advertising exposure. Creative humor cannot equalize all advertising factors such as product popularity or media weight.

For example, McCulloch chainsaws used a live beaver with an animated mouth talking about "what I know best," cutting wood. In one particularly memorable commercial, Barney the beaver and his brother are considering buying a chainsaw for their father's birthday because he's getting so old. But when consumers were asked to identify the name of the advertised brand, 55% believed it to be Homelite, 25% didn't know any name and only 20% correctly identified the sponsor.

James Garner freely admits that half the time people believe he and Mariette Hartley are doing commercials for Kodak.

Stroh's beer commercials show men in desperate situations, like a man crawling across the desert suffering from terrible thirst. But when help comes and he is offered a bottle of cold beer, he refuses it because it isn't Stroh's. Nearly 60% of those interviewed believe the beer was Budweiser (brand #1) or Miller's brand (#2).

7. *Write humor directed at the heavy user.* Humor has different appeals to different age ranges; it appeals more to males than females, and it is influenced by geographic locations, ethnic backgrounds and economic strata. Youth humor doesn't work as well for business equipment as it does for beer. Sophisticated wit and satire are not needed for fast food operations. They do better for business air travel and books. The biggest problem for humor writers is that, out of necessity, humor comes from their own background, personality and experiences. The product profile may not match the writer. Don't let somebody over 50 write humor for products designed for college students. Even professors are not in tune with their student's humor — and youngsters are turned off by adults who attempt to use rock expressions and drug humor. As in music, modeling, or photography, there are specialists within the specialty. And that's another reason why the ad humor field is so filled with opportunity for those writers who can develop a defined skill. Somewhere, every day, somebody needs you!

8. *The product must perform in a realistic, honest way.* It is tempting, since comedy uses wild exaggeration, to use the same brush on the product ("Aw, they knew I was kidding"), but even in humor there is no justification for misrepresentation. Again, the product must be the star. Unless the product itself is based upon novelty or whimsy, the spot should never perceive it to be something funny or silly. You can, however, have fun with the product. And that is something else. Bill Cosby and his child friends have fun eating Jell-O and watching the gelatin shimmer and shake. That's fun and it's honest.

9. *Cluster your humor.* Since humor can distract attention from selling information, it is important not to mix the two. Laughing, even reflective thinking about one facetious play-on-words or satirical remark, causes subsequent information to be missed. In a 30-second commercial there is no time for "laugh pauses" which are built into sitcoms, plays and films. Humor should be used either in the beginning of a commercial to attract attention or to close off the spot with a pleasant witticism.

10. *Choose your spokesman carefully.* Humor should be presented with warmth, not jokes. Bill Cosby's personal sincerity and his rapport with children encouraging their natural and funny expressions was the principal reason Jell-O commercials consistently won the "most fun to watch" laurels. More importantly, they boomed Jell-O sales. In his highest rated humor spot, Cosby teaches the children how to eat Jell-O Pudding and the children respond by bursting out laughing at his antics. No jokes. Just warmth and believability.

If you use a celebrity, the product must fit in with his image. Jack Benny played off the theme of parsimony as part of his on-stage personality. So it was logical to use him in commercials when the point of view was economy.

Victor Borge is an authority on piano music, Dean Martin on alcohol, Billy Martin on baseball and Howard Cosell on everything. One of the exceptions to this theory is that Hertz rent-a-car has been using O. J. Simpson for over eight years, and while I personally think the tie-in is meaningless, O. J. Simpson's affiliation with the client has been one of the most lasting of all celebrity endorsements. But I continue to wonder just what expertise does Simpson convey when somebody who can fly through airports really needs a rental car. (A new pair of wings every once in a while, but cars?) Then note that Simpson flies through the sunroof and lands forcefully down in the seat. One day I look forward to his missing the seat by a few inches and landing smack on the gear shift — which is why, I presume, the name of the company is Hertz. Another testimonial I could not fathom was Mr. Magoo for G. E. lightbulbs. The company used this nearsighted, bumbling martinet for years. Since he can't see very well, I often wondered why his delight with one lightbulb over another would have any credibility at all.

Test out celebrities for public acceptance as advertising spokesmen, not only for their popularity.

Spokesmen like Cosby, Garner and Hartley have consistently tested out high.

Bob Hope, Mel Brooks and George Burns are so strong that they frequently overpower the product. The public remembers the star, not the product. ("I saw that funny Bob Hope commercial last night!")

If the client's service is an important part of the product, do not be afraid to let the client, himself, play the fall guy.

Most clients can't act, but that helps the humor. Most clients are also strong egoists (which frequently helped make their business successful) and a high percentage would jump eagerly at the chance to "be on camera." When the client does his own commercials, he gets a closer identity with his product. The idea works better with owners of retail establishments, service firms, products with the owner's name in the title, restaurants and car dealers, than it does with chief executives of manufacturing, financial or transportation corporations where the product is far more important than the personality of the individual. But then again, Frank Borman of Eastern Airlines and Lee Iacocca of Chrysler don't do humor . . . intentionally!

11. *Do not fight logical consumer preferences.* For example, there is always a temptation to do something different in food ads — all of which have a common look of a four-color photo of delicious food ready to be served on a plate. While many other types of food ads have been attempted, survey after survey finds women readers prefer traditional food ads which feature the visual appeal of the food just as it is ready to be admired by those at the table.

If you try humor here it must include the beauty shot and the recipe instructions. And women readers are very selective about their choice of a "role model." They do not seem to care about any models who portray any of their own negative characteristics or those who are depicted in less than a flattering way.

12. *Humor should be written by specialists.* Jingles are written by musical composers, and comic illustrations are drawn by top cartoonists. So, too, should humor be put under the direction of skilled professionals with a successful comedy track record. Funny costs money. Most top agencies agree with this theory. It is encouraging to those interested in becoming a specialized free-lance humor writer to know that there is a void in the advertising marketplace that needs to be filled. It might as well be you as someone else.

About the only reason Madison Avenue copywriters are willing to go along with calling in free-lance humor writing "experts" is that it takes the onus off them if the commercial fails; and about 80% of all advertising fails. Humor ads do not have a greater failure rate, just a greater impact when they are successful.

13. *Don't follow the latest humor fads*! Novelty is part of the creative approach. The problem is that the advertising business is a rat race (and frequently the rats win). One successful creative approach, particularly humor, immediately breeds a dozen imitators. Rarely does the second and third entry do as well as the first, and more frequently they only remind the consumer that "Oh, this commercial is a copy of the funny . . . one!" Copying is an indication of mental bankruptcy. While there are formulas for humor ads, they are not a license for unadulterated imitation.

HUMOR IN PRINT ADVERTISING

There are five major ways in which print advertising utilizes humor:

1. Use of play-on-words or pun headline.
2. Use of an anecdotes in narrative copy.
3. Use of a professional comedian in a testimonial.
4. Use of a humorous photograph.
5. Use of a cartoon or short comic strip.

You can't reason with people who aren't paying attention.

The first purpose of a humorous headline is to stop the reader from glancing at the illustration and then turning the page. It's the sugar-coated hook that intrigues the reader to go on to the body copy.

Many copywriters play down body copy as being statistically insignificant. Research shows that only 10 to 15% of all readers actually take the time to read the full ad after noting the headline. Therefore, some believe, 90% of the impact of an ad is the responsibility of the headline and illustration. Clever writing from then on just doesn't count.

There are a few things wrong with that bizarre rationale. Not only is the arithmetic faulty, but the small percent who do read all your ad are the heavy users, the ones most likely to buy and your client's most desirable customers. The object of the humor headline is to build interest in the body. Every line has two objectives: (1) to sell the project and (2) to sell the next line of copy.

Humor must be consistent throughout the ad. Otherwise the reader feels he's been subtly tricked. Most humor ads are like rating a racehorse: fast start, no finish. With that kind of reputation, the horse would have a very short racing career.

Humor, however, is much more difficult in print than broadcast because there is no preparation time in print — the humor is immediately effective or it isn't.

The most frequent, and the most simple, method of using humor is the headline pun or what is known as the play-on-words. It works most effectively in print. The result of a good pun gets a smile of comprehension and sometimes even a grunt of approval from readers, while the same pun told verbally would, at best, elicit a groan. Why we groan and frequently add, "that's terrible" when we hear a pun, I haven't the "soggiest" idea. Punny is not very funny. It's a Pun-Dora's Box. It's a clever and witty bubble that is bright for only a moment — then pops off into oblivion.

But many creative directors stake their reputation on this method. The line "Our team always does well on the road" over a group photo of National Car Rental reservation clerks seated in a yearbook team setting, is typical of this play-on-words humor.

The headline may run above or below the picture, depending on what you want the reader to see first. Most art directors prefer having the play-on-words appear above the three-quarter-page illustration. Then when you see the product, the cliche or pun becomes obvious. By putting the line under the picture, you are encouraging the reader to already start to form the idea in his mind," "Oh, that's a group of reservation clerks." Then, the headline teases the reader into understanding something more than what he first observed. Both ways work. The first utilizes the humor technique of using the picture as the surprise. The second uses the headline like a surprise caption in a cartoon.

Another example is one of Doyle Dane Bernbach's Volkswagen ads.

"What is the use of saying all the right things in the world if nobody is going to read them? And nobody is going to read them if they are not said with freshness, originality and imagination," said William Bernbach.

So the most famous of Volkswagen ads simply showed the car with the headline, "LEMON." The copy described how a careful VW inspector had examined and considered this car a "lemon" because it had a blemish in the glove compartment chrome. Suppose they had merely said, "Every VW must pass rigid inspection." How many ads and how much money would it have taken to make the same point that was made in one creative stroke with the one word headline "LEMON"?

"The difference between the right word and almost the right word is the difference between lightning and the lightning bug," said Mark Twain.

CARTOON ADS

The popularity of comic strips and cartoons in general has encouraged some advertising people to use these devices extensively in print ads.

Cartoons are a medium for which there is universal appeal. Since 1932, research continues to prove that next to the front page, newspaper readers prefer cartoons more than any other section or service.

Cartoon ads also get high scores in recall studies. A cartoon suggests fun, and America is a land of balloon readers.

Another group that likes black and white cartoon ads are frugal clients because cartoons cost much less to produce than four-color illustrations.

Leading the pack in use of cartoons are advertisers from banks (who have discovered that money can be funny), oil companies (Mobil, Shell), airlines (United), utilities (Bell, American Electric Power), office equipment (Xerox, General Electric, Pitney Bowes, Western Electric, Kodak), liquor (Chivas), magazines (*Barron's, People*), food (Starkist), and 85% of children's cereals. Some cartoonists refuse to draw for cigarettes, nuclear power and insurance companies, although New England Life ads, by Rowland Wilson, are among the most memorable and have run for years. The senior citizen of cartooning ads is Chivas Regal, which first commissioned cartoons in 1963 and is still running them.

The agency comes up with the first idea and writes a caption. Then the cartoonist starts, working somewhere between the creative platform of the ad agency and the independent free-wheeling ideas of the artist. "If they didn't like my ideas, they shouldn't hire me in the first place," said one cartoonist. "Frankly, a lot of ads would be better if they gave the artist more freedom."

New Yorker cartoonists are the most avidly used but clients are not allowed to reprint *New Yorker* cartoons in advertising material. In order for *New Yorker Magazine* to keep their editorial matter "pure," they even forbid any advertiser to use the magazine's type style for captions.

Name cartoonists love the opportunities for work outside the traditional magazine and newspaper markets. One artist, who makes many times his *New Yorker* income by developing advertising material and greeting cards, is George Booth, referred to as the wackiest of cartoonists. His stock in trade is complacent cats, dour dogs and eccentric-looking characters. His goal "is to make people smile . . . and maybe even chuckle once in a while. The need is great," he notes. Booth's tools are simple: a Bic ball point pen, a felt-tipped marker and a pad of 9 x 12 ledger paper. The most important tool of his trade, however, is his imagination. Booth averages $600 for a *New Yorker* cartoon, but gets a fee from $1,500-$3,000 for a finished cartoon ad. Once one agency offered him $750 for a simple cartoon ad because that was all they had in the budget. "That is also my fee," said Booth.

In advertising, the caption is generally where the humor lies. The drawing, while fun to look at, should neither be outrageous nor wacky. It features the client product, but frequently the product is presented in an incongruous setting.

Herb Valen, a former gag writer, is an agent who represents 18 *New Yorker* cartoonists in their dealings with ad agencies. He also handles less famous cartoon illustrators.

"Sometimes cartoonists go too far or almost too far in trying to be funny," he said. "It can be like overacting. It can border on being grotesque, I guess, but then life is grotesque."

In a sense, cartoon advertising is borrowing interest because the cartoon style promises the reader that he will be amused instead of merely being sold something. Businessmen seem more comfortable being personified in cartoons. They expect the drawings to depict them as happy, witty and friendly. They poke fun, but in a gentle way. Cartoonists can draw an affluent corporate executive and make you feel tremendous empathy for him.

Cartoons are best used to lead into the ad text and make it more inviting. But an advertising cartoon must not use the switch. It should not betray the confidence or injure the sensibilities of the reader by springing a gag which has nothing to do with the real purpose of the ad.

A humorous cartoon ad should admit from the start that it is an ad. Trick headlines for cartoons can have no other purpose than to deceive the reader.

If a cartoon is too flip, it may get a reaction, "That's cute." But it will not make a sale.

Cartoon characters in ads should portray positive identity. Readers do not want to identify themselves with weirdos or monsters.

One way clients evaluate the effectiveness of a cartoon is to try to imagine the scene by just reading the caption. If their mental image is better than the illustrator's, it's back to the drawing board.

ADVANTAGES OF HUMOR IN ADVERTISING

Good humor advertising not only can run for years, it is in a high percentage of the most famous ad campaigns of all times. In celebration of its 75th anniversary, the Chicago Ad Club selected "The greatest ideas in Chicago advertising history." Nearly 25% of them were based on humor: "Good things from the garden of the Jolly (ho, ho, ho) Green Giant"; 9 Lives Morris the Cat; Fibber McGee & Molly for Johnson's Glo-Coat; "Put a tiger in your tank" for Exxon; and "When it rains it pours," for Morton Salt.

One of the most successful adult ads using humor and animation (the combination has been used since 1950 in children's ads for

Kellogg's Rice Krispies — "Snap, Crackle, and Pop") was the series designed by Ed Graham, Jr., for Piel's Beer. It used Bob Elliot and Ray Goulding as the voices of the ficticious brothers, Bert and Harry Piel.

The commercials have been regarded by many as the best example of lighthearted commercials of all time.

But in 1961, after seven years and the most favorable reviews, Piel's suddenly discontinued them because, they claimed, the advertising was being noted but was not increasing Piel's sales.
The facts, however, were that the audience loved the commercials but hated the taste of the beer. Bert and Harry fans raised such a hullabaloo about the disappearance of the commercial that after two years the company decided that they had made a mistake in "killing" them and brought them back with great fanfare.

Here's an example of their "truth in advertising" commercial, an indication of why the public felt so sympatico with their humor.

HARRY: I'm Harry Piel. You know, it's not an accident that Piel's beer has a reputation for "fresh-poured flavor."
BERT: Er, wait a minute, Harry. Er, yeah, that's all right.
HARRY: Just pour a glass of today's Piel's and you'll notice its long-lasting head. . . .
BERT: Er, probably.
HARRY: Now that's a big reason why Piel's tastes extra good.
BERT: Er, virtually.
HARRY: . . . keeping flavor and freshness from escaping.
BERT: We certainly hope . . . heh.
HARRY: And that's why Piel's fresh-poured flavor lasts all the way down.
BERT: Many impartial people have stated that.
HARRY: Why do you keep qualifying everything I say, Bert?
BERT: Well, no exaggerated advertising claims for us. I'm taming down your pitch.
HARRY: But why? Every word was true.
BERT: Look, Harry. . . . An honest, ordinary description of Piel's beer sounds like an exaggeration. If I'd never tasted it, I'd assume you were talking through your hat . . . figuratively speaking.
HARRY: Well, if that's true, everyone who hasn't, please try today's Piel's immediately, and then you'll know I'm not exaggerating.
BERT: Most likely.
HARRY: Oh, now, Bert. . . .
BERT: All right — definitely!

Few humor commercials have had the constant appeal of the Polaroid camera spot featuring James Garner and Mariette Hartley. The two spar like a typical married couple — with banter that permits the wife to put down the celebrity husband. Now, that's normal!

Introduced by the team in 1976, the OneStep Plus camera became the fastest selling camera in the U.S., instant or conventional. So popular were Garner-Hartley (he continued to get top billing) that they were elected "Star Presenters of the Year" by *Advertising Age* in 1979.

The important lesson from these classical commercials is that the audience feels they are spending a few minutes with Garner and his "family" on one of their days off.

SCENE: JAMES GARNER AND MARIETTE HARTLEY IN PATIO SETTING
GARNER: This is Polaroid's new OneStep Plus.
HARTLEY: Plus what?
GARNER: Plus an electronic cue light. It always give you the exact light you need.
HARTLEY: How does it know?
GARNER: It has its own electric eye that tells it.
HARTLEY: What if it sends out too much?
GARNER: It can't. It reads the light and stops when it's enough. (GARNER TAKES FLASH PICTURES) So you can get beautiful pictures in minutes every time.
(RAPID DEVELOPMENT OF POLAROID PICTURE)
GARNER: Look, you can't beat that light.
HARTLEY: Beautiful, but I don't think that's the way it works.
GARNER: How do you think it works?
HARTLEY: Some other way (she giggles).
GARNER: Get the OneStep Plus.

THE HUMOR OF SEX ADVERTISING OR GRIN AND BARE IT

Sex is not only the most important subject of humor, it outranks all other subjects combined.

But its use in quality advertising, especially humorous sexual satire, is highly controversial. Controversy or not, it is conspicuous and you had better know how to handle it.

Most commercials which use alluring sex symbols, double entendres, touching of bodies, exposed decolletage and suggestive silhouettes and leers are such obvious infantile parodies that they could never stimulate erotic thoughts or behavior.

Examples are numerous:

> A whole stable of designer jeans commercials which focus mainly on denim-clad behinds. "The tighter they are," said Calvin Klein, "the better they sell." Bottoms are big business. They are also the place where designers put their name in logos.

★ ★ ★

> Harvey's Bristol Cream Sherry, in which a forthright woman invites a man to her apartment for a drink. So what's new? Didn't they call Mae West a comedienne?

★ ★ ★

> Noxzema shaving cream once featured a commercial with Farrah Fawcett, who helps a lonely woodsman shave. After he remarks happily, "I haven't seen a woman in nine years," a can of shaving cream bursts not-so-subtly through the earth's crest. That was known as a hard act to follow.

Although there is no question that it gets immediate attention, sex in advertising is the last taboo to fall. Yet, while it is called "new wave" advertising, there is nothing new about using humorous sex to sell goods. Like cultural pap, it plays to the vicarious child in everybody.

For years print ads have featured well-endowed young women sprawled across the hoods of sportscars. In tobacco advertising, attractive girls with hypnotic, sensuous poses urged Chesterfield smokers to "blow some my way."

The "cheapest shots" are the thousands of double entendre headlines, such as the Campari "The first time is never the best," or the "I do it every day" headline for Buf-puf. Some see these "play on words" as humorous. Others, like Wilson Byron Keyes, find subliminal sex in every word, every photograph, every glance — even in ice cubes.

Frank Perdue, the chicken distributor, declared in some commercials that "my legs aren't moving as fast as my breasts."

The California Avocado Commission, to show how avocados are helpful to diet-conscious people, used Angie Dickinson sprawled sexily across a two-page spread of recipes under the headline, "Would this body lie to you?"

In the October 1981 issue of top fashion magazines, Arpege Perfume ran a two-page spread of one of the most humorous sex ads of the year. The left-hand picture shows a young woman, seated luxuriously on a chaise lounge in a softly lighted living room. Beside her is a champagne bucket. The caption: "The Promise Made." The picture on the right hand side seems identical, except it is obviously hours later. There are only a few changes — a jacket and earrings removed, two empty champagne glasses, the bottle turned upside down in the bucket, the telephone off the hook. On her face, a Mona Lisa smile of satisfaction. This time the bottom caption reads: "The Promise Kept."

A subtle message of desire fulfilled employing subtle humor and good taste. That's fun!

HUMOR ADVERTISING FOR RADIO

In 1973 Bert Berdis, a former comedy writer for Jackie Gleason, joined his partner Dick Orkin, an actor, to form a team that won more advertising Clios and other industry awards than all other independent producers put together.

Before they split in 1982, Dick and Bert championed one of the best formats for radio humor — the 60-second playlet that involves a conflict and a resolution. There are two options for this miniature story: (1) humorous characters who appear in a normal situation, or (2) a humorous incident that revolves around normal people.

Their commercials had the rare property of making listeners both laugh and buy.

Like carefully scripted plays, their technique encouraged the listener to believe he is eavesdropping on a private conversation. There is a bit of voyeurism in all of us. "Their work is instantaneously recognizable," said *Newsweek,* "not only for their playlet formula approach, but for the 60-second descent into absurdity, a riotous glimpse of the dark side of the marketplace."

"There really isn't anything you can't sell with humor," Berdis claims. "An important must, however, is a client with a strong sense of humor about himself. We never make fun of the product, but we do have fun with the product — that's a big difference most copywriters fail to see. The image of the product does not take a beating. Rather the product and the advertiser acquire likeability."

Using the imagination that it provides, radio is the most powerful medium for humor. It is the most accurate because a listener's imagination is perfect. When you tell me that the girl in the spot is the most beautiful I have ever seen, my mind conjures up what I believe to be exquisite beauty. No actress could achieve such perfection. My wife, maybe — but an actress, never.

Here's one of Dick and Bert's final scripts — as recorded:

MAN 1 – Welcome back from vacation, boss.
MAN 2 – Oh, thanks Glubman. How did everything go here at the warehouse?
1 – Oh, fine. No problem.
2 – The big shipment of eggs got out all right?
1 – Eggs? Oh, eggs all gone. Yes sir. One little problem though, our lift-truck broke down. (sounds of chicks)
2 – What was that?
1 – I said our lift-truck broke down.
2 – Do you have a chickie in here?
1 – No, no, she's outside typing.
2 – Well, I hope you called Caterpillar to rent another lift-truck.
1 – Caterpillar rents lift-trucks?
2 – Yes, for breakdowns or seasonal overloads, your Caterpillar lift-truck dealer rents almost any kind of late model lift-truck. They'll deliver them fast and on time. (sounds of chicks again) Do you hear that?
1 – Oh, yes, you said for breakdowns or for seasonal overloads Caterpillar rents lift-trucks.
2 – (Chicks sound) Not that. THAT! You have a baby chick in your lunchpail.
1 – What do you know? One of the eggs must have hatched.
2 – I think there are more in your drawers!
1 – Aw, it doesn't feel like there's any . . .
2 – Not those drawers. THOSE drawers! Just exactly how many eggs hatched?
1 – Just a couple, sir, but don't open the drawer . . . I don't think you'd . . .
2 – And what do you call this?
1 – Well, this one's called Fluffy. And this one's called Pinky. And this one . . .
2 – No! Glubman! Glubman! . . .
ANNCR – Announcer: Whatever your lift-truck problems, your Caterpillar lift-truck dealer can quickly rent you the solution . . . and without a peep! (Sounds of chicks fades off.)

THE BASIC RADIO FORMULA

A commercial that tries to do too much is confusing. Pure and simple, according to Hank Seiden, is the essence of all advertising, and humor advertising even more so. That is why this seven-point formula for radio humor seems so patently simple. The key exclamations that tell the whole story are only eleven words.

1. Hey!
1. Oh!
3. That's me!
4. Get him!
5. No kidding?
5. Wow! -
7. Say goodbye!

Let's have a more detailed look at this formula.

1. *HEY!* Since radio is a medium which is used as a background companion while each individual is doing some other activity — driving, studying, housework, loving — it is first necessary to attract his attention so he turns from hearing to listening. The script must call for some audio device that not only attracts attention (like a telephone ring, street noises, an unusual voice, musical intro) but immediately separates the commercial from any previous programming sound. Humor spots using voices do better on radio stations that have a heavy music format.

2. *OH!* In the first three to five seconds of a radio commercial you must clearly establish the locale and the major characters. The audience must not need more information or ask themselves questions like, "What in the hell is going on?" You are working in fractions of seconds and anything that impedes comprehension encourages the listener to mentally tune out and go back to his primary activity. Unlike students, listeners are not being rewarded for close attention, and even students are notable for daydreaming. I never teach class before ten in the morning, because I like to work in front of a live audience.

3. *THAT'S ME!* The listener must empathize with the situation or the characters. Dick Orkin thinks that the listener must say, "Oh, I've been in that spot myself before." If not personally, he should at least believe that the situation could happen. If this part of the formula is done successfully, the audience is interested in knowing how cleverly the hero (or fall guy) is going to work himself out of the embarrassing situation. And since humor depends so much on surprise endings, you have set up a perfect humor platform.

This is why most situations utilize stereotyped characters. Farmers in ads talk like farmers in *Reader's Digest.* Used car salesmen machine-gun their delivery and, unfortunately, housewives shouldn't sound like PhD's.

4. *GET HIM!* That's not a command, but an exclamation of derision. This is the humor part in most commercial. It can be clustered in one section or more frequently stirred in the scene throughout the commercial. The fall guy is unwinding the rope which is about to hang him. It is important that the audience quickly identifies the fall guy, or the competitive product at which we will be laughing. It also must know the proper way for the bumpkin to act or talk, utilizing the superiority theory of humor. In this scene the outline of the problem or the conflict is completed leaving only the resolution in doubt.

5. *NO KIDDING?* This is the sell portion of the commercial, sometimes known as sponsor's prime time, which, like humor, can come as one copy block or can be shuffled in small doses. The straightman goes over all the product benefits that strategy indicates and in these few precious seconds you frequently win or lose the value of the commercial. It is important that the sales talk not come on so blatantly that the listener feels mousetrapped into an unwelcome pitch. A disillusioned listener will become embarrassed at his own gullibility and in defense will usually direct his anger at the product. It may be wise to insert one or two expressions of skepticism in the hard sell, as Mariette Hartley does in the Polaroid spots, to keep the audience in a superior point of view. After all, no skeptic is converted in a few seconds, so a continuation of facetious "prove it to me" questions or statements confirms what the listener is thinking anyway. The fact that performance humor is based upon a suspension of disbelief doesn't mean that humor advertising can benefit from that association.

6. *WOW!* This is the commercial pay-off. It is frequently no more than a few words, certainly no more than one or two lines. It must resolve the conflict or problem, say something positive about the product and still maintain the mood of the commercial. It is the surprise curve at the end of the straight ball pitch, although it should be something very warm and charming that subtly says to the listener that you'll be a warm, charming and happy person if you'll only follow our advice.

7. *SAY GOODBYE!* George Burns' famous exit line in his Burns and Allen routines was, "Say goodnight, Gracie!" And Gracie would say, "Goodnight everybody," and the audience loved them both. Strangely enough, most people don't know how to say goodbye. They stumble, mumble, and squirm. This applies to boyfriends on a first date and to lecturers getting off the stage. In advertising the formula is simple and effective. In both radio and tv, a distinctively different voice-over or musical jingle is heard, which gives the full name of the product and adds a five- to ten-word tag. It is frequently done vice versa, but I prefer the former choice. Sometimes copywriters like to insert a final bit of humor following the tag — a delayed word of

the fall guy. But this technique immediately takes the listener's mind off the name of the product in exchange for a cheap one-more-time shot at humor. It should be avoided. Like commercial sex, too much can be dangerous to your wealth.

THE DISSECTION OF A RADIO COMMERCIAL

Here is how the above seven ingredients work in an actual radio spot produced by Dick and Bert for a local auto dealer in Libertyville, Illinois.

HUMOR FORMULA

SHEILA:	Sam, you're ready for any pushy car salesman they got here.	*"HEY"* - woman's character voice
SAM:	But I'm still practicing my answers.	*"OH"* - intro of characters and locale
SHEILA:	O.K. When the car sales person first comes up, you say what?	*"THAT'S ME"* - how to handle a pushy car salesman
SAM:	"I'm just looking."	
SHEILA:	O.K. and when he comes around a second time, you say what?	
SAM:	"I haven't made my mind up yet."	
SHEILA:	Good. And when he comes up to you a third time . . . ?	
SAM:	"Beat it, buster, before I break your nose."	
SHEILA:	Ooooh, you're gonna be perfect. This time no salesperson is gonna talk you into the first car you see . . .	
SAM:	But, Sheila, I . . .	

278   COMEDY TECHNIQUES

SHEILA:	Just open the door . . . (Beautiful music, birds chirping)	*"NO KIDDING?"* - Intro of friendly atmosphere and product sell which alternates throughout spot.
BOTH:	Oh, my!	
SALESMAN:	Hello. Welcome to Weil Olds in Libertyville.	
SHEILA:	Sam. Isn't this gorgeous here?	
SALESMAN:	Is this your wife?	
SAM:	No, I'm just looking.	*"GET HIM!"* - Incongruous dialogue
SALESMAN:	Would you like a cup of coffee ma'am?	
SHEILA:	Yes, please.	
SALESMAN:	How do you take it?	
SAM:	I haven't made my mind up yet.	
SHEILA:	Sam, this is marvelous. No pressure. No hyper at Weil, It's a very friendly atmosphere.	*"NO KIDDING?"* -
SALESMAN:	How about coffee for you, sir?	
SAM:	Beat it buster, before I break your nose.	*"GET HIM!"* - Incongruous dialogue
SHEILA:	Hey, relax. You want coffee?	
SAM:	Yeah!	
SHEILA:	Well, tell him what you want in it!	
SAM:	Power steering, power brakes, stereo (fad-	

	ing), reclining steering wheel, clock . . .	
CHORUS:	(Singing)	*"SAY GOODBYE"* -
	Weil Olds in Libertyville	jingle and tag
	Is a beautiful place in the country.	
	Weil Olds in Libertyville	
	Is a beautiful place in the country.	

In 1976, *Time* management felt the magazine was suffering from an image of stuffiness and asked Dick & Bert to try humor to alleviate the ailment. But as in the Caterpillar case history, the orders were that comedy could not degrade the magazine. One result is the commercial below.

Notice the same humor formula: immediate identification of scene, characters and conflict; humor based upon incongruity and ridicule of a fall guy. Note the heavy middle section where the schlemiel almost sings the praises of the product. And finally, to say goodbye, an announcer's voice acts like a coda to remind listeners that the entertainment they have just heard was a commercial for *Time* magazine.

"Puffy Sleeves" was named one of the top ten commercials of the year and is still one of the most frequently played radio commercials because its humor can be repeated endlessly without encountering listener fatigue.

BERT:	Pardon me, sir. Would you step over here to the patrol car please?
DICK:	Oh, h-hello, Officer.
BERT:	Do you have business in this neighborhood, sir?
DICK:	Yes, I live f-four blocks from here . . . It's the brick colonial with the crack in the driveway.
BERT:	What are you doing out this time of night sir?
DICK:	Well, I got all ready for bed and, darn it, if I didn't forget to pick up a copy of *Time* magazine at the newsstand today.
BERT:	What type of coat would you call that, sir?
DICK:	Th-this? This is a h-housecoat. See, I spilled cocoa on mine and I just grabbed my wife's. I guess the puffy sleeves look a little silly. (LAUGH)
BERT:	Want to get in the car, sir?
DICK:	In the car . . .? (DOOR OPEN)
DICK:	See, I just don't go to bed without a *Time* movie re-

280   COMEDY TECHNIQUES

BERT: view or something from the "Modern Living" section . . .
BERT: Yes, sir.
DICK: I tried reading something else but there isn't anything like *Time*. Do you know, Officer, how many editorial awards *Time* magazine has won?
BERT: No, sir.
DICK: And *Time* is so respected — and I'm a firm believer — along with Winston Churchill . . . that you are uh . . . what you read. (PAUSE) Oh, please don't send me up the river just for wearing puffy sleeves.
BERT: You're home, sir.
DICK: I'm home — Oh . . . I thou — thank — God bless you . . . (DOOR OPENS)
DICK: Okay — Bye.
ANNCR: *Time* magazine — the most colorful coverage of the week. Pick up a copy.

BLUE NUN — MAYBE SHE'S SEASICK?

The most famous case history of humor effectiveness in radio advertising is that of Blue Nun, a German white wine imported by Schieffelin & Company.

The wine had been assigned to one of New York's most audacious admen, Jerry Della Femina, in the late 1960's with a miniscule ad budget of approximately $200,000. Femina created the slogan: "Blue Nun. The wine that goes with every meal." The comedy team of Jerry Stiller and his wife, Anne Meara, were engaged for a series of irreverent commercials that spoofed the Blue Nun name by getting it confused with sisters of the church.

The radio commercials were 60-second vignettes in which two single people meet and decide to have a bottle of wine. Stiller played the part of a pseudo-sophisticate who wouldn't know Dom Perignon from Morgan David, and Meara played a simple, practical gal on a blind date.

The commercials were targeted for the mass audience of "gourmet" aficionados who are firmly convinced that red wine goes with meat, white wine with fish. Not so, the client wanted the world to know! White wine is correct with any dish. But rather than intimidate an audience who does not know how to order wine in either a retail store or in a restaurant, the humor message was directed at a gullible girl.

Here are two examples: When it comes to radio humor, they are works of art.

THE RESTAURANT

ANNCR: Stiller and Meara
STILLER: Good evening, Miss. Will you be dining alone?
MEARA: (IN TEARS) Yes.
STILLER: What can I get you?
MEARA: Manicotti.
STILLER: Oh, I'm sorry we're all out.
MEARA: No, I mean Carmine Manicotti. He just broke our engagement. He had his mother call and tell me.
STILLER: Oh, the swine.
MEARA: No, she was very sweet about it.
STILLER: No, I meant Carmine. Anyway, may I suggest the Surf and Turf tonight?
MEARA: Is that some new singles bar?
STILLER: No, the Surf and Turf is our new delicious combination of lobster tail and filet mignon. Perhaps to raise your spirits, a very special wine.
MEARA: Can I get a wine that goes with seafood and meat?
STILLER: Certainly. May I bring a little Blue Nun to your table?
MEARA: I'm sure she'd be very sympathetic, but I'd much rather be alone.
STILLER: No, Miss, Blue Nun is a wine. A delicious white wine that's correct with any dish. It goes as well with meat as it does with fish. And, perhaps after dinner, cantaloupe.
MEARA: I don't see cantaloupe on the menu.
STILLER: No, that's me. Stanley Cantaloupe. I get off at eleven. Maybe we could go out on the town.
ANNCR: Blue Nun, the delicious white wine that's corect with any dish. Another Sichel wine, imported by Schieffelin and Co., New York.

THE CRUISE SHIP

STILLER: Excuse me, the cruise director assigned me this table for dinner.
MEARA: Say, weren't you the fella at the costume ball last night dressed as a giant tuna? With scales, the gills and the fins?
STILLER: Yeah — that was me.
MEARA: I recognized you right away.
STILLER: Were you there?
MEARA: I was dressed as a mermaid so I had to spend

most of the night sitting down. Did you ever try dancing with both legs wrapped in aluminum foil?
STILLER: No, I can't say I have. Did you order dinner yet?
MEARA: I'm having the filet of sole.
STILLER: Hmmm. The filet mignon looks good. Would you like to share a bottle of wine?
MEARA: Terrific.
STILLER: I noticed a little Blue Nun at the Captain's table.
MEARA: Poor thing. Maybe she's seasick.
STILLER: No, Blue Nun is a wine. A delicious white wine.
MEARA: Oh, we can't have a white wine if you're having meat and I'm having fish.
STILLER: Sure we can. Blue Nun is the white wine that's correct with any dish. Your filet of sole. My filet mignon.
MEARA: Oh, it's so nice to meet a man who knows the finer things. You must be a gourmet?
STILLER: No, as a matter of fact, I'm an accountant. Small firm in the city. Do a lot of tax work . . . (fade out)
ANNCR: Blue Nun. The delicious white wine that's correct with any dish. Another Sichel wine imported by Schieffelin & Company, New York.

IN COMEDY, NEW IS SPELLED "NU?"

The selection of which humor format to use must be based upon public curiosity and novelty. In Yiddish, the expression is "Nu?"

For example, to demonstrate the simplicity of office dictating equipment it would be obvious to have a discussion between a boss and an efficiency-minded secretary. But if there is to be humor in the commercial, there must be incongruity — something which makes the secretary different and the boss memorable. In the first attempt, Ann Meara plays a female secretary who works nights as an auto mechanic. The situation is artificial and therefore the humor sounds forced. However, in the second commercial, the secretary is Jerry Stiller, an ex-pro football player, and his boss is a modern female corporate executive. In a contemporary world filled with new situations, this playlet starts off with tension as well as intrigue.

THE AUTO MECHANIC

ANNCR: Here's Stiller & Meara for Lanier Dictating Equipment.
MEARA: Hi. I'm Donna Sue Billie Jean Garbonzo from Dial-a-Secretary.
STILLER: You're dressed like a mechanic.
MEARA: I work nights in a body shop.

STILLER: Great. I needed a secretary. Listen, wash your hands. Put your tool kit in the corner. Sit here. Take a memo.
MEARA: Take it where? I'm not a messenger.
STILLER: You don't take dictation?
MEARA: You don't use dictation equipment?
STILLER: This is a small company.
MEARA: Maybe it's small because you don't use Lanier dictating equipment. I know, I've been around.
STILLER: I can see that.
MEARA: You could take Lanier's pocket-sized portable with you on trips and work while you're away from work. Lanier's standard cassette units could help you and your secretary get more done while you're in the office.
STILLER: With Lanier, I won't need you. But maybe you could take a look at my car.
MEARA: I already did. It looks like it was attacked by sharks. You need our weekend special. I'll do your points, plugs, shocks, and throw in a lube job — $800.
ANNCR: You can get more done with Lanier Business Products. Look for Lanier in the Yellow Pages under dictating machines.
STILLER: Get outa here! Hey! You got grease all over my lap!

THE PRO FOOTBALL PLAYER

ANNCR: Stiller and Meara for Lanier Dictating Equipment.
MEARA: I have your secretarial application right here, Mr. Piltown.
STILLER: Call me Craig.
MEARA: Well, sit down, Craig.
STILLER: I am sitting.
MEARA: Oh, of course you are. My you're huge.
STILLER: I played fullback for the Pennsylvania Anthracites.
MEARA: How did you get into secretarial work?
STILLER: Well, I was a receptionist, then one of the girls got pregnant so they just moved me up.
MEARA: Uhhh.
STILLER: It's not easy being a secretary. I was the only one around that could handle those old-fashioned belted dictating machines. Boy, are they hard to load! You see, that's my speciality.
MEARA: You won't be needing that Craig. We use Lanier Cassettes. You've heard of Lanier Cassettes?

STILLER: He played with the Texas Cowboys.
MEARA: (laughter) No, Lanier makes cassette dictating equipment. Cassettes are easier to load and they sound better.
STILLER: No belts? Then, you don't need me.
MEARA: Oh yes, I need you. I need you, Craig.
STILLER: Hey lady, you blew in my ear.
MEARA: (sigh) It's lonely at the top.
STILLER: I'm not that kind of a guy.
MEARA: (chuckle) You'll learn. (laugh)
ANNCR: Put standard cassettes' speed and efficiency in your dictation. Give Lanier a hearing. We're in the yellow pages under Dictating Machines.

CAN YOU OVERDO IT? YES, YOU CERTAINLY CAN

The fun goes out when one humor idea is overdone. Here's a script that knocked out the writers when they first conceived it, but repeat performances can give you a pain in the — can.

(SFX: TELEPHONE RINGING:)

WOMAN: Hello. Agency Clearance.
MAN: Hi. We're doing a commercial for Bon Jour jeans. Can we use the word "can" in our commercial?
WOMAN: Of course you can.
MAN: Well, I don't want to open a can of worms . . . but Bon Jour makes tight fitting jeans for young gals . . . so the can we're thinking of . . . probably isn't the can you're thinking of.
WOMAN: Oh! Then I have to can that can.
MAN: Oh, just listen to our commercial . . . and then let us know whether we can . . . or can't.
WOMAN: I bet the melody is the "Can-Can."
MAN: You're uncanny!
MUSIC: (MELODY OF "CAN-CAN" TO DISCO ARRANGEMENT) No jeans fit you in the can-can like
Bon Jour jeans can-can,
like Bon Jour jeans can.
Bon Jour jeans fit you in
the can-can like
no others can-can like no
others can.
No jeans fit you in the can-can like
Bon Jour jeans can-can.
Like Bon Jour jeans can.

(MUSIC UNDER — AS A BED FOR THE BAL-
ANCE OF THE COMMERCIAL)
MAN: So . . . can I?
WOMAN: You certainly can. And can you tell me where I can get Bon Jour jeans.
MAN: I can't do that. But he can!
ANNCR: Bon Jour Jeans for gals.

Here's the right way to use word distortions, close to Spooner-isms, to make an ending funny and contain a bit of surprise. It's for the Minolta copier. Note how Minolta gets mentioned the recommended average six times in a 60-second spot.

WAITER: I got an order for you, chef.
CHEF: What is it?
WAITER: Table six wants the blimp cocktail.
CHEF: You mean shrimp cocktail.
WAITER: And the bean soap.
CHEF: Bean soup!
WAITER: And a bowl of the beef glue.
CHEF: What? Let me see the menu.
WAITER: Okay.
CHEF: Who made this copy. It's all smeared and wrinkled. I can hardly read it.
WAITER: Booth four wants chicken frisbee.
CHEF: Fricassee.
WAITER: What the heck is corn on the cat?
CHEF: Oh, these copies are terrible.
WAITER: What do you want from me, our copier jams up all the time.
CHEF: Get me a Minolta.
WAITER: I don't see Minolta on the menu. Oh, you mean the minestrone.
CHEF: I mean the Minolta EP 310 copier.
WAITER: Ahhh.
CHEF: The Minolta EP 310 has this incredibly short paper path that virtually eliminates paper jam.
WAITER: No kidding.
CHEF: And the Minolta EP 310 even has a self-diagnostic system.
WAITER: How about the bowling banquet in the back room.
CHEF: Yeah?
WAITER: They want the nude cake.
CHEF: You mean nut cake.
WAITER: No, nude cake, where the girl jumps out at the . . .
CHEF: Oh, that.

WAITER: Yeah.
ANNCR: The Minolta EP 310 copier. A business partner you can depend on.

BOY, WERE YOU DRUNK LAST NIGHT!

A frequent humor bit builds into a horror story as the drunk awakes and is told by his friend what he did last night.

Using humor classics in advertising commercials has two advantages: the audience knows the plot so you can skip through such a routine in 30-60 seconds and the audience delights in the misfortune of others — a basic humor condition.

An example of this approach is this script from a Prudential Insurance commercial:

MAN: Hi, Honey. What's new?
WOMAN: Well, the fire's out.
MAN: Fire?
WOMAN: We'll have to re-do the kitchen. Oh, oh, they're coming for the car.
MAN: Car? What car?
WOMAN: Our car.
MAN: Honey . . .
WOMAN: But at least the plumber's ankle is okay.
MAN: The plumber's ankle?
WOMAN: Yeah. He was fixing the broken faucet when the fire broke out.
MAN: Honey . . . honey . . . call . . . call Prudential!
WOMAN: Life insurance?
ANNCR: Now a Prudential agent can provide insurance for your car and your home. Same Prudential planning and service.
WOMAN: It's all taken care of.
ANNCR: Most claims are settled with a phone call. And some people even save money by changing to Prudential for car and homeowner's insurance.
WOMAN: It's nice to save money.
MAN: With someone you know.
WOMAN: By the way, guess who bit the mailman?

COMEDIANS AS SPOKESMEN

As in print advertising, one of the most acceptable tv humor formats is using established comedians as spokespersons. While the benefits are unnecessary to repeat, we might devote some space to some of the problem areas and how to avoid them.

If you use comedy stars, they will fight to get their own professional humor writers to do the material. Being funny is their life's reputation, and they properly feel that their own writers know their style best. They like endorsing products as long as they can endorse a check first, but what is more important to them is the need to continually satisfy their fans. Therefore, they will fight for laughs ("if it's funny, leave it in") more than for what's beneficial for the product.

One of the most difficult to control is Bob Hope, one of the most important people in the United States. That's not only my opinion, it's his, too. He is not beyond ad-libbing in his live commercial spots no matter what the client thinks.

Once he asked the audience to be sure to buy Jell-O. "It may be only a dessert to you, but it's bread and butter to me."

One of his gems was for (or against) Beechnut gum: "I've been chewing Beechnut gum for 25 years. Its price has never changed. It is either a big bargain now, or it was a big gyp then."

Some critics claim that comedians are risky spokesmen since, as Howard Spielman pointed out, "they are not to be taken seriously."

They are also so strong a spokesman that they have the danger of overshadowing your product more than other celebrities. For 11 years, Jonathan Winters, dressed in an all-white sanitation outfit, talking like an Englishman, said, "Hefty." Trouble was, he admitted, people kept asking him if he liked doing those Glad bag commercials. "It tells you something about the bag, or it tells you something about me," Winters said sadly.

Tv commercials generally require a team of two — a copywriter and an art director. They say a story conference is a meeting between two or more creative people, each of whom hopes the other guy has a bright idea.

And if no advertiser buys your material, all is not lost. Comedians have often made commercials the butt of their humor, and they're a market, too.

Steve Martin once devoted an entire hour tv program to ridiculing ad commercials. He would pick odd-ball combinations, like "Honeymoon Butter made with love because it is churned at Motel Dairy Farms in honeymoon suite waterbeds." He opened the program with an invitation: "Who wants to sit around watching other programs where people sing, dance or get shot when you can watch our program and see real people solve real programs — like stains, smells and that embarrassing itch?"

One of the best advertising parodies was a commercial for "Shimmer," a new wild product, on *Saturday Night Live:*

    WOMAN: New Shimmer is a floor wax.
    MAN: No, new Shimmer is a dessert topping.
    WOMAN: It's a floor wax!
    (angry)

MAN: It's a dessert topping!
(angrier)
WOMAN: It's a floor wax, I'm telling you!
(yelling)
MAN: It's a dessert topping, you cow!
ANNCR: Hey, hey, hey. Calm down you two. New Shimmer is a floor wax AND a dessert topping. Here, (to woman) I'll spray some on your mop and (to man) some on your butterscotch pudding.
MAN: Hmmmm. Tastes terrific.
WOMAN: Just look at that shine. But will it last?
ANNCR: Hey. Outlasts every other leading floor wax two to one. It's durable and it's scuff resistant.
MAN: And it's delicious!
ANNCR: Sure is. It perks up everything from an ice cream sundae to a pumpkin pie.
WOMAN: Made from an exclusive non-yellowing formula.
MAN: I haven't even touched my pudding and I'm ready for more.
WOMAN: But what about black heel marks?
ANNCR: Dirt, grime, even black heel marks wipe clean with a damp cloth.
MAN: Hold steady, honey, I'll clean that up.
WOMAN: No problem, sweetheart, not with new Shimmer.
ANNCR: Ha, ha, ha, ha, ha. New Shimmer, for the greatest shine you ever tasted.

WHEN THEY'RE GOOD, THEY'RE GREAT

According to the advertising contest directors, the number of humor commercials winning "best of . . ." category awards is increasing. This success record must be mitigated by several facts: good humor spots are usually more original than straight sell commercials, and each creative director is always trying to impress his peers. Also, each award ceremony is intended to be as much an entertainment evening as it is an industry tribute, and humor commercials always get the biggest audience response.

More importantly, radio comedy well done forces the listener to become involved and think about what is being said. This involvement increases the odds of memorability. And familiarity with a brand name makes the consumer confident when it comes time to purchase that category of product. Humor works! . . . But not for everybody!

HUMOR IN TV COMMERCIALS

The scene is a small western town. The old man looks up the road and suddenly starts yelling, "He's coming. He's coming." Townspeople dash for safety. Several run into the bar. The barber puts up his "closed" sign and pulls down the window shade. One man dives under a horse and wagon. Another goes flying through the hotel window. The scene cuts to the edge of Main Street. The villain is standing menacingly in the middle of the dusty road, bowler hat tilted confidently to one side, his unshaven, scarred face punctuated by the stump of an unlit cigar dangling out of the left side of his mouth. He carries a 20-foot bull whip tightly in his left hand as he walks unchallenged down the middle of the road into the center of town.

Suddenly from the opposite corner comes the handsome sheriff, six guns loose in the gun belt holsters crossed over his hips. While the townspeople watch every move, the sheriff walks up to the outlaw: "Bowl-a-matic 300?" he challenges. "Bowl-a-matic 300," snaps back the villain. "Sheriff," he roars, "I'll have you rolling in the gutter."

"Not if I strike first," calmly answers the sheriff. The camera pans down to discover a tabletop family bowling game, and follows the details as the announcer takes up the story, "Bowl-a-matic 300, the exciting new bowling game by Coleco. It works just like a real bowling game: strikes, spares and an automatic pin setter."

The villain throws his last ball. It's a strike. He turns to the sheriff with a smug smile. "You'll need a turkey to beat me!" The sheriff calmly takes up his ball and rolls it. Strike! He throws a second ball. Strike! And a third. Strike! For the first time, a smile of victory spreads across the sheriff's face.

The villain throws his cigar butt away in disgust, "You're the first straight bowling sheriff I ever met."

"The sheriff won!" yells the old man. "The sheriff won!"

The street corner suddenly comes alive with deliriously happy townspeople rushing from their hiding places and converging on the victorious sheriff.

A sweet young girl looks up to the sheriff.

"Sheriff, why do they call it Bowl-a-matic 300?"

The sheriff pauses for a moment and then drawls confidently, "'Cause that's the name of the game."

As the crowd continues to shower the sheriff with praise, the announcer signs off: "Bowl-a-matic 300 by Coleco. For good guys who finish first."

This 60-second adaptation of "High Noon" is an example of perfect humor advertising on tv.

In 60 seconds the advertiser achieved the following benefits:

1. A dramatic demonstration of the important play features of the game.

2. The name of the product "Bowl-a-Matic 300" was mentioned

specifically five times (note that in the script, the villain and the sheriff square off just by mentioning the name of the game, it is mentioned twice by the voice-over announcer and highlighted by the pointed question asked by the pretty girl). In addition, the name of the game is prominently displayed on screen during several of the bowling duel scenes and once again in a final beauty shot of the game silhouetted over a frozen long shot of the western town.

3. While the audience quickly understands that the game is meant for teens and pre-teens, the fact that two grown men are engaging in a serious game of skill improves the chances that parents will consider its purchase as a family game. In other words, the commercial upgraded the market for the game.

4. The western "High Noon" plot and the stereotyped characters were familiar and, therefore, a comfortable climate for the viewer. He immediately understood the scenario and the satire. As a humor base, the hoary plot permitted the viewer to feel superior to the action and the dialogue. It was another case of "ritual familiarity." The viewer knew how the story would turn out. He could concentrate on the product story, which was the only unique subject in the plot.

5. The setting for the play of the bowling game was incongruous and thus memorable. It would have been too obvious if the setting had been a bowling alley and the script called for a championship bowler to walk over and join his son in a challenge match. The son wins and the father beams as he says something about how much fun the game was. The audience would immediately spot the phoniness. How can a bowling game for children compete in fun and realism with a real bowling game at a full-size bowling alley? By comparison the toy would have been overwhelmed. And what's so memorable about that commercial? In the western town, however, the humor impetus springs from incongruity and permits the audience, once again, to enjoy the satire, the play-on-words and the slapstick by its "willingness to suspend disbelief."

Although the Bowl-a-matic spot is exceptional, it is just an example of what copywriters of humor tv spots set as a goal: a product demonstration story that is interesting, memorable and has impact. How much impact? Well, the commercial ran each pre-Christmas season for three years without change. The final figures show that it sold over 500,000 units of the $30 retail game for Coleco Industries, at that time a small New England game manufacturer. That's 15 million dollars. That's impact!

COMPARING TV AND RADIO HUMOR

Television is quickly surpassing radio as humor's best medium. The public, when queried, lists humor spots as their favorite type of commercial.

It is necessary to compare radio and tv, as far as humor writing goes, because you must write for each medium differently.

For example:

Radio is a "background" medium used primarily for mood and companionship. Information and entertainment values rank second and third. On the other hand, tv is firstly an entertainment medium. News and information rank second in importance and background companionship has only minor value.

Radio sound offers the humor writer the opportunity to encourage the listener to use his own "perfect imagination" to fill in the details of a suggested scene of description. TV permits the visual verification of a stated fact (such as a shirt with dirt around the collar). By its very nature, it has more effective power and immediacy than any other in-home medium.

Both radio and tv encourage the writer to weave in a story to carry the message. Harry McMahan claims that "from the beginning of communication, man has found that a story (as in the Bible or in *Aesop's Fables*) helps the reader to remember the moral, and in advertising *moral* is spelled *copy claim*."

All notable tv humor stories are based on two elements: conflict and resolution, and both must be visual — the acne skin that magically becomes clear and kissable.

In addition, tv provides these unique opportunities for good advertising humor:

The appearance of the product can be enhanced by lighting tricks, hidden supplemental features can be animated, explanation can be detailed by stop motion, and benefits can be highlighted by slow motion or freeze frame.

The product action has a wide spectrum of possibilities: everything from slapstick frenzy to charming movements like jiggling Jell-O.

The humor of tv action can be exaggerated without destroying the "I see it, thus I believe it" credibility.

Tv has greater impact than any other ad medium because for 30 seconds or more it has a "captured" audience, a term obviously qualified by the frequency of hunger pains, toilet training or the transfer of vital bodily hormones.

It is the definition of a "mass medium," since it offers, through network advertising, the ability to have your message exposed to 98% of the American homes.

Here are a few examples:

To humorously demonstrate their product, Volkswagen came up with a unique demonstration and a memorable commercial. The spot simply showed a man coming out of his home on a dark, cold, wintry morning. He climbs into his Volkswagen, starts the motor and plunges along the heavily snow-covered city streets. The voice-over announcer asks: "Did you ever worry how the man who drives the snowplow drives *to* the snowplow?" Just then, the car drives up to a giant snowplow parked outside a municipal garage. The man gets out of his car, climbs into the snowplow cab and drives off. The voice-over ends up: "This one drives a Volkswagen, so now you can stop worrying."

To demonstrate that the less expensive Granada looked remarkably like a Mercedes, a Ford commercial showed the Granada in a parade containing many different models of cars. The Inquiring Reporter asked people in the crowd to try and guess the car brand and then permitted them to argue among themselves as to whether the car they saw was a Ford or a Mercedes.

The demonstration of Samsonite luggage durability is famous for its torture tests. The luggage has been pounded by a group of linemen from the Pittsburgh Steelers and thrown out of airplanes from 30,000 feet without smashing — the idea, suggested by Alan King, is that flying in a Samsonite suitcase is safer than a plane.

Tv humor can also be used for product comparison formats — the newest fad in advertising theory. Another Volkswagen commercial photographed two identical surburban homes side by side. Into the driveway on the left drives an attractive sedan. The driver gets out of his car and walks into the house, as the voice-over announcer explains that Jones has just bought himself a brand new Buick. Then a Volkswagen sedan enters the driveway on the right. From a distance, it looks attractive and not much smaller than the Buick. The driver gets out and directs a moving van to stop behind him. By slowing the camera speed, men are shown rushing into the house with a number of uncrated household appliances and furnishings. Of course, the voice-over claims, as his voice slowly trails off, that "the savings on the Volkswagen permitted Smith (the neighbor on the right) to not only get a new car but a tv set, a refrigerator, a deep freeze, a hi-fi, a. . . ."

Another value of tv humor is as a memorable introduction of line extensions — new products which contain the corporate logo and an affiliation with a popular consumer brand: i.e., Campbell's spaghetti sauce, Arm & Hammer underarm deodorant or Jell-O pops. Mrs. Paul's Kitchens, whose main product is frozen fried fish, decided to enter the frozen fried chicken business. The new chicken commercial utilized a humorous approach, ending with the line, "Even if you don't like fish, you can still love Mrs. Paul's."

While most advertising experts believe that humor should never be directed at the in-line extension product, in fairness it must be reported that this theory is one of the most controversial in advertising humor writing. Corbett Monica, both a comedian and a tv commercial producer, strongly argued that it is really just the opposite — you make fun of the product, never the people who use the product. He pointed out that the famous Volkswagen commercial always suggested that the car owner was a smart money-saver who was wise enough not to be a status seeker. At the same time, he pointed out, the client permitted the commercials to call his car, in one commercial, a lemon, in another, a bug, and in a third, a beetle.

"The worst tv commercials you'll ever see," he said, "are those where the user is a funny fat lady, a man with a funny accent, a nasty housewife or anybody falling on their face."

He pointed out, as an example, that a commercial for Adler Elevator Shoes, which helps make the wearer look taller, made so much fun of the guys who needed to buy the shoes, "Nobody was willing to go into a shoe store and take the jokes along with the shoes."

In addition, one agency, Wells Rich Green, created a series of tv commercials introducing Benson & Hedges 100 mm cigarettes in the early 70's showing "the disadvantages of a long cigarette." Users were shown getting the cigarette caught in closing elevator doors, car windows and crushed in long encounters of the first kind. The humor theme was used in both print and tv and helped the brand grab a significant share of the market quickly.

Humor doesn't have to carry the creative load by itself — it works well in combination with other emotions, too. Just as many situation comedies use serious problems to set up tension-relief comedy, so too have advertising pros used humor as part of the emotional mixture.

An example was the Bell Telephone commercial series, "Reach out and touch someone." Designed to increase the use of long distance lines by stressing the emotional benefits of calling family and friends, the campaign combined humor with visuals, music and sentimental situations. It continued to achieve one of the best recall scores year after year.

Products that have been on the market for many years can benefit from humor because it is an effective way to put new life and memorability in an old story.

Most industry experts agree, however, that humor is better for selling a low-priced product than for a high-priced one. The rationale is that when people make a major buying decision they are likely to want more reasons than a funny commercial to justify that decision.

THE FINAL A, B, C's OF RESEARCH

A humor commercial isn't finished until it's researched for the following three points.

(a) *Is this a product that consumers are willing to accept as fun?*

(b) *Has the humor hit the real target audience?* Only post-research will prove this after the pre-research has helped you focus on this target group. The following story may not be true, but it does illustrate this point:

One day, supposedly, Heinz researchers turned up some interesting information: men loved catsup, used it generously on hamburgers, steaks and many other dishes in restaurants. Heinz catsup is one of the few bottles of packaged food acceptable on the table in medium quality restaurants. But, the researchers claimed, wives who considered themselves decent cooks would never bring out the catsup until asked, for fear it would cover up the flavor of the food they had worked so hard to prepare.

So the Heinz agency came up with an ad featuring a well endowed waitress carrying a tray of a hamburger, a beverage and a large size bottle of Heinz under the headline "She knows more about your husband than you do." The copy explained the research. The ad ran successfully in the U.S., but when the agency tried to run it in Canada, one magazine protested that the suggestive headline would be misinterpreted in French-speaking Quebec. "Change the headline to what you think best, we're on publication deadline," came the order back from the American agency. "Just send us an advance proof."

Back came the ad in French, too late to be stopped. Everything was the same: a photo of a buxom waitress, a tray with food and the bottle of Heinz catsup. The only difference was the headline, which claimed, "He gets it downtown. Why don't you give it to him at home?"

(c) *How long will the humor stand up?* Since it is generally planned that each ad will be seen several times, how effective is the humor the fourth or fifth time? Woody Allen once said, "The structure of the joke is the juxtaposition of the trivial and the mundane." His example:

"Why does man kill? He kills for food. And not only for food. Frequently, there must be a beverage, too."

But here's the double-edged sword. A joke whose humor comes from a surprise ending also has a shortened life expectancy . . . and if the humor is predictable, it's not funny at all. Therefore, ad humor should be pegged a few steps lower than hilarious and sidesplitting. If you laugh loudly the first time, you certainly won't laugh as much the fourth or fifth time. Ergo, in your mind, the fun has gone out of the humor. But if, the first time, the advertising produces a warm feeling, a smile or a mild chuckle — and it continues to make you grin over a reasonable period — then it is an ad or commercial that you welcome and has a longer life expectancy.

INDEX

Abbott and Costello, 153
Ace, Goodman, 100, 115, 207
Ace, Jane, 207
Adams, Don, 101
Addams, Charles, 229-30
Adler, Bill, 133
ad-libs, 44
advertising, 257-95
Aesop's fables, 71, 291
agents, 116, 211-23, 242-45
aggression, 33-35, 47-48, 51-52
Agnew, 27
Alda, Alan, 8
All in the Family, 113, 115, 191-93
Allegory, 76
Allen, Fred, 94, 171, 209, 212
Allen, Gracie, 276
Allen, Melanie, 93
Allen, Steve, 92, 99, 102
Allen, Woody, 8, 23-26, 28, 30, 35, 39,
 42, 66, 69, 95, 99, 102-3, 105, 108,
 119, 125, 172, 294
Altman, Robert, 99
ambivalence, 20
Amin, Idi, 62
anarchism, 61
Andrews, Bert, 191
anecdotes, 169-70
Animal House, 57
animals in humor, 134
antonyms, 88
anxiety, 24, 30
Aristophanes, 35, 70
Aristotle, 17
Armour, Richard, 93, 98, 110, 171
Arnez, Desi, 193
Auchincloss, Louis, 262
audiences, 27, 35, 45-47, 103, 111,
 157-62, 177-78
authority, 26-28, 61-62, 120
Aykroyd, Dan, 56, 58, 62

Backus, Jim, 209
Baer, Arthur, 69
Bain, 18
Baker, Herbie, 95, 106
Baker, Russell, 99
Ball, Lucille, 193, 195
Bancroft, Ann, 105
Barnes, Clive, 31
Barth, John, 70
Beattie, 19
bedpan humor, 128-29

Beerbohm, Max, 27, 103
beginning writers, 92-93, 141-45
Belkin, Gary, 115
Belushi, John, 57, 60-61
Benchley, Robert, 25, 69
Benny, Jack, 102, 127, 262
Berdis, Bert, 273, 277, 279-80
Bergson, 17-19
Berle, Milton, 27, 127, 172
Bernbach, Doyle Dane, 267
Bernbach, William, 267
Bier, Jesse, 49
biological humor theories, 18, 52
bisexuality, 26
Bishop, Joey, 131, 177
black humor, 66
Blacks and humor, 33, 186-88
Blue Nun commercials, 280-82
Bob and Ray, 67
Booth, George, 268
Borge, Victor, 32, 263
Brenner, David, 81, 90-91, 104
Brooks, Mel, 8, 44, 93, 95, 99, 104-5,
 107, 118-19, 121, 131, 137, 266
Bruce, Lenny, 126
Buchwald, Art, 35, 94-95, 98
Buckley, Tom, 35
Bunker, Archie, 68, 104, 124, 193
Burns, George, 127, 265, 276
Burrows, Abe, 27-28, 34-36, 44, 95, 102,
 107, 109, 116, 201
Byron, 76

Caesar, Sid, 118, 125
Cambridge, Godfrey, 80
Caples, John, 259
Carlin, George, 126
Carpenter, Don, 107
Carroll, Bob, 115
Carson, Johnny, 7, 27, 56, 102, 127,
 131, 138-40, 155, 257
Carter, Jack, 177
Carter, Jimmy, 56
cartoon ads, 268-69
cartoons, 226-45
Carver, Ron, 176
celebrities, 27, 112, 121, 265
censors, 75
Chaefsky, Paddy, 98
Chaplin, Charlie, 31, 34, 44, 108
Charles, Ray, 58
Chase, Chevy, 55-56, 58
Cheech & Chong, 31-32

cleverness, 80
clichés, 36, 76, 79, 81-82, 85, 87, 100, 232-38
climax, 43
Cobb, 76
Cocteau, 52
collaborators, 106-8
comedians, 27, 39-40, 286-87
configurational theories, 20-21
Connelly, Marc, 69
contracts, 224-25
The Cool Fire, 116
Copyright Handbook, 225
Coren, Alan, 26
Cosby, Bill, 264-65
Cosell, Howard, 67, 127, 264
A Couple of Comedians, 107
Coward, Noel, 24, 101
Craig, C. Samuel, 259
Crosby, Norm, 204, 209
Crystal, Billy, 104
Curtin, Jane, 57

Dana, Bill, 94-95, 101, 106, 261
Dangerfield, Rodney, 35, 86, 172
Davis, Herman, 260
Davis, Madelyn, 115
Davis, Sammy, 35
Davis, William, 40
death, 30, 51-52
Decker, Richard, 228
Dee, Sylvia, 170
deflation, 50
Defoe, 77
Derman, Lou, 114
DeVries, Peter, 69, 171
dialogue in sitcoms, 204-8
Diamond, Selma, 109, 116, 199
Dickinson, Angie, 272
Diller, Phyllis, 111, 145, 166-67, 171
dimensional humor, 81-83
disguise, 75
double entendre, 48, 68, 121-25
Douglas, Jack, 94-95, 102, 110-11
dramatic irony, 75
Durante, Jimmy, 130

Eastman, Max, 94
Ebel, Fred, 157
Ebert, Roger, 114
Elinson, Jack, 95-96, 98, 101, 107
Elliot, Bob, 270
Encyclopedia of Black Humor, 186
Encyclopedia of One-liner Comedy, 154
English humor, 185-86
epigram, 74

Erasmus, 76
ethnic humor, 32, 36, 183-89
exaggeration, 38-40, 48, 67, 74

family humor, 28, 99
Far Eastern humor, 186
Farris, Joe, 230
Fawcett, Farrah, 272
Feiffer, Jules, 114
Feinberg, Leonard, 71, 72-75
female comics, 109
Femina, Jerry Della, 280
Ferre, Nels F. S., 169
Fields, W. C., 170
fillers, 173-75
Fisher, Rhoda and Seymour, 39
Flesch, Rudolph, 163
Flippen, Ruth, 95
Flugel, 26, 34
foods in humor, 124-25
Ford, Gerald, 55-56, 60, 112
formula joke, 101-2
Foxx, Redd, 33, 186
Freberg, Stan, 257, 259
Freud, 21, 24, 31-32, 40, 57, 75, 81, 137
Fry, William Jr., 93, 101
funny words, 118-40

Gable, Clark, 126
Galbraith, John, 259
Garel, Leo, 230
Garner, James, 265, 271
Garnett, 72
Garvey, Daniel, 200
Gelbart, Larry, 36
Gene Perret's Roundtable, 93
Gestalt psychology, 21
Glascow, Arnold, 143
Gleason, Jackie, 166, 273
Glenn, John, 31
Gobel, George, 177
Gogol, 76
Goldberg, Rube, 31
Golden, Harry, 110
Goulding, Ray, 270
Graham, Ed Jr., 259, 270
Green, Kathy, 109
Greene, Shecky, 105
greeting cards, 246-56
Gregory, 20, 23-24, 40
Gretsky, Wayne, 108
grotesque, 32
Gulliver's Travels, 66

Hammerquist, Bob, 246
hardcore language, 126-28

Hart, Moss, 137
Hartley, Mariette, 265, 271, 276
Hawn, Goldie, 42
HEARTS Theory, 23-24, 47-48, 89
Helitzer, Mel, 104
Heller, Joseph, 70
Henry, Bob, 107
Hercer, Ed, 93, 159
Herman, Lenny, 233
Hershfield, Harry, 32
Hiken, Nat, 95
Himelfarb, Marvin, 115
Hite, Shere, 25
The Hite Report on Male Sexuality, 25
Hitler, 27
Hobbes, 18, 76, 82
Hodgart, 71-72
Holberg, 77
Holman's Handbook to Literature, 70
Holmberg, Dee, 94, 99, 110, 112
homonyms, 88
homosexuality, 26
Hope, Bob, 7, 95, 103, 112, 131, 138, 144-45, 162, 164, 177, 265, 287
Horatian satire, 71
hostility, 25-33, 47-48
How the Great Comedy Writers Create Laughter, 93
How to Make Love to a Man, 25
Huggins, Andy, 134-35
Hugo, 77
humorists, 170-71

I Love Lucy, 192-93
Ibsen, 76
Idle, Eric, 40, 106
improvisation, 44
incongruity, 19, 36, 69, 74
Indian humor, 186
invective, 70
Irish humor, 185
irony, 65-66, 72
The Irony of American History, 65
Italian jokes, 184

Jackson, Reggie, 172
Jagger, Mick, 58
jeremiad, 70
Jerome, Jerome K., 90
Jessel, Georgie, 127
Jewish humor, 119, 133, 187-88
Johns, Al, 227
Johnson, Samuel, 142
Josefberg, J. Milton, 95
Juvenilian satire, 71

Kanin, Garson, 44
Kanter, Hal, 93-94, 105, 108
Karp, Richard, 261
Kaufman, George, 108-9
Keith-Spiegel, Patricia, 17
Kerr, Jean, 112
Keyes, Wilson Byron, 272
King, Alan, 125, 128-29, 177, 292
King, Martin Luther, 69
Klein, Marty, 93, 104
Koestler, 19
Kroll, Jack, 36
Kronenberger, Louis, 24
Kropotkin, Peter, 61
Kuavis, Paul, 258

La Rochefoucauld, 27
Lachman, Mort, 107, 113
lampoon, 71
Landers, Bill, 69
Lavant, Oscar, 89
Leacock, Stephen, 19, 36, 171
Lear, Norman, 95, 104, 108, 112, 115-16
Leonard, Jack E., 177
Leonard, Sheldon, 190, 192
Levin, Martin, 110
Lewis, Joe E., 29
Lewis, Sinclair, 70
Lincoln, Abraham, 170
Linkletter, Art, 117, 127
Little, Marion, 93
Little Moron jokes, 184
Lloyd, Harold, 31, 95
localizing humor, 160-62
Love and Death, 30
Ludovici, 18, 52
Lynch, Daniel, 149

Machiavelli, 77
Maier, 21
Make 'em Laugh: Life Studies of Comedy Writers, 93
malapropisms, 68, 204-5, 209
The Man Who Came to Dinner, 128
manufactured words, 68
Marcus, Jerry, 230
marketing cartoons, 239-45
marketing humor, 110-13, 142-43, 210-13, 224-45
Markow, Jack, 226, 239
Marshall, Gary, 191, 196, 198
Martin, Billy, 264
Martin, Dean, 264
Martin, Steve, 58, 60, 93-94, 103, 106, 109, 113, 119, 127, 164, 287
Martins, John, 257

Marx, Chico, 89-90
Marx, Groucho, 50, 89
M*A*S*H, 195, 198
mask-persona, 75
Mason, Jackie, 26
Maugham, Somerset, 33
Mauldin, Bill, 23
de Maupassant, Guy, 75
McCormick, Pat, 112
McMahan, Harry, 292
Meader, Vaughn, 177
Meara, Ann, 280-84
Mencken, H. L., 71, 74
Mendelssohn, 34
Michaels, Lorne, 60
Millard, Oscar, 211
Miller, Norma, 186
Mills, Bob, 105, 110, 117
misperceptions in sitcoms, 202, 208
Mizerany, Steve, 258
A Modest Proposal, 74
money in humor, 28-29
Monica, Corbett, 292
Montesquieu, 77
Monty Python's Flying Circus, 56
Moore, Gary, 209
Moore, Mary Tyler, 197
morality in humor, 32, 54-62, 195-96
Morris, Garrett, 56-57
Mr. Ace and Jane, 207
Mull, Martin, 131
Murphy, Maureen, 121
Murray, Bill, 56, 62
myth, 71

Nader, Ralph, 259
Nash, Ogden, 31
National Lampoon, 26-27, 121
Nazis, 57
Nelson, Roy Paul, 65, 168
Nessen, Ron, 60
The New Yorker, 71, 110, 268
Newhart, Bob, 160
Newman, Loraine, 57
Newman, Randy, 58
Nichols, Mike, 109
Niebuhr, 65
nihilism, 54-62
Nixon, 26, 55-57
Nobile, Philip, 170
non sequiturs, 102, 207
nuclear war, 31
numbers in humor, 130-31

obscenity, 72
O'Connor, Edwin, 68

The Odd Couple, 109
O'Donnohue, Michael, 56
old age, 30
Olgilvy, David, 261
one-liners, 24, 102, 113-14
Orben, Robert, 27, 93, 95, 99, 103, 108, 111, 131, 152
Orkin, Dick, 273, 277, 279-80

Paar, Jack, 110
Panneborg, 76
paradox, 74
Parker, Dorothy, 38, 50
parody, 66, 75, 206, 253
Partch, Virgil, 234
Passell, Peter, 29
pathos, 65
Penney, Alexandra, 25
Perdue, Frank, 258, 273
Perret, Gene, 93-95, 98, 101, 103-4, 106-8, 110-13, 116, 141, 159
Pielke, Robert B., 54
Piel's beer commercials, 270-71
places in humor, 131-33
plotting sitcoms, 150-53
poetic license, 38
Polaroid commercials, 271
Polish humor, 36, 184
political humor, 26, 56, 59-60
Polykoff, Shirley, 257
Pope, 76
practical joke, 69, 76
Prather, Hugh, 142
Prescott, Peter, 24
presidential humor, 120
pretense in satire, 76
Priestley, 19
print advertising humor, 266-67
Pryor, Richard, 58, 126
psychoanalytic theory, 21
Pudgy, 43
Pumpian, Paul, 95
punchline, 40, 47, 101-2, 157
puns, 67, 89, 155, 206, 209, 267

quips, 159

radio advertising, 274-81
Radner, Gilda, 54, 109
Reader's Digest, 173-75
Reagan, Ronald, 7, 35, 120, 144
realism, 36-38, 47
reductio ad absurdum, 74
Reeve, Lloyd Eric, 100
Reiner, Carl, 44, 94-95, 100, 108, 115, 125, 131, 137

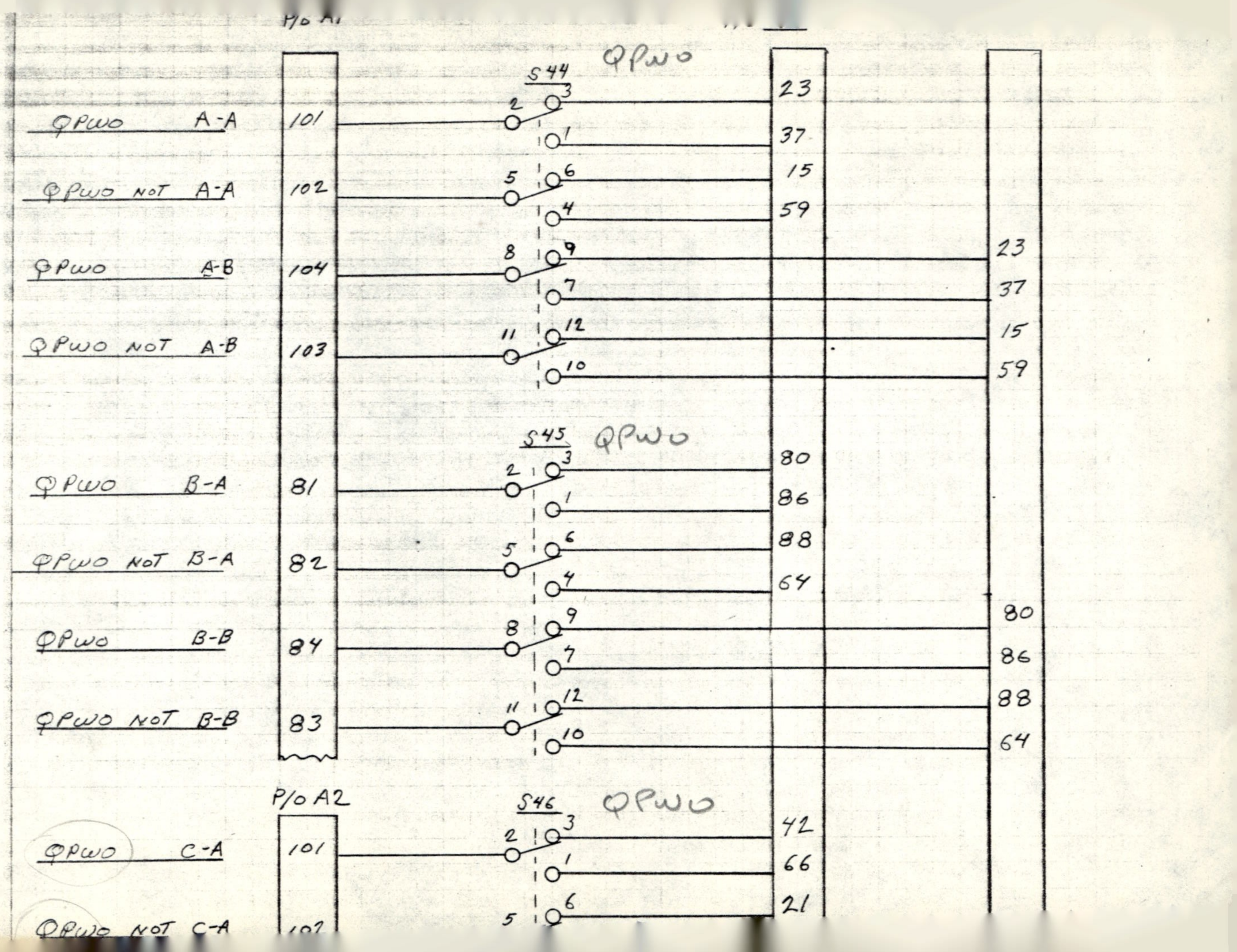

relativism, 54
release theory, 20, 24, 32, 34, 40
religion in humor, 52-53, 60, 133
Repplier, Agnes, 44
Reston, James, 35
reverse, 84, 227
Rickles, Don, 35, 43, 177
ridicule, "rid-a-cruel," 23-24
Rivers, William L., 200
roasts, 86, 127, 161
Robinson, Larry, 258
Rockefeller, Nelson, 61
Rogers, Will, 188, 258
role reversal in sitcoms, 203, 208
rolling laugh, 97, 102, 130
Roman, Ken, 262
Rooney, Andy, 7, 259
Rooney, Mickey, 112
Roosevelt, Teddy, 122
Rosen, Arnie, 106-7
Ross, Stanley Ralph, 100
routining jokes, 181
Rudner, Rita, 132

Salinger, J. D., 122
Sandman, Larry, 252
sarcasm, 70, 161
satire, 24, 27, 66, 70-78, 206
Saturday Night Live, 54-62, 287
savers, 103, 155, 158
Schiller, Bob, 115
Schlesinger, Arthur Jr., 67
Schopenhauer, 19
Schwartz, Sherwood, 102
Scott, Sir Walter, 67
Screenwriter's Handbook, 214
Segal, George, 31
Seiden, Hank, 274
Seigel, Bugsy, 90
self-deprecation, 35
"Seven Dirty Words," 126
sex in advertising, 271-73
sexual humor, 25, 121-28, 188
Shakespeare, 35
Shanks, Bob, 116
Shanks, George, 227
Shaw, George Bernard, 127, 170
Sheridan, Richard, 68
Shows, Charles, 93, 114, 116
Shulman, Max, 95, 100
sick humor, 49-53
Simmons, Ed, 113
Simmons, Matty, 26
Simon, Danny, 95
Simon, John, 68
Simon, Neil, 42, 99, 103, 109, 118

simple truth, 83
Simpson, O. J., 264
Sinatra, Frank, 27, 35, 105
sitcoms, 114-16, 190-209
situations in sitcoms, 202-3
sketches, 113-14
slapstick, 24, 34
Smith, Sidney, 106
speechwriting, 149-69
Spielman, Howard, 287
splitting quotes, 43
spokesmen in commercials, 264, 286-87
Spooner, Rev. William A., 69
spoonerisms, 68-69, 206, 209, 285
stage fright, 27, 45, 166
stand-up comedy, 41, 105, 112, 176-82
Stein, Benjamin, 114
Stein, M. L., 169
Steinberg, 229
Stendahl, 74
stereotypes, 32-33
Sternthal, Brian, 259
Stiller, Jerry, 280-84
Stoppard, Tom, 81
straight line, 100, 102
Strindberg, 76
Sullivan, Frank, 69
Sully, James, 23
The Sunshine Boys, 118
superiority theory, 18, 76
surprise, 19, 36, 42, 44-49, 74-76, 106, 171-72, 230
Swift, Jonathan, 66, 71–74
switching, 79, 84-85, 90, 102
symbol, 75
synonyms, 88

taboo, 34
take-off, 84
taste, 55, 104
Taylor, R., 228
Taylor, Robert Lewis, 170
technology, 30-31
television, 31
television commercials, 289-93
tension, 40-42, 48-49
Three's Company, 201-205
Thurber, James, 74, 227
Tolkin, Mel, 137
Tom Swifties, 67
Tomlin, Lily, 123
topper, 42, 45, 102-3
tragedy, 25, 65
travesty, 71
triple, 41-42, 130, 154
Trueblood, Ellen, 171

truism, 37, 82, 88, 162
Twain, Mark, 25, 128, 267
"Two Thousand Year Old Man," 44, 131, 137

Uncle Remus, 55
understatement, 74, 227

Valen, Herb, 270
Van Doren, Mark, 24
Van Loon, Hendrik Willem, 67
verbal irony, 75
Vernon, Jackie, 160, 177
Vietnam, 27
Voltaire, 77
Vondel, 77
vulgarity, 33

Walpole, Horace, 3, 25
Watergate, 27
Wayne, John, 162
Weiskopf, Bob, 115
White, Barry, 56
White, E. B., 23

White, Slappy, 162
Whol, Robert, 131
Who's on First?, 153
Wilde, Larry, 93, 183
Wilde, Oscar, 127
Wiley, Max, 95, 98
Williams, Dylan, 70
Williams, Robin, 131, 193
Wilson, Earl, 172
Wilson, Rowland, 268
Winwood, Robb W., 239
Winters, Jonathan, 86, 287
wisecracks, 38, 183
wit, 21, 24, 33, 38
word play, 82
Wouk, Herman, 94
The Writer's Handbook, 170
The Writer's Market, 239, 242

Yiddish, 124, 133
Youngman, Henny, 28-29, 148, 209

Zinsser, William K., 29, 39, 170